THE COMPLETE MEDITERRANEAN DIET COOKBOOK

BY ANTHONY MILLER

Over 500 Tasty, Quick & Easy Recipes Designed for People Who Don't Have Time to Cook but Want to Eat Well, Healthy and Lose Weight with Balanced Dishes.

© Copyright 2021 All rights reserved.

This document is geared towards providing exact and reliable information in regards to the topic and issue covered. The publication is sold with the idea that the publisher is not required to render accounting, officially permitted or otherwise qualified services. If advice is necessary, legal or professional, a practiced individual in the profession should be ordered.

From a Declaration of Principles which was accepted and approved equally by a Committee of the American Bar Association and a Committee of Publishers and Associations.

In no way is it legal to reproduce, duplicate, or transmit any part of this document in either electronic means or in printed format. Recording of this publication is strictly prohibited, and any storage of this document is not allowed unless with written permission from the publisher. All rights reserved.

The information provided herein is stated to be truthful and consistent, in that any liability, in terms of inattention or otherwise, by any usage or abuse of any policies, processes, or directions contained within is the solitary and utter responsibility of the recipient reader. Under no circumstances will any legal responsibility or blame be held against the publisher for any reparation, damages, or monetary loss due to the information herein, either directly or indirectly.

Respective authors own all copyrights not held by the publisher.

The information herein is offered for informational purposes solely and is universal as so. The presentation of the information is without a contract or any type of guarantee assurance.

The trademarks used are without any consent, and the publication of the trademark is without permission or backing by the trademark owner. All trademarks and brands within this book are for clarifying purposes only and are owned by the owners themselves, not affiliated with this document.

Table Of Contents

What Is The Mediterranean Diet?	9
Healthy Fats in the Mediterranean Diet	10
Plant-Based Food in the Mediterranean Diet	10
Herbs and Spices in the Mediterranean Diet	10
Protein in the Mediterranean Diet	12
Wine in the Mediterranean Diet	13
8 Tips to QuickStart your Mediterranean Diet Journey	15
The Key to Making Mediterranean Diet Work:Embrace Life	15
Pantry Essentials	17
Grocery Store Guide: How To Shop	18
The Processed Food Puzzle	19
Your Basic Tools	20
BREAKFAST RECIPES	**23**
Pomegranate and Peaches Avocado Toast	24
Oatmeal Banana-Nut	24
Greek-Style Homemade Yogurt	24
Casserole for Breakfast	25
Almond Butter and Banana Toasts	25
English Muffin with Berries	26
Healthy English Muffin Lox	26
Bowl Protein	26
Berries Deluxe Oatmeal	27
Apples and Cinnamon Oatmeal	27
Oatmeal Energy	28
Anna's Organic Granola	28
Hot Quinoa and Berries	28
Fruity Milk Parfait	29
Yogurt with Banana Almond	29
Open-Faced Sandwich for Breakfast	30
Broccoli Omelet	30
Veggie Frittata and Caramelized Onions	31
Mediterranean Scramble Eggs	31
Veggie Omelet	32
Apple Oatmeal with Cinnamon	32
Egg White Omelet with Vegetables	32
Green Fruity Smoothie	33
Breakfast Salad with Fruit and Yogurt	33
Pumpkin Pancakes Spiced	34
Muffins of Lemon-Zucchini	34
English Muffin Breakfast	35
Tartine with Strawberries and Cream Cheese	35
Broccoli and Pepper Jack Omlet	36
Granola Make It Your Way	36
Oatmeal with Apple and Spice	36
Whole-Wheat Strawberry Pancakes-Maple Compote	37
Blueberries and Yogurt Cornmeal Waffles	37
Banana-berries smoothie	38
Smoothie of Chocolate-Peanut Butter	38
Kale and Apple Smoothie	38
Lassi mango	39
Papaya and Coconut Breakfast Shake	39
Cappuccino At-Home	40
Green Tea Gingered	40
Crepes Buckwheat	40
Muffins with Carrots	41
Oatmeal Pineapple	41
Muffins with Spinach	42
Breakfast Blend for Chia Seeds	42
Fruit Dishes for Breakfast	42
Pumpkin Cookies for Breakfast	43
Scramble Veggie Version	43
Mushrooms and Tea with Turkey	44
Delicious Omelet	44
Simple Waffles Omelet	44
Jared Omelets	45
Mushrooms and Omelets Cheese	45
Egg White Mix for Breakfast	46
Omelet with Pistachio Pesto	46
Cashews and Salad with Blueberries	46
Bowls of Quinoa	47
Sandwich with Strawberrys	47
Quinoa Apple Muffins	48
Superb Quinoa Hash Browns	48
Quinoa Bars for Breakfast	48
Quinoa Quiche	49
Egg Muffins and Quinoa	49
APPETIZERS	**51**
Spicy Hummus	52
Almond & Parmesan Stuffed Cucumbers	52
Jalapeno Poppers Stuffed with Hummus	53
Sweet Curried Almonds	53
Baileys Ice Coffee	54
Truffle Popcorn	54
Eggplant Dip with Mayonnaise	54
Garlic Lentil-Walnut Spread with Cilantro	55
Cucumber Bites	55
Curly Kale & Artichoke Flatbread	56
Artichoke & Bean Spread	56
Garbanzo Patties with Yogurt Sauce	56
Cheesy Grilled Asparagus	57
Thyme Artichoke with Aioli	57
Anchovy & Pepper Tapenade	58
Roasted Carrot Ribbons with Mayo Sauce	58
Roasted Pepper Hummus	58
Spanish-Style Avocado Dip	59

Parsley Lamb Tagliatelle	59
Cheese & Cucumber Mini Sandwiches	60
Almond Spinach with Chickpeas	60
Italian Eggplant Balls	60
Cream Cheese & Tomato Toast	61
Chili Butternut Squash with Walnuts	61
Grilled Eggplant Rounds	62
Pepper & Tomato Dip	62
Garlic Lentil Dip	63
Cucumber & Prawn Bites	63
Spicy Caper & Eggplant Spread	64
Gluten-Free Pizza Caprese	64
Light & Creamy Garlic Hummus	64
Creamy Potato Spread	65
Parmesan Potatoes	65
Homemade Salsa	66
Flavorful Roasted Baby Potatoes	66
Garlic Pinto Bean Dip	66
Jalapeno-Chickpea Hummus	67
Healthy Kidney Bean Dip	67
Healthy Spinach Dip	68
Tomato Cucumber Salsa	68
Rosemary Cauliflower Dip	68
Easy Tomato Dip	69
Spicy Chicken Dip	69
Olive Eggplant Spread	70
Paprika Cauliflower	70
Crispy Potato Chips	70
Healthy Trail Mix	71
Citrusy Watermelon & Cantaloupe Balls	71
Caper & Olive Snack	72
Party Nut Mix	72
Greek-Style White Bean Spread	72
Cucumber Tzatziki Dip with Walnuts	73
Greek-Style Potato Boats	73
Herby Vegetable Medley with Marsala Sauce	74
Lamb Arancini	74
Bell Pepper & Eggplant Dip	74
Cheesy Meatballs	75
Parmesan Trail Mix	75
Za'atar Yogurt Spread	76
Speedy Shallot & Kale Spread	76
Basil & Tomato Bruschetta	76
Feta & Olive Stuffed Cherry Tomatoes	77
Scallion & Goat Cheese Dip	77
Spicy Baba Ganoush	78
Avocado Boats	78
Tuna-Zucchini Rolls	78
Prosciutto Wrapped Pears	79
Yogurt & Walnut Dip	79
Parsley Ricotta Cheese Dip	80
Vegetable Cakes	80
Dilled Salmon Rolls	80
Eggplant Fries	81
Balsamic Beet Bites with Feta	81
Arugula & Pesto Dip	82
Olive & Cucumber "Pasta"	82
Feta-Stuffed Zucchini	82
Ricotta Stuffed Potatoes	83
Baked Sweet Potatoes	83
Perfect Queso	84
Cucumber Tomato Okra Salsa	84
Creamy Artichoke Dip	84
Delicious Eggplant Caponata	85
Perfect Italian Potatoes	85
Creamy Eggplant Dip	86
Tasty Black Bean Dip	86
Creamy Pepper Spread	86
Kidney Bean Spread with Lemon	87
Spicy Berry Dip	87
Tomato Olive Salsa	88
Balsamic Bell Pepper Salsa	88
Slow Cooked Cheesy Artichoke Dip	89
Pepper Tomato Eggplant Spread	89

FISH &SEAFOODS 91

Roasted Salmon Parcels	92
Salmon with Shrimp Tomato Sauce	92
Roasted Salmon with Asparagus	92
Saucy Thyme Salmon	93
Fried Salmon with Escarole & Olives	93
Chili Salmon with Fennel & Peppers	94
Mustard Salmon with Walnuts	94
Paprika Cod with Cabbage	94
Balsamic Salmon with Haricots Vert	95
Avocado Salmon Tartare	95
Eggplant & Salmon Rolls	96
Smoked Trout Dip	96
Rosemary Trout with Roasted Beets	96
Trout & Farro Bowls	97
Pan-Seared Trout with Tzatziki	97
Oven-Baked Rainbow Trout	98
Roasted Cod with Mozzarella & Tomatoes	98
Turmeric Cod	98
Lemon Cod with Rice	99
Cod Fillets with Cherry Tomatoes	99
Cod with Paprika and Mushroom Sauce	100
Herby Cod Skewers	100
Cod & Calamari with Mango Sauce	101
Haddock Fillets with Capers	101
Haddock in Tomato Sauce	102
Wine Poached Haddock	102
Tomato Tilapia with Parsley	103
Tilapia & Brown Rice Pilaf	103
Garlic & Lemon Sea Bass	104
Tuna Burgers with Green Olives	104
Tzatziki Tuna Gyros	104
Basil Tuna Skillet	105
Herby Flounder	105
Halibut Cream Soup	106
Barramundi with Dates & Hazelnuts	106
Mackerel Fillets in Hot Tomato Sauce	107

Sardine Patties	107
Quick Shrimp Rice	108
Anchovy & Avocado Dip	108
Crispy Baked Pollock	109
Chili Anchovies	109
Roasted Shrimp with Veggies	110
Rosemary Shrimp in Lemon Sauce	110
Butter & Garlic Squid & Shrimp	111
Tiger Prawns with Mushrooms	111
Sicilian Prawns with Capers & Lemon	112
Sour & Tasty Prawn	112
Awesome Calamari in Cilantro Sauce	112
Chili Squid Stew with Capers	113
Andalusian Squid with Zucchini	113
Citrus Squid with Olives	114
Creamy Basil Scallops	114
Tuscan-Style Scallops with Kale	114
Mayo Scallop & Veggie Mix	115
Pancetta-Wrapped Scallops	115
Crab Patties with Radicchio Salad	116
Drunken Mussels with Lemon-Butter Sauce	116
White Wine Mussels	116
Mussels with Leeks	117
Basil Clams with Snow Peas	117
Clam & Chickpea Stew	118
Italian Seafood Stew	118
Fish & Vegetable Stew	118
Seafood Soup	119
Seafood Special Spaghetti	119

SOUPS 121

Cheesy Keto Zucchini Soup	122
Mint Avocado Chilled Soup	122
Spring Soup Recipe with Poached Egg	123
Swiss Chard Egg Drop Soup	123
Delicata Squash Soup	124
Apple Pumpkin Soup	124
Cauliflower and Thyme Soup	124
Chicken Kale Soup	125
Chicken Mulligatawny Soup	125
Traditional Chicken Soup	126
Chicken Cabbage Soup	126
Keto BBQ Chicken Pizza Soup	126
Spicy Halibut Tomato Soup	127
Fall Soup	127
Sausage & Spinach Chickpea Soup	128
Veggie & Chicken Soup	128
Chicken Soup with Green Beans & Rice	128
Turkey & Rice Egg Soup	129
Oregano Chicken & Barley Soup	129
Slow Cooked Hot Lentil Soup	130
Italian Cavolo Nero Soup	130
Vegetable Soup	130
Tasty Zuppa Toscana	131
Spinach & Lentil Soup	131
Super Bean & Celery Soup	132

Power Green Soup	132
Tomato Beef Soup	132
Easy Vegetable Soup	133
Chicken & Eggplant Soup	133
Cold Prawn Soup	134
Soup with Spinach & Orzo	134
Spicy Chicken Soup with Beans	134
Leftover Lamb & Mushroom Soup	135
Spring Soup with Poached Egg	135
Easy Butternut Squash Soup	136
Cauliflower, leek & bacon soup	136
Mushroom Spinach Soup	136
Broccoli Soup	137
Keto French Onion Soup	137
Homemade Spicy Chicken Soup	138
Chicken Veggie Soup	138
Buffalo Ranch Chicken Soup	138
Chicken and Egg Soup	139
Green Chicken Enchilada Soup	139
Salmon Stew Soup	140
Italian Chicken & Veggie Soup	140
Rosemary Soup with Roasted Vegetables	140
Spicy Lentil Soup	141
Basil Meatball Soup	141
Basil Tomato & Roasted Pepper Soup	142
Pork & Vegetable Soup	142
Herbed Bean Soup	142
Quick Chicken & Vermicelli Soup	143
Cannellini Bean & Feta Cheese Soup	143
Italian Sausage & Seafood Soup	144
Cauliflower Soup with Pancetta Croutons	144
Cheesy Tomato Soup	144
Pork Meatball Soup	145
Turkey & Cabbage Soup	145
Green Lentil & Ham Easy Soup	146
Soup With Lamb & Spinach	146
Lemon Chicken Soup	146
Spanish Chorizo & Bean Special Soup	147
Turkish Chicken Soup with Buckwheat	147

BEANS, RICE & GRAINS 149

Flavors Taco Rice Bowl	150
Cucumber Olive Rice	150
Cheese Basil Tomato Rice	151
Fiber Packed Chicken Rice	151
Bulgur Salad	152
Herb Polenta	152
Quinoa & Black Bean Stuffed Sweet Potatoes	152
Quinoa Buffalo Bites	153
Raw Tomato Sauce & Brie on Linguine	153
Red Wine Risotto	154
Seafood Paella with Couscous	154
Spanish Rice Casserole with Cheesy Beef	154
Stuffed Tomatoes with Green Chili	155
"Mari & Monti" Fried Rice	155
Turkey and Quinoa Stuffed Peppers	156

Veggies and Sun-Dried Tomato Alfredo	156
Sausage & Bean Casserole	157
Moroccan Spiced Couscous	157
Parmesan & Collard Green Oats	158
Vegetable Rice Bowl	158
Italian Cannellini Beans with Egg Noddles	158
Awesome Chickpea & Spinach Bowl	159
Cavolo Nero & Pea Farro Pilaf	159
Lentil & Potato Stew with Goat Cheese	160
Spanish Rice with Chicken	160
Chicken & Olive Rice	160
Lima Bean Stew	161
Garbanzo Bean & Pork Stew	161
Caper & Brown Rice Pilaf	162
Valencian Mussel & Rice Stew	162
Chili Zucchini Millet	162
Couscous with Apricots & Chickpeas	163
Basil and Pecorino Risotto	163
Risotto Milanese	164
Thyme Pork with Rice	164
Asparagus Brown Rice	164
Feta Couscous with Kale & Cucumber	165
Mediterranean-Style Quinoa	165
Hot Vegetarian Two-Bean Cassoulet	166
Bulgur Tabbouleh	166
Italian Barley with Artichoke Hearts	166
Cherry Tomato Ricc Pilaf with Pistachios	167
Spicy Garbanzo Bowl with Feta Cheese	167
Lemony Shrimp & Quinoa Bowl	168
Harissa Farro & Chickpea Stew	168
Greek Lentils with Chicken	168
Caper & Tuna Pearl Barley	169
Slow-Cooked Bean & Pork Cassoulet	169
Pressure Cooker Pork with Rice	170
Veggie Brown Rice Bowl	170
Feta & Chard Couscous	170
Parmesan & Sage Faro	171
Lemon Chickpeas with Carrots & Capers	171
Cannellini Beans with Cherry Tomatoes	172
Lamb with Mint	172
Cheesy Mushroom Wild Rice	172
Ricotta & Rice Stuffed Peppers	173
Lamb & Mint Risotto	173
Hot Vegetable Stew with Green Beans & Rice	174
Parmesan Mushroom Pilaf	174
Tasty Greek Rice	174
Perfect Herb Rice	175
Quinoa and Three Beans Recipe	175
Raisins, Nuts and Beef on Hashweh Rice	176
Red Quinoa Peach Porridge	176
Rice & Currant Salad Mediterranean Style	176
Shrimp Paella Made with Quinoa	177
Squash and Eggplant Casserole	177

PIZZA &PASTA 179

Asiago & Artichoke Pizza	180
Balsamic-Glazed Pizza with Arugula & Olives	180
Pepperoni Fat Head Pizza	180
Extra Cheesy Pizza	181
Spanish-Style Pizza de Jamon	181
Spicy & Smoky Pizza	182
Turkey Pizza with Pesto Topping	182
Baby Spinach Pizza with Sweet Onion	182
Italian Mushroom Pizza	183
Broccoli-Pepper Pizza	183
Caramelized Onion and Goat Cheese Pizza	184
Vegetarian Spinach-Olive Pizza	184
Chicken Bacon Ranch Pizza	184
Tagliatelle with Sardines & Capers	185
Fall Baked Vegetable with Rigatoni	185
Broccoli Pesto Fusilli	186
Pasta Salad	186
Fettuccine a la Puttanesca	186
Walnut Pesto Pasta	187
Broccoli Pasta with Basil Pesto	187
Garlic Shrimp with Tie Pasta	188
Creamy Salmon Fettucine	188
Beef Carbonara	189
Pork Loin with Green Beans & Fettuccine	189
Garlic-Butter Steak Bites with Fusilli	190
Beef Ragu with Veggies	190
Tuscan Chicken Linguine	190
Beef-Asparagus Rotini Pasta	191
Classic Beef Lasagna	191
Cauliflower Casserole with Macaroni	192
Mussels with Spaghetti	192
One-Pot Spicy Pasta	192
Spicy Veggie Pasta Bake	193
Tomato Kale Chicken with Pappardelle	193

MAIN COURSES 195

Peppered Pork & Parsnip Bake	196
One-Pan Lamb with Cherry Tomatoes	196
Tomato & Dill Lamb	196
Easy Lamb Stew	197
Creamy Lamb with Pears	197
Juicy Pork Chops	198
Balsamic Lamb with Walnuts	198
Hot Pork Meatballs	198
Peppercorn Pork Chops	199
Orange Lamb with Dates	199
Rosemary Lamb with Broccoli	200
Slow Cooker Pork with Pearl Onions	200
Slow Cooker Pork & Mushroom Stew	200
Saffron Pork with Green Onions	201
White Wine Leg of Lamb	201
Minty Lamb Chops with Bell Peppers	202
Baked Lamb Ribs	202
Jalapeño Lamb	202
Cilantro Lamb	203
Spicy Lamb in Peach Sauce	203
Bell Pepper Pork Chops	204

Lamb with Eggplants	204
Moroccan Lamb Stew	204
Beef & Mushroom Stew	205
Grilled Beef Meatballs	205
Pork Stew with Apricots	206
Lamb & Fig Stew	206
Parsley Pork with Olives & Capers	206
Creamy Pork with Green Sauce	207
Saucy Dill Pork	207
Simple Pork Stew	208
Cheesy Pork Meatloaf	208
Pork with Capers & Ricotta	208
Braised Beef & Vegetable Stew	209
Chili Beef with Zucchini	209

DESSERTS & SNACKS — 211

Apple Tart	212
Fresh Parfait	212
Delicious Peach Pie	213
Simple Brownies	213
Easy Chocolate Cake	214
Apple Pancakes	214
Easy Fudge	215
Black Bean Brownies	215
Banana Cake	216
Chocolate Pudding	216
Coconut Mousse	216
Mango Pudding	217
Rhubarb Pie	217
Fruit Skewers	218
Berries Mix	218
Blueberry Compote	218
Summer Strawberry Stew	219
Lemon Apple Mix	219
Minty Rhubarb Drink	220
Nigella Mango Sweet Mix	220
Blueberry Curd	220
Lemon & Coconut Cream	221
Almond Peach Mix	221
Fruits Stew	222
Easy Pomegranate Mix	222
Black Rice Pudding	222
Peach Stew	223
Coconut Cream	223
Strawberries and Avocado Salad	224
Blueberry Cream	224
Apple Coconut Cupcakes	224
Cinnamon Apples	225
Pumpkin Bars	225
Cold Cashew and Berry Cake	226
Cold Carrot and Mandarins Cake	226
Green Tea Cream	226
Chickpeas and Pepper Hummus	227
Lemony Chickpeas Dip	227
Chili Nuts	228
Protein Bars	228
Red Pepper Muffins	228
Nuts and Seeds Mix	229
Tortilla Chips	229
Kale Chips	230
Potato Chips	230
Peach Dip	230
Cereal Mix	231
Goji Berry Mix	231
Artichoke Spread	232
Avocado Salsa	232
Onion Spread	232
Simple Salsa	233
Spinach Dip	233
Avocado Dip	234
Chives Dip	234
Dill Dip	234
Chickpeas Salsa	235
Cilantro Dip	235
Yogurt and Dill Dip	236
Broccoli Dip	236
Easy Salmon Spread	236

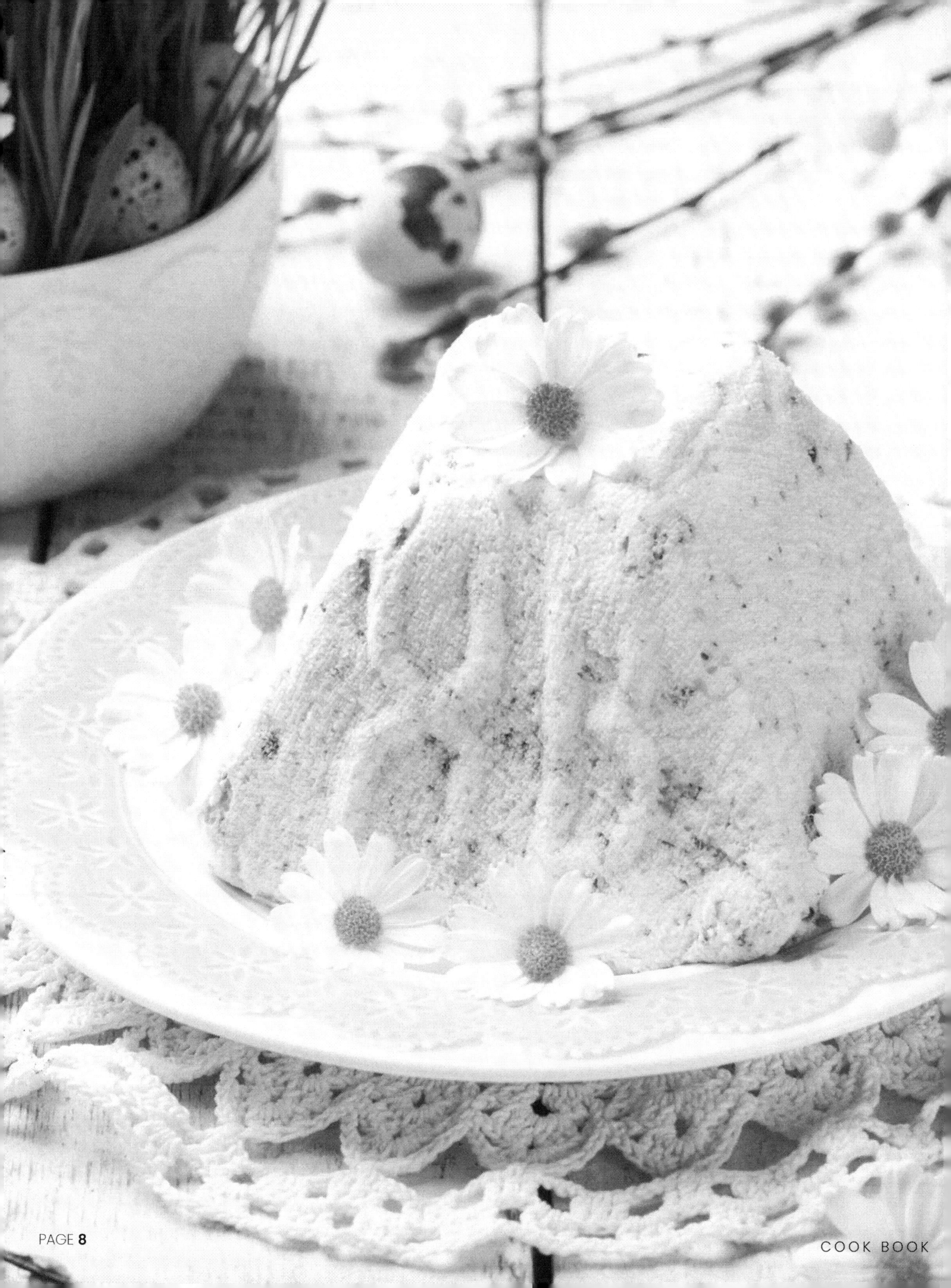

What Is The Mediterranean Diet?

The locus of this diet is centered around fruits and vegetables, healthy fats, and lean protein. The basic principles are as follows:

- Use olive oil as the primary source of fat

- Use an abundance of fruits, vegetables, whole grains, nuts, and legumes

- Consume yogurt and cheese in moderate amount every day

- Fish and lean meat should be consumed in a low amount a few times a week

- Red meat should be consumed rarely and in small portions

- Consume fresh fruit for dessert; foods with added sugar must be eaten only a few times per week

- Wine should be consumed in moderate amounts, preferably with meals

COOK BOOK

Healthy Fats in the Mediterranean Diet

The Mediterranean diet is unique in that it doesn't promote a low-diet eating lifestyle. Instead, it focuses on consuming more healthier fats such as monounsaturated fat and polyunsaturated omega-3 fatty acids and less saturated fats and omega-6 polyunsaturated fatty acids. Healthy fat sources include olive oil, canola oil, soybean oil, flaxseed oil, nuts, and avocados. Animal fats, on the other hand, are dense in saturated fats. Under the Mediterranean diet, 35% to 40% of calories can come from fat.

One of the significant advantages of consuming healthy fat is that, along with protecting your heart, it also makes you feel full for more extended periods. So you are less likely to snack throughout the day and tack on unnecessary weight.

Plant-Based Food in the Mediterranean Diet

Fresh fruits, vegetables, legumes, and whole grains are the anchor of this diet. Those who live in the Mediterranean tend to eat up to ten servings of fruits and vegetables daily. Legumes and whole grains are also staples of this diet. Foods in this group are naturally low in calories and full of essential nutrients, which makes losing weight and staying healthy easy to do.

Some of the plant-based food that is heavily used in this diet includes:

- Legumes : Chickpeas and lentils

- Fruits : Grapes, persimmons, olives, pomegranate, figs, and oranges

- Vegetables : Artichokes, broccoli, asparagus, tomatoes, eggplant, and green beans

- Grains : Wheat, rice, barley, and corn

- Nuts : Pine nuts, almonds, walnuts, and hazelnuts

Herbs and Spices in the Mediterranean Diet

Herbs and spices are chock full of nutrients and jam-packed with flavors and aroma to make the dishes more decadent. Here are the most popular herbs and spices used in the Mediterranean diet:

- Basil : This contains an essential oil called Eugenol that blocks inflammation-causing enzymes. It also contains zeaxanthin, a flavonoid that protects the eyes from harmful UV rays and slows down the formation of macular disease.

- Cilantro : Also known as coriander, cilantro is often added to salads, salsa, and soups to add flavor and for a crunchy texture. It is rich in phytonutrients.

- Cinnamon : Cinnamon is shown to help curb the levels of blood glucose in patients with diabetes. It has an active compound named coumarin, which gives it its anti-clotting and anti-inflammatory properties.

- Dill : This is a fantastic source of antioxidants and calcium, which together help reduce the risk of bone-related diseases and calms intestinal distress.

- Garlic : Garlic is often blamed for bad breath, but research shows that 1200 grams of aged garlic help prevent plaque build-up, lowers cholesterol and blood pressure, and lowers heart disease risk. It contains phytonutrients, which has antiviral and antibacterial properties.

- Lemon : Lemon is a powerful source of Vitamin C, and its juice, zest, and rind are used in pasta, rice, soups, and fish-based dishes.
- Mint : Mint is considered to be a decongestant and is used to treat digestive disorders. It is full of Vitamin A and C, which strengthens the immune system and boosts eye health.

- Pepper : Cayenne, bell pepper, red pepper flakes are all excellent sources of capsaicin, which is a compound that shields against heart disease and inflammation and also boosts metabolism.

- Saffron : Saffron contains a carotenoid named crocus, a precursor to Vitamin A, and helps keep your eyes healthy, immune system robust, and fights against cancer.

- Thyme : Thyme is a powerful source of minerals, such as potassium, which controls blood pressure, and iron, which boosts the formation of red blood cells.

Protein in the Mediterranean Diet

When it comes to protein, there are several days where protein is altogether skipped. When it is consumed, it's done so in moderate quantities and with lots of vegetables. Here are some high-quality protein sources you should consider adding to your diet.

- Fish : Include fishes high in omega-3 fatty acids, such as salmon, halibut, and haddock.
- Legumes : Lentils and beans
- Whole grains : Quinoa
- Nuts and seeds: Hemp seeds, squash and pumpkin seeds, peanuts, almonds, pistachios
- Vegetables : Broccoli and Brussels sprouts

Wine in the Mediterranean Diet

Red wine is allowed in the Mediterranean diet. Those who are not fans of red wine can replace it with juice made from Concord grapes or just eat purple grapes. Red wine contains antioxidants that are derived from flavonoids found in the skin of grapes. Flavonoids are shown to protect the heart by reducing bad cholesterol, increasing good cholesterol, and lowering the risk of blood clot formation. A flavonoid known as resveratrol is shown to inhibit tumor development in certain types of cancer.

Benefits of the Mediterranean Diet

The Mediterranean Diet is popular due to its eclectic array of health benefits that span both the body and mind.

In the body, following the Mediterranean diet is shown to prevent heart disease and strokes by limiting refined and processed food like red meat and breads.

It protects against type 2 diabetes and metabolic syndrome by introducing foods full of fiber, which digests, slows, and prevents huge swings in blood glucose.

The Mediterranean Diet promotes longevity by lowering heart disease and cancer risk. It also keeps you agile because the nutrients you consume through Whole Foods reduces the risk of muscle weakness and general frailty.

In the mind, good cholesterol, balanced blood sugar levels, and improved vascular health, all combined, diminish your risk of developing Alzheimer's and dementia. And the high levels of antioxidants gained from this diet prevents oxidative stress, which in turn significantly lowers your risk of developing Parkinson's disease.

8 Tips to QuickStart your Mediterranean Diet Journey

- Use olive oil for cooking or sautéing your food instead of butter or other oils.
- Eat more salads as your side dish or starter to your main meals as they're naturally high in vegetables.
- Substitute whole grains for pasta, bread, or rice as much as possible.
- Switch fish for red meat at least two times a week
- Limit dairy consumption by buying low-fat yogurt or skim or 1% milk.
- Instead of snacking on chips, crackers with processed dips, try carrots and celery with salsa dips.
- Instead of eating stir-fried meat with rice, try quinoa with stir-fried vegetables.
- Instead of ice cream, snack on fruits for dessert or pudding made with skim milk.
- Limit soda and processed juice. Replace it with sparkling water, plain water, or grape juice.

The Key to Making Mediterranean Diet Work:Embrace Life

Mediterranean diet is not just about eating good food; it's also about living life to the fullest with plenty of physical activity that keeps the heart rate up and pumping and increases muscle strength. Walking is a good exercise that combines aerobic and strength training. Try to walk every day and see if you can walk places instead of always relying on the car.

Get plenty of sunshine and get your family and community involved. Invite them for meals or go on hikes with them. Building and embracing the community and relishing its spirit is a massive part of Mediterranean culture and essential to keep stress at bay. That, combined with its dietary aspect, will help you get the maximum out of the Mediterranean Diet.

The Mediterranean Lifestyle

It's easy to be healthy when you live in a sunny country on the Mediterranean Sea. With the ocean breeze, sunshine, and good wine, how could you be stressed out and lack energy? Part of the Mediterranean Diet means adopting a bit of a vacation-mode attitude, at least for several minutes throughout the day. Here's how:

Slow down at mealtimes.

Time the length of one of your regular family meals. Then, try stretching it out just 10 minutes longer, to include conversation with the folks at your table. And yes, please eat at a table with all TVs, phones, and electronics off. You'll be on your way to the relaxed meal that's a signature of Mediterranean regions.

Savor a glass of wine.

Savoring wine with a meal helps slow down your dinners. Serve wine (it doesn't have to be an expensive bottle) on the nights you have time to appreciate it, or serve it with a leisurely lunch on the weekends. It's customary to enjoy wine only when food is also being served.

Move that body more often.

You could have the healthiest diet in the world, but

without moving your muscles, your body won't be truly fit. Keeping your muscles strong helps prevent injured backs and shoulders and makes it easier to do just about everything. Think of daily physical activity as insurance against aches and pains. It is also an amazing way to relieve stress. Even 10-minute spurts of activity several times throughout the day lead to better health.

Get a good night's sleep. Aim for seven to eight hours of sleep nightly. We can't stress this enough. We know people who have changed their entire lives just by regularly getting enough sleep. Even with the best diet and exercise plan in the world, your body will not work as efficiently without enoug h sleep. Make it a priority.

The Mediterranean Kitchen

You may already have a Mediterranean kitchen and not even know it. There's no need to buy a lot of expensive ingredients, as many Mediterranean staples, like beans, canned tomatoes, and tuna, are probably in your pantry right now.

Pantry Essentials

Olives: If your grocery store has an olive bar (often near the deli department), sample different varieties to find your favorites. Then buy that variety in a jar, as they are usually less expensive than at the olive bar. Start tossing olives into soups, salads, sandwiches, pastas, potatoes, or almost any dish in which you'd use salt.

Beans (canned and dried): You can feed a crowd of 10 with one bag of dried beans, which costs about $1.50. Get in the habit of cooking up one batch a week. Dried lentils cook even faster. You also can't go wrong with any can of beans; drain and rinse them to remove about 40 percent of the sodium.

Nuts and seeds: Go nuts over seeds and nuts. Sprinkle a tablespoon or two over any dish to add flavor, crunch, and a dose of good fats. Almonds, pecans, peanuts, pistachios, walnuts, chia seeds, ground flaxseed, pumpkin seeds, and sesame seeds are all nutrition boosters.

Whole grains and brown rice: Whole grains are the foundation of the Mediterranean Diet. Luckily, delicious whole grains like sorghum, quinoa, spelt, and farro are now easier to find. To begin to enjoy whole grains you might be unfamiliar with, combine the new whole grain with rice.

Pasta: Pasta is a healthy, low-glycemic-index food. (The glycemic index rates how fast a carbohydrate-rich food is digested and affects your blood sugar levels.) The way dried pasta is made actually reduces its glycemic index. To get more fiber in your diet, choose whole-grain pasta more often.

Canned fish: We serve budget-friendly canned tuna or salmon a couple of times a week. (Go for the kind packed in olive oil for extra flavor.) Drain sardines or anchovies and mash into tomato sauce for extra nutrients and richness.

Canned and jarred vegetables: Canned, no-salt tomato products are a pantry necessity—especially because the tomato season is short in most parts of the world. Jarred roasted bell peppers, artichoke hearts, and capers are veggie staples you can use daily while eating the Mediterranean way.

Olive oil and vinegar: If you have these two staples on hand, you can flavor any dish (Deanna has 8 to 10 bottles in her pantry!). We like to use extra-virgin olive oil for cooking and drizzling. It has the most health benefits, and a high enough smoke point to be practical when sautéing. Balsamic vinegar and red wine vinegar are two of our favorites and are typical staples in the Mediterranean Diet.

Kosher or sea salt: You might be surprised to see salt on two dietitians' pantry lists, but remember that the majority of sodium in our diets doesn't come from table salt. That said, the larger grains of these salts means there's less in your measuring spoon, but they still deliver a big flavor punch to dishes.

Grocery Store Guide: How To Shop

Don't follow the old rule that you should only shop the perimeter of the grocery store. Today's supermarkets have Mediterranean Diet staples in every aisle—including the middle ones. While shopping, picture the Mediterranean Diet Pyramid inside your shopping cart: Half your cart should be fruits, vegetables, and plant-based foods, then fill up the rest with seafood, and so on.

Fresh produce section: What's in season? Seasonal fruits and vegetables are usually less expensive. Don't forget fresh herbs: Parsley, cilantro, basil, and mint can be budget-friendly ways to eat more always-in-season greens.

Fish counter: Ask questions. The fishmonger behind the counter is happy to steer you to inexpensive choices; he or she can also be a great source for recipes and cooking tips.

Canned fish aisle: There are lots of new additions here, including packets of tuna and salmon that are ready to eat with a fork. Most of the choices are simple and sustainable. Just pick your favorite or try something new, like sardines.

Frozen food aisle: The frozen food aisle is an ideal place to finish filling your cart with fruit and veggies. In general, frozen fruits and vegetables are just as nutritious as fresh, as they are frozen at the peak of freshness. Choose any vegetable without sauce. We buy frozen fruits to go into every breakfast, from cereal to yogurt. Frozen fish fillets are healthy, convenient choices, and because they're often frozen individually, you can cook just what you need.

Rice and grains aisle: In general, you'll find most whole grains here, in the natural foods aisle, or in the bulk food section. To make sure the grains are whole, search for these words on the Nutrition Facts label: oats, bulgur, wheat berries, rye berries, or whole [name of grain], such as whole wheat. Look for farro, bulgur, quinoa, sorghum, spelt, barley, brown rice (instant and regular), and wild rice without any added flavors or seasonings.

Bulk food section: This area, with foods in open bins, makes food shopping fun. Here's where you can buy small amounts of things to taste, without spending a lot on full packages of whole grains, beans, and dried fruits.

Dairy case: From low-fat to full-fat, we promote eating the type of milk, cheese, or yogurt that you prefer. Products with more fat will have more calories, but we find that they are more filling and flavorful, and often you can use less in a recipe. When it comes to yogurt, we prefer plain, but if you are buying flavored yogurt, compare the amount of added sugar to other flavored yogurts and go with the lowest number. (The total sugar amount on the label also includes the lactose and fructose —those naturally occurring sugars found in dairy and fruit.) Or better yet, buy the plain and add your own fruit.

The Processed Food Puzzle

These days, the term "processed food" is often associated with negative qualities, when in reality, a processed food is any food that has been changed in some way before consumption. This includes all frozen, canned, cooked, or fortified foods. And while there are certainly processed foods we'd recommend eating less of, there are also many staples in the Mediterranean Diet that go through some kind of processing for preservation and food safety, like dried grains, frozen produce, and canned beans.

Typically, the processed foods that are more problematic have long lists of ingredients, including many terms you might not even recognize. Many are high in sodium, saturated fat, artificial flavors, and other undesirable ingredients we want to eat less of and even avoid when possible. When in doubt about a food, check the label for the amount of added sugar, sodium, saturated fat, and extra ingredients.

To help you when shopping, here's a basic list of minimally processed foods that we recommend and a list of overly processed foods to eat less of.

Minimally processed:

- Canned fish
- Dried pasta, grains (without any additional ingredients)
- Frozen fish, vegetables, and fruits
- Plain yogurt
- Extra-virgin olive oil
- Canned beans, vegetables, and fruits
- Bagged produce

Highly processed (depending on the brand, some of these items may be less processed than others):

- Frozen dinners
- Frozen pizzas
- Fast food
- Deli meats, sausage, and bacon
- Salad dressings, condiments, and sauces
- Crackers and chips
- Shelf-stable baked goods

Your Basic Tools

The recipes in this book use basic kitchen equipment you probably already have. Here's a list of the kitchen tools we use most often.

• Chef's knife

• Paring knife

• Two (12-by-18-inch) half sheet pans, also known as rimmed baking sheets (in the recipes, this is what we'll call a large rimmed baking sheet)

• Large (10- or 12-inch) nonstick skillet with a lid, or cast iron skillet (in the recipes, this is what we'll call a large skillet)

• 8-quart covered stockpot for soups and stews (in the recipes, this is what we'll call a large stockpot)

• 4-quart covered saucepan or pot to cook whole grains or vegetables (in the recipes, this is what we'll call a medium saucepan)

• 9-by-13-inch baking pan for roasting vegetables (in the recipes, this is what we'll call a baking pan)

• Meat thermometer

• Ruler

• Kitchen brush

• Microplane zester for grating citrus

• Two mixing bowls: one large and one medium

• Measuring cups and spoons

• Fine mesh strainer for straining citrus juice

• Colander for draining canned beans, pasta, and grains

• Two cutting boards—one for produce and one for meat, poultry, and fish

• Glass containers for food storage and leftovers

• Blender and/or immersion blender

• Food processor

About the Recipes

Friends and family—from novices to experienced cooks—helped us test the recipes in this book. While each of these recipes takes around 30 minutes or less, keep in mind that the prep and cooking times are our best estimates. Different people (and different ovens) do things at different speeds. And we often are prepping ingredients while something is cooking in the oven or on the stove, which is reflected in the cooking times.

We always recommend that you first read the recipe all the way through and get all your ingredients out before diving in. This will ultimately save you time in the kitchen—and make sure your dinner is done in around 30 minutes or less!

If you're cooking for family or guests with varied tastes or special dietary needs, we've got you covered. Look for the following labels:

• Dairy-free

• Nut-free

• Gluten-free

• Egg-free

• Vegetarian

• Vegan

• 5 ingredients (not including water, salt, pepper, oil, and nonstick cooking spray)

• One pot (the recipe can be cooked in a single pot or pan or baking dish)

• Half the time (15 minutes or less from start to finish, including all the prep and cooking)

Remember to always check labels while you shop, though. For example, some ingredients like oats are naturally gluten-free but processed in factories with cross contamination. If gluten or nuts are a concern for you, be sure to look out for labels on packaging before you buy or use anything.

And if you remember only one thing, remember this: The Mediterranean Diet is NOT a strict diet.

It's a pattern of eating based on vegetables, fruits, whole grains, fish, beans, nuts, olive oil, and some dairy and meat. Please swap ingredients in and out of our recipes based on your preferences.

What we mean is, use brown rice if you don't have quinoa. Use spinach if you don't like kale. Almonds will work instead of walnuts. And even though some produce (pineapples), whole grains (wild rice), nuts (pecans), and seafood (salmon) aren't really grown or harvested in the Mediterranean region, that doesn't mean you shouldn't happily swap them into recipes to make them your own.

One last note: Make this book messy! Dog-ear the pages and write notes in the margins. These recipes are a starting place to build your confidence in cooking the Mediterranean way, using what you have on hand and what tastes good to you and your family.

Now, let's get into the kitchen!

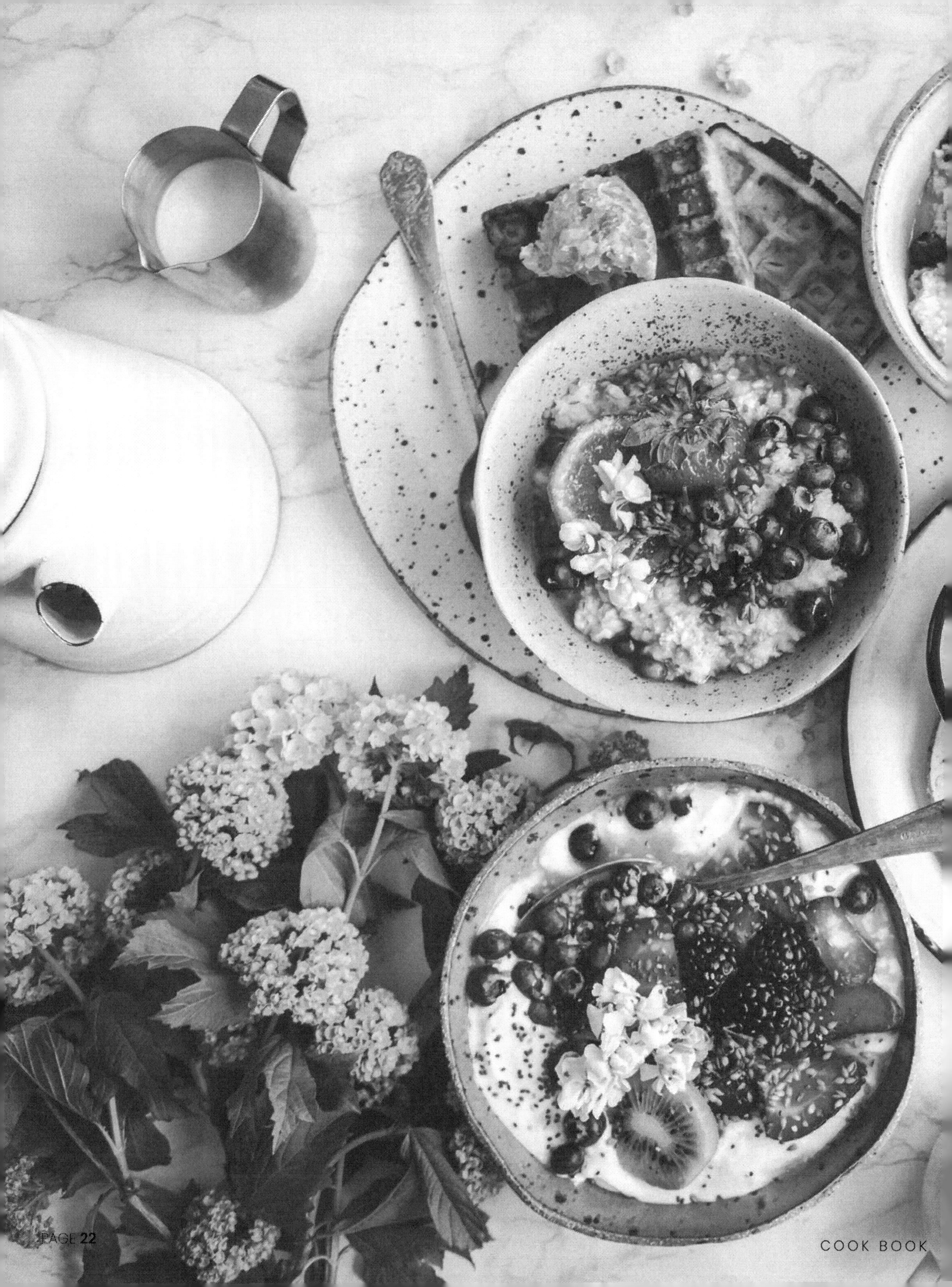

BREAKFAST RECIPES

COOK BOOK

PAGE 23

Pomegranate and Peaches Avocado Toast

Ready in 10 Minutes |Servings: 1|Difficulty: Normal

Nutrition Info: 335Calories, Sodium, 7 mg, Proteins 11 g, Carbohydrates 34g, Fat5 g, Sugars 34 g

INGREDIENTS

DIRECTIONS

1 slice whole grain bread
1/2 avocado
1 tsp ricotta
pomegranate seeds, small handful
honey, drizzle

1. Toast the whole grain bread in the oven or toaster.
2. Spread avocado onto the toast, as smooth or coarse as you prefer.
3. Spread a dollop of ricotta across the avocado.
4. Drizzle a bit of honey over the avocado mixture.
5. Sprinkle pomegranate seeds on top and enjoy.

....

Oatmeal Banana-Nut

Ready in 15 Minutes|Servings: 4 |Difficulty: Normal

Nutrition Info: Calories: 310Calories, 365 mg of sodium, Proteins 11 g, Carbohydrates 42 g, Fiber in the diet 6 g, Fat 9 g

INGREDIENTS

DIRECTIONS

One cup of oats cut with steel
One banana, pureed
1/3 of a cup of walnuts, sliced
Two cups Skim Milk
Two cups of water
1/3 of a cup of honey
Two Cinnamon tsp
1/2 nutmeg tsp
One vanilla extracts tsp
1/2 of a teaspoon of salt

1. Add all ingredients in a slow baking oven. Mix gently, cover, and simmer for eight hours on low heat.
2. Offer on top of added sliced bananas and walnuts.

....

Greek-Style Homemade Yogurt

Ready in 12 Minutes|Servings: 8 (size 1 cup) |Difficulty: Easy

Nutrition Info: Calories: 143, Fat Total 3.5 g, Sodium 159 mg, carbohydrates 19 g, Fiber Diet 0 g, Proteins 18 g

INGREDIENTS

DIRECTIONS

1/2 gallon of 2% milk
One cup of condensed milk (this is voluntary but thickens the yogurt)
1/2 cup live culture of yogurt (can use pure regular yogurt)
Thermometer
Little blanket
For stretching cheesecloth

1. 1. Add milk to a slow cooker. Stir in the milk powder. Heat your milk slowly; Cook till it reaches 180 ° F (approximately 1-2 hours, based on your cooker). Turn the slow cooker off and cool the milk to 110 degrees F. Mix in the live yogurt Culture and mix once completely merged. Wrap the slow cooker (which has been turned Off) to retain the heat inside a blanket. Let's hang there for 6-8 hours.
2. 2. Remove the slow-cooker cover. You may need to soak to make thick, Greek-style yogurt to create from the yogurt, the whey (the substance on top of the cream). Place a number in order to do this; in a colander, layers of cheesecloth. Over a wide cup, put the colander. Add yogurt to the colander and let it drain for a few hours in the refrigerator before it is drained. The continuity you need has been hit. You've got delicious Greek yogurt now!
3. 3. In mason jars (or other containers) pour the yogurt and position in the refrigerator for from 7-10 days.

Casserole for Breakfast

Ready in 13 Minutes| Servings: 8 |Difficulty: Normal

Nutrition Info: 328 Calories, Fat 12 g, sodium 335 mg, potassium 31 g

INGREDIENTS

- Frozen hash browns for 4 cups
- Twelve eggs
- 1/2 cup milk lower in fat
- Ten ounces of Prepared, low-sodium sausage
- Cheddar cheese • 8 ounces, shredded
- Two cloves of Garlic, diced
- One onion strong, minced
- 1/2 bell pepper red, minced
- Black pepper freshly ground

DIRECTIONS

1. Sprinkle with cooking spray on the rim of a slow cooker.
2. Beat the eggs into a big tub. Stir in milk, and mustard, black pepper, and swirl until well mixed.
3. Placed on the bottom of the slow cooker with 1/2 hash browns. Cover with 1/2 of each of them: sausage, bell pepper, Cheese, Garlic, onion. Insert the second layer of browns, sausage rolls, hash browns, bell pepper, Cheese, Garlic, and onion.
4. Place over the layers of the beaten egg. Cover and simmer for 4 to 5 hours or on low heat for 4 to 5 hours. Up to 2 to 3 hours before the eggs are ready.

Almond Butter and Banana Toasts

Ready in 7 Minutes|Serving 1 |Difficulty: Easy

Nutrition Info: 484 Calories, Fat 21 g, sodium 402 mg, potassium 56 g

INGREDIENTS

- 2 slices of 100% whole wheat bread
- Almond butter 2 tbsp
- One tiny banana, cut
- 1/8 cinnamon ground teaspoon

DIRECTIONS

1. Toast the bread and sprinkle almond butter on each piece. On top, place the banana slices and sprinkle them with Cinnamon.

English Muffin with Berries

Ready in 10 Minutes|Serving 1 |Difficulty: Normal

Nutrition Info: Calories 231, Total Fat 4 g, Sodium 270 m, Protein 8 g, Calcium 5%

INGREDIENTS

DIRECTIONS

100 percent English muffin whole wheat, cut in half

One cup of cream cheese and reduced fat

Four strawberries, cut thinly

1/2 cup of crushed blueberries

1. 1. Toast the English halves of muffins. Spread the cream cheese on each toasted half, equally, and cover with the fruit.

....

Healthy English Muffin Lox

Ready in 15 Minutes|Serving 2 |Difficulty: Normal

Nutrition Info: Calories 192, Fat 8 g, Cholesterol 8 mg, Protein 14 g

INGREDIENTS

DIRECTIONS

One 100 percent English muffin whole wheat, cut in half

1/4 of a teaspoon of fresh dill, finely chopped

One-third of a teaspoon of pure lemon juice

Two cups of cream cheese low in fat

One (four-ounce) of water should be wild salmon, no salt added, washed,

Six thin, unpeeled cucumber slices

Six thin Roma tomato slices

Black crushed pepper

1.Toast the English halves of muffins. In a wide tub, meanwhile, chopped dill and lemon juice are mixed equally into the cream. Cheese.

2. Pour the mixture of cream cheese uniformly on each side, Around a toasted muffin.

3. Rinse the salmon under flowing water in order to Drop the canned liquid and then uniformly scoop the fish, Onto the muffin halves in English. If the salmon is too heavy, mash it up. First, with a fork.

4. Cover with slices of cucumber and onion, and sprinkle with pepper to taste.

....

Bowl Protein

Ready in 12 Minutes|Serving 1 |Difficulty: Easy

Nutrition Info: Calories 346, Total Carbohydrate 47 g, Sugars 8 g, Protein 28 g

INGREDIENTS

DIRECTIONS

3/4 cup low-fat cottage cheese

1/2 huge banana, sliced thinly

One tablespoon almond butter

1/4 cup undercooked old-fashioned oats

1. 1. In a little tub, mix all the ingredients combined, and enjoy Instantly.

Berries Deluxe Oatmeal

Ready in 10 Minutes|Serving 2 |Difficulty: Easy

Nutrition Info: Calories 261 Total Fat 10 g, Carbohydrate 63 g, Sugars 9 g, Protein 7 g

INGREDIENTS

- One 1/2 cup pure almond milk unsweetened
- 1/8 Teaspoon Extraction of Vanilla
- 1 cup old-fashioned oats
- 3/4 cup blend of blackberries, blueberries, and coarsely minced Strawberry
- Two tablespoons toasted pecans

DIRECTIONS

1. In a shallow saucepan, heat the almond milk and vanilla on Average warmth.
2. Insert the oats and mix for about four minutes, or before much of the liquid is drained, so the solution starts simmering.
3. Stir in the berries.
4. Scoop 2 bowls of the blend, and finish with toasted pecans.

....

Apples and Cinnamon Oatmeal

Ready in 12 Minutes|Serving 2 |Difficulty: Easy

Nutrition Info: Calories 377, Fat 16 g, Carbohydrate 73 g, Protein 13 g

INGREDIENTS

- One 1/2 cup pure almond milk unsweetened
- Old-fashioned oats for 1 cup
- One big unpeeled apple Granny Smith, cut into cubes
- 1/4 teaspoon Cinnamon ground
- Two tablespoons toasted walnut bits

DIRECTIONS

1. Put the Milk over medium Heat to a boil, then incorporate the oats & apple.
2. Mix until much of the liquid is absorbed, around four minutes.
3. Stir the Cinnamon.
4. Scoop the oatmeal combination into two compartments, then cover with walnuts.

....

COOK BOOK

Oatmeal Energy

Ready in 12 Minutes|Serving 1 |Difficulty: Normal

Nutrition Info: Calories 270, Fat 4 g, Carbohydrate 60 g, Sugars 7 g, Protein 23 g.

INGREDIENTS

DIRECTIONS

1/4 cup water
1/4 cup of milk low in fat
Old-fashioned oats, Half cup
Four Whites Eggs, Pounded
1/8 tsp ground cinnamon
1/8 tsp ground ginger
1/4 cup blueberries

1. In a small pot, heat the water and milk to a boil on a moderate flame.
2. Incorporate the oats, stirring continuously, or until much of the moisture is drained, for around four minutes.
3. Apply the beaten egg steadily, stirring continuously.
4. Bake for the next five minutes just until the eggs are not runny anymore.
5. Through the oatmeal mixture, whisk the Cinnamon and ginger and sweep the mixture into a cup.
6. Cover with berries and immediately serve.

Anna's Organic Granola

Ready in 13 Minutes|Servings 12 (Makes 5-6 cups) |Difficulty: Hard

Nutrition Info: Calories 262, Fat 11 g, Sodium 6 mg, Carbohydrate 52 g, Sugars 12 g, Protein 6 g

INGREDIENTS

DIRECTIONS

Three Cups of Old-Fashioned Oats
1/4 cup Flaxseeds
One cup diced almonds
1/2 tsp ground cinnamon
1/4 tsp ginger ground
1/4 cup brown sugar
1/4 cup honey or maple syrup
1/4 cup extra virgin olive oil
1/2 tsp almond extract
1 cup of golden grapes
A mist of olive oil

1. Preheat the furnace to 250 ° F.
2. In a spacious cup, combine the very first 6 items and blend to integrate effectively.
3. Place the maple syrup or honey, oil, and almond extraction in a different, shallow dish.
4. Drop the wet ingredients into the dry ingredients and combine when there are no longer dry areas, uniformly with a spatula.
5. Put into 2 greased sheet plates. Cook for around 1 hour and 15 minutes, swirling once 15 minutes to produce an even hue.
6. As you whisk, split up bits of granola to the perfect consistency. Remove from the oven, and transfer to a large bowl.
7. Stir in the raisins so they disperse uniformly.

Hot Quinoa and Berries

Ready in 15 Minutes| Serving 2 |Difficulty: Hard

Nutrition Info: Calories 476, Fat 17 g, Carbohydrate 70 g, Sugars 7 g, Protein 14 g

INGREDIENTS

DIRECTIONS

One cup uncooked quinoa
One cup coconut milk unsweetened
One cup of water
1/2 cup of assorted blackberries
Two tablespoons of sliced toasted pecans
Two tsp raw sugar, additional

1. 1.Rinse the quinoa (if not pre-rinsed).
2. 2. Put the quinoa, coconut milk, and water to a simmer on elevated heat in a small covered kettle.
3. 3.Reduce the heat to low and boil for 10 to 15 minutes just until the fluid has been consumed.
4. 4.Cooked quinoa should be mildly al dente; it is able since most of the grains have uncoiled, and you'll see the unwound germ.
5. 5.Let the quinoa sit in the covering pot for about five minutes.
6. 6. Fluff softly with a spoon and sweep into two serving containers, and cover with blackberries, pecans, and honey (if utilizing).

Fruity Milk Parfait

Ready in 7 Minutes|Serving 1 |Difficulty: Easy

Nutrition Info: Calories 388, Fat 212 g, Total Carbohydrate 41 g

INGREDIENTS

One cup simple low-fat Greek yogurt

1/4 cup blueberries

1/4 cup Kiwi fruit cubed

1/4 Cup of cubed strawberries

1 tsp of flaxseed ground meal or flaxseed meal

1/2 cup (or Anna's Homemade Granola) low-calorie granola

DIRECTIONS

1. Scoop half the yogurt into a shallow glass container or parfait tray.

2. Cover with a light coating of blueberries, flaxseed meal, kiwifruit, strawberries, and granola.

3. Layer and top the leftover fruit, flaxseeds, and granola with the leftover yogurt.

....

Yogurt with Banana Almond

Ready in 8 Minutes| Serving 1 |Difficulty: Easy

Nutrition Info: Calories 337, Fat 12 g, Carbohydrate 48 g, Sugars 11 g, Protein 25 g

INGREDIENTS

1 tsp raw, crunchy almond butter, unsalted

3/4 cup of plain Greek low-fat yogurt

1/4 Cup of old-fashioned, undercooked oats

1/2 big, trimmed banana

1/8 tsp cinnamon powder

DIRECTIONS

1. In the oven, melt the almond butter for 15 seconds.

2. Scoop the yogurt into a cup and mix in the almond butter, oats, and bananas.

3. Sprinkle Cinnamon on the highest part.

Open-Faced Sandwich for Breakfast

Ready in 10 Minutes|Serving 1 |Difficulty: Normal

Nutrition Info: Calories per Servings: 310 Kcal,Fats: 19 g ,Carbs: 5 g ,Protein: 25 g

INGREDIENTS

One 1/2 teaspoons of pure quality olive oil
Two egg whites, pounded
Spinach 1/2 cup
Broken black pepper, to satisfy
1 tsp of mustard brown
One strip of 100% entire wheat bread
Two large tomato cuts
One small, low-fat cheddar cheese slice

DIRECTIONS

1. Preheat oven or toaster oven to 400 º F. Warm a smaller Non-adhesive pan over medium flame.

2. Apply the oil to the frying skillet and then add the egg whites when the oil is hot.

3. When frying, crumble the eggs, then introduce the spinach and sprinkle with pepper to taste.

4. Spread the mustard on the bread and insert the tomatoes and the scrambled eggs, and cover with cheese.

5. Warm till the cheese is melted, around two minutes in the oven.

••

Broccoli Omelet

Ready in 8 Minutes|Serving 1 |Difficulty: Normal

Nutrition Info: Calories 493, Fat 41 g, Carbohydrate 6 g, Sugars 0 g, Protein 29 g

INGREDIENTS

Two whites of eggs
One entire egg
2 tablespoons of Pure Olive Oil
1/2 cup broccoli minced
1 big clove of Garlic, chopped
1/8 teaspoon of chili flakes and pepper
1/4 cup low-fat feta cheese
Broken black pepper

DIRECTIONS

1. In a shallow cup, stir in the egg whites and the egg. Heat a small Non-adhesive pan over medium flame. Put 1 tablespoon of oil to the hot skillet, and introduce the broccoli whenever the oil is hot.

2.Cook for Two Minutes until inserting Garlic, flakes of chili pepper, and black flakes, black pepper to try.

3. Cook for two min further, then eliminate the broccoli solution in a large bowl from the pan.

4. Switch the Heat to medium, add the remaining tablespoon of oil and the additional tablespoon of oil,

5.Whenever the oil is hot, add the whisked eggs. When they start to bubble and draw away from the ends, maybe 30 seconds, turn the omelet over, and quickly scoop the broccoli mixture and feta cheese. On one half of the omelet, pull over the omelet, turn off the fire, and shield the pan with a lid for two min.

6.Remove from Heat, coat with feta, and cover till feta is ready.

7.Instantly serve.

Veggie Frittata and Caramelized Onions

Ready in 12 Minutes|Serving 6 |Difficulty: Normal

Nutrition Info: Calories 197, Fat 14 g, Carbohydrate 6 g, Sugars 2 g, Protein 14 g

INGREDIENTS

1 tbsp extra virgin olive oil
One tiny white onion, finely sliced
1/4 tsp brown sugar
1/8 tsp crushed black pepper
FRITTATA
2-3 tbsp of Organic Olive Oil
1 1/2 cups Sawed zucchini
1 clove, Garlic, minced
One cup of cremini mushrooms cut finely
2-3 tbsp of fresh basil thinly sliced
1 tbsp sliced fresh parsley or 1 tsp dry parsley
Spinach in two cups
Four complete eggs
Five Egg Whites
1/2 a cup of 1% milk
1/2 cup low-fat pepper jack cheese shredded
1/8 tsp sea salt
Broken black pepper
Heat up the furnace to 350 degrees F.

DIRECTIONS

1. To caramelize the onions, warm a medium saucepan over Reasonable temperature.
2. Introduce the oil and whenever the oil is hot, incorporate the onion, sugar, and pepper.
3. Just let onion "sweat," pushing it to avoid burning once every moment, before light brown and softened, perhaps ten minutes.
4. Switch off the heat and protect the pan. When going to serve,
5. Begin by warming a big skillet over medium heat to begin the frittata. And then the oil is added.
6. Toss in the zucchini, and bake for around one minute. Insert the Garlic, and fry 2 to 3 more minutes before adding the mushrooms, basil, and parsley.
7. Cook the veggies for another minute, spray the vegetables with salt and pepper (the mushrooms will produce water and are not tan. If you add the salt Straight away). Comb, turn the heat off and add the spinach in a big cup, stir together all the eggs, egg whites, milk, shredded cheese, salt, and pepper.
8. Sprinkle a 9-inch circular cake pan with olive oil spray. Pour in the sautéed components, and then the egg mixture.
9. Put the pan on the middle rack of the cooker, and bake for 20 to 25 minutes, or when it comes out of a knife implanted in the center clean. (Eggs will easily overcook, so keep a close watch!)

Mediterranean Scramble Eggs

Ready in 12 Minutes|Serving 1 |Difficulty: Easy

Nutrition Info: Calories 424, Fat 37 g, Carbohydrate 5 g, Sugars 1 g, Protein 21 g

INGREDIENTS

Two tablespoons of Pure Olive Oil Extra

1/8 cup red onion minced

One Garlic with a moderate clove, diced

1/4 cup of red bell pepper cut

1/4 of a cup of rinsed and discarded canned artichoke hearts, minced

Two white eggs

One egg as a whole

1/8 dried oregano tsp

1/8 Smashed Black Pepper Tsp

1/8 cup of feta cheese with reduced fat

DIRECTIONS

1. On medium fire, heat a mini non-stick pan.

2. Apply oil to the warm pan and introduce the onion and Garlic while the oil is hot. Cook for 1 minute Prior to inserting the strips of bell pepper and artichoke, hearts. Sauté the veggies for a further three minutes, just until the bell pepper is smooth, and the onion is translucent.

3. In a small pan, stir the egg whites and eggs in a container and season with the oregano and black pepper.

4. Drop in the eggs and blend them with a combination of Spatula. Run for 3 to 4 minutes, or till no more eggs are runny.

5. It's going to melt. Instantly serve.

COOK BOOK

Veggie Omelet

Ready in 10 Minutes|Serving 1 |Difficulty: Normal

Nutrition Info: Calories 279, Fat 20 g, Carbohydrate 6 g, Sugars 0.8 g, Protein 20 g

INGREDIENTS

DIRECTIONS

- One tablespoon of Pure Olive Oil Extra
- 1/4 of a cup of coarsely sliced broccoli
- Two tablespoons of red onion minced
- One clove, Garlic, minced
- Sawed 1/4 cup zucchini
- Two eggs whites
- One egg as a whole
- 1/8 cup low-fat cheddar cheese sliced
- 1/8 tsp salt from the sea
- 1/8 Smashed Black Pepper Tsp

1. Over low pressure, heat a medium-sized non-stick bowl, and add oil as the pan is heated.
2. Insert the broccoli whenever the oil is hot.
3. Prior to introducing the Onion, Garlic, &zucchini, Sauté for between 3 and 4 minutes. Stir in a little mug, Egg whites and entire eggs combined, and salt seasoning orchili.
4. Switch the Heat to low and add the eggs to the Container of vegetables to make sure that the container is angled so that the eggs wrap the vegetables uniformly.
5. Switch the Heat off after 30 seconds, Rotate the omelet, and spread half of the omelet with the cheese.
6. Fold the other half over the cheese, and shield the pan with a Lid. Let it steam, or till the melty cheese, for 1 to 2 minutes.
7. Instantly serve.

···

Apple Oatmeal with Cinnamon

Ready in 7Minutes|Servings: 8 |Difficulty: Easy

Nutrition Info: Calories 312, Protein 9 g, Carbs 60 g, Fat 7.5 g, Sugar 23 g.

INGREDIENTS

DIRECTIONS

- 2 cups oats steel cut
- Water Eight cups
- Cinnamon • 1 teaspoon.
- 1/2 tsp of allspice
- Nutmeg 1/2 tsp
- 1/4 cup of sugar brown
- 1 teaspoon extraction of vanilla
- Two apples, sliced
- 1 cup of raisins
- 1/2 cup of unsalted walnuts, fried, diced

1. Spray the non-stick cooking spray on a slow cooker.
2. Insert all the slow cooker items except for the walnuts. Mix enough to make a paste.
3. Set the slow cooker to a low temperature and cook for eight hours.
4. Offer with diced walnuts.

···

Egg White Omelet with Vegetables

Ready in12 Minutes|Servings: 2 |Difficulty: Hard

Nutrition Info: Calories: 145, Sodium: 77 mg, Protein: 8.5 g, Carbs: 19 g, Fat: 4.5 g

INGREDIENTS

DIRECTIONS

- Six white eggs
- One spoonful of water
- Two tablespoons of olive oil
- 1/2 onion yellow, sliced
- 1 tomato, which is sliced
- 2-3 stalks of asparagus, sliced into small parts
- 3-4 cut mushrooms

1. In a medium cup, whisk the egg whites, insert a tablespoon of water, and stir. With a fork until it mixes well.
2. Heat 1 teaspoon of oil in a medium-sized skillet over medium-high heat. Adding Onions, tomatoes, asparagus, and mushrooms and sauté until the vegetables are tender approximately 3-4 minutes. Remove from pan and dismissed.
3. Introduce another teaspoon of oil to the pan and let itheat for a minute or two. Bring beaten eggs to pan, spinning pan as required, so eggs cover the complete pan. Let eggs established along the edges of the pan, it should only take a few moments if the pan is warm enough. Utilizing spatula, slide eggs away from the edges of the pan and flip the pan to enable more egg mixture to circulate to the pan surface. Reiterate until eggs are almost finished but still soft in the middle.
4. Introduce vegetable blend to the middle of the omelet. Fold one side of omelet over Seasonings. Slide onto a plate. Voila, it is safe to serve.

Green Fruity Smoothie

Ready in 12 Minutes|Servings: 1 |Difficulty: Normal

Nutrition Info:Calories: 235, Sodium: 64 mg, Protein: 5 g, Carbs: 56 g, Fat: 1.5 g, Sugar: 3.7 g

INGREDIENTS

- Two cups of new leafy spinach
- One banana medium, stripped
- Strawberries 7-8, chopped
- 1/2 of a cup of orange juice
- 1 cup of ice smashed

DIRECTIONS

1. In a blender, put all components and mix thoroughly.
2. In a tall glass, serve.

Breakfast Salad with Fruit and Yogurt

Ready in 15 Minutes|Servings: 6 |Difficulty: Hard

Nutrition Info: Calories: 190, Sodium: 118 mg, Protein: 4 g, Carbs: 40 g, Fat: 1 g.

INGREDIENTS

- 2 cups of water
- 1/4 of a teaspoon of salt
- 3/4 cup of brown rice fast cooking
- 3/4 Bulgur cup
- One big, hulled and diced apple
- One big, hulled and minced pear
- One orange, peeled, cut into pieces
- 1 dry cup of cranberries
- 1 box (8 ounces) of Greek style low-fat or non-fat yogurt, simple

DIRECTIONS

1. Heat water over high heat in a big pot until it boils.
2. Integrate salt, rice, and bulgur into the mixture. Reduce the heat, cover, and simmer to l for ten minutes. Remove from the Heat and encourage to sit for 2 minutes, covered.
3. Place the grains in a large bowl and chill in the fridge until they are chilled.
4. Let the cold grains out of the freezer. Attach strawberries, pears, bananas, bananas, and more. Cranberries that are dry. Fold and blend softly in the yogurt until the grains and fruit are set. Wrapped completely.
5. In bowls, serve.

COOK BOOK

PAGE **33**

Pumpkin Pancakes Spiced

Ready in 10 Minutes|Servings: 10 |Difficulty: Hard

Nutrition Info: Calories: 150Sodium: 360 mg, Protein: 6.6 gCarbs: 32 gFat: 2 g

INGREDIENTS

Two cups of total wheat flour
Two teaspoons of flour for baking
One teaspoon of soda for baking
One cinnamon teaspoon
1/2 tsp nutmeg field
1/2 teaspoon ginger ground
1/4 cup of sugar brown
1 yolk egg
One canned pumpkin cup
Two spoonfuls of coconut oil
Skim milk Two cups
Two whites of egg

DIRECTIONS

1. Flour mixture, baking powder, baking powder, and baking soda together in a mixing cup. Nutmeg, Cinnamon, and ginger.

2. Blend the brown sugar, egg yolk, pumpkin, and egg yolk together in another dish.Stir the Milk.

3. Pour the milk mixture with the dry ingredients into a pan.Mix until just Merged. Do not stir too much.

4. In a pan, pound the egg whites until smooth. Fold whites of eggs into pancake Batter.

5. Over moderate heat fire, Heat a non-stick grill pan or wide skillet. Spray with non-stick cooking.

6. When the griddle is heated, 1/4 cup of ladle batter is applied to the skillet. Cook for a while before the batter begins to boil, flip, and cook until browned gently.

Muffins of Lemon-Zucchini

Ready in 10 Minutes| Servings: 12 muffins |Difficulty: Normal

Nutrition Info: Calories per Servings: 310 Kcal,Fats: 19 g ,Carbs: 5 g ,Protein: 25 g

INGREDIENTS

All-purpose flour • 2 cups
1/2 of a cup of sugar
1 tsp flour for baking
1/4 of a teaspoon of salt
1/4 cinnamon teaspoon
1/4 cup of nutmeg
1 cup zucchini shredded
3/4 cup milk that is nonfat
Olive oil, 2 teaspoons
Lemon juice for 2 tablespoons
egg
Non-stick mist for cooking

DIRECTIONS

1. Preheat the oven to 400 º F. By spray gently, ready the muffin tray or cooking spray or muffin liner.

2. Integrate the flour, sugar, baking powder, salt, Cinnamon, etc. in a blending cup with nutmeg.

3. Integrate the zucchini, milk, oil, lemon juice, and egg in a different dish. Stir well.

4. Apply the zucchini solution to the combination of flour. Stir before they're all mixed. Do not Stir over.

5. Onto packed muffin cups, add batter. Bake for 20 minutes or until lightly browned.

English Muffin Breakfast

Ready in 8 Minutes|Serving 1 |Difficulty: Normal

Nutrition Info: (1 serving) 166 calories, 21 g protein, 17 g carbohydrates, 2 g fat, 2 g fiber, 8 mg

INGREDIENTS

1/2 English muffin whole-wheat

One piece of lowered-fat (2% milk) Swiss cheese, cut into pieces to suit the muffin Olive oil in a sprayer with pumps

1/2 cup of liquid egg replacement seasoned

1 1/2 teaspoons of coarsely diced (green part only) scallions

DIRECTIONS

1. Toast the English muffin in a broiler or microwave toaster. Switch the toaster off

2. Cover the muffin with slices of cheese and leave to stand till the cheese is Started to melt by Heat generated for approximately 30 seconds. Move to a dish.

3. In the meantime, brush the oil with a small non-stick skillet and cook over medium heat.

4. Apply the egg substitute and cook for about 15 seconds before the edges are fixed.

5. Using a heat-resistant spatula, raise the sides of the replacement for the egg so that the uncooked liquid underneath will flow. Keep cooking, raising the edges roughly every 15 Seconds before the egg combination is ready, around a total of 1 1/2 minutes. Using your spatula,

6. In order to produce a rugged "patty," fold the sides of the beaten egg into the core 3 inches wide, approx.

Tartine with Strawberries and Cream Cheese

Ready in 10 Minutes|Serving 1 |Difficulty: Hard

Nutrition Info: (1 serving) 167 calories, 9 g protein, 27 g carbohydrates, 3 g fiber, 4 mgCholesterol.

INGREDIENTS

One whole-grain bread slice

Two tablespoons of fat-free, spreadable cream cheese

Two big crewed and chopped strawberries

Honey for 1 teaspoon (optional)

DIRECTIONS

1. In a toaster, toast the bread.

2. Layer with the cream cheese and finish with the cream cheese on top with strawberries.

Broccoli and Pepper Jack Omlet

Ready in 10 Minutes | Serving of 1 | Difficulty: Normal

Nutrition Info: (1 serving) 145 calories, 18 g protein, 5 g carbohydrates, 4 g fat, 1 g fiber

INGREDIENTS

- In a pump sprayer, olive oil
- 1/2 cup of liquid egg substitution seasoned
- One lowered-fat (2% milk) pepper Jack cheese cut, torn into a few 1/4 cup bits
- Broccoli (defrosted frozen broccoli is fine), fried and sliced, heated in a microwave,

DIRECTIONS

1. Sprinkle a small non-stick skillet over medium heat with oil and Heat. Add the eggs, then
2. Replace them and cook for about 15 seconds before the edges are set. Use a heatproof spatula
3. Raise the edges of the egg substitute so that the uncooked fluid will flow below.
4. Keep cooking, raising the sides every 15 seconds or so, till the omelet is set around 1 1/2 minutes overall.
5. Distance away from the Heat. Disperse over the top of the rest of the cheese and broccoli Omelet. Marginally turn the pan and use the spatula to make the omelet fold again and again and in thirds. (From the Heat of the omelet, the cheese will melt.)
6. Slide out. Put on a tray, and then serve.

Granola Make It Your Way

Ready in 7 Minutes | Servings: 10 | Difficulty: Normal

Nutrition Info: (1 serving) 165 calories, 3 g protein, 35 g carbohydrates, 2.5 g fat, 3 g fiber, 0 mg cholesterol

INGREDIENTS

- 1/4 cup of medium brown sugar, wrapped
- Two spoonsful of water
- One tablespoon oil for vegetables
- One cinnamon ground teaspoon
- One tsp maple or vanilla extract flavoring
- Four cups of old-fashioned oats (rolled)
- One cup of medium grapes
- 1/2 cup of dates chopped
- 1/2 cup of milk, fat-free, for serving
- Preheat the furnace to 300 °F.

DIRECTIONS

1. Stir the brown sugar, water, oil, Cinnamon, and maple together in a wide dish.
2. Flavoring till it dissolves the sugar. Insert the oats and blend once covered slightly. On a wide cookie sheet, spread uniformly.
3. Bake, mix regularly, and push the toasted sides into the middle of the Granola, for about 40 minutes, till the oats are uniformly crisp. Remove that from the oven and mix in the dates and raisins. Enable it to cool fully.
4. Stock in an airtight place Up to 2 weeks in a jar.
5. Chuck 1/2 cup of granola into a container for each portion and apply milk.

Oatmeal with Apple and Spice

Ready in 12 Minutes | Serving 1 | Difficulty: Normal

Nutrition Info: (1 serving without milk) 190 calories, 5 g protein, 39 g carbohydrates, 2.5 g fat.

INGREDIENTS

- One sweet, trimmed, hulled apple, like Gala or Golden Delicious, and cut to 1/2-inch
- Dice 2/3 cups of water
- 1/3 cup (rolled) old-fashioned oats
- Pinch of Cinnamon Ground
- Chopped fresh nutmeg pinch
- A couple of grains of kosher salt
- 1/2 cup of milk, fat-free, for serving

DIRECTIONS

1. Integrate the apples, water, oats, Cinnamon, nutmeg, and salt in a shallow saucepan.
2. Under moderate flame, bring to a simmer, turn the heat down to minimum, and cap. Simmer for about four minutes before the oats are tender.
3. In a 1-quart microwave-safe dish, mix the apple, water, Cinnamon, oats, nutmeg, and salt. Using plastic wrap and microwave on maximum power for about four minutes before the oats are tender.
4. Carefully reveal, mix, let it stand for 1 minute.
5. To a bowl, move the oatmeal, drop in the milk, and serve.

Whole-Wheat Strawberry Pancakes-Maple Compote

Ready in 6 Minutes|Servings 6 |Difficulty: Easy

Nutrition Info: (1 serving: 2 pancakes with compote) 267 calories, 8 g protein, 45 g carbohydrates, 7 g fat, 3 g fiber, 34 mg

INGREDIENTS

Compote
Fresh strawberries, one pound (1 quart) cored and finely sliced 1/4 cup Maple Syrup
Pancakes
One cup of pastry flour whole-wheat
1/2 cup all-purpose flour superfine
Sugar for 1 tsp
1 1/2 tsp of powder for baking
1/4 kosher salt tsp
1 1/2 cups of low-fat (1%) milk
1 huge egg plus 2 large white eggs
In a pump sprayer, Two teaspoons of canola or corn oil and more

DIRECTIONS

1. Compote: In a moderate bowl, combine the strawberries and maple syrup.
2. Let the strawberries stay at room temperature to allow the fluids to be released at ambient temperature. A minimum of 1 hour and up to four hours.
3. To produce the pancakes: preheat the 200 ° F furnace. In a medium bowl, blend the mixture with the Full-wheat pastry flour, unbleached flour, sugar, salt, and baking powder.
4. Mix the milk, egg and egg whites, and the 2 tbsp Oil. Drop in the dry ingredients and mix until they are just blended.
5. Over medium-high fire, Heat a grill pan (ideally non-stick). Sprinkle it with some oil.
6. For each pancake, add 1/4 cup of the batter onto the grill pan. Cook till the top is finished.
7. Each pancake's surface is coated with a bubble for around two minutes. Flip Up With a large spatula, pancakes, and cook for a few minutes until the lower parts are Golden brown, 1 minute longer, approximately.
8. To a baking tray, move the pancakes and keep the leftover pancakes hot in the oven before making them.

Blueberries and Yogurt Cornmeal Waffles

Ready in 10 Minutes|Servings 8 |Difficulty: Normal

Nutrition Info: (1 serving) 233 calories, 9 g protein, 38 g carbohydrates, 5 g fat, 2 g fiber

INGREDIENTS

One cup all-purpose unbleached flour
One cup of cornmeal that really is yellow
Sugar 2 teaspoons
1 1/2 tsp of powder for baking
1/4 kosher salt teaspoon
1 3/4 cups of low-fat (1%) milk
1 tbsp of butter that is unsalted, melted
1 tbsp canola or corn oil, plus further in a pump sprayer,
Two major egg whites
Two cups plain low-fat yogurt for serving, at room temperature,
Two (6-ounce) blueberry containers (approx. 2 2/3 cups), at ambient temperature, for serving.

DIRECTIONS

1. Preheat the furnace to 200 ° F. Preheat a waffle iron non-stick as per the Directions from the maker.
2. In a big bowl, stir together all the flour, cornmeal, sugar, baking powder, and salt.
3. Mix together milk, melted butter, and the 1 tablespoon oil in a small bowl Drop in the dried ingredients and mix with a wooden spoon till the products are dry.
4. Just slightly mixed with flour streaks; must not overmix.
5. Pull the egg whites with an electric stick blender in a separate bowl on high Speed only till stiff, and not dry, peaks.
6. Into the batter, bring the whites. Spray oil on the waffle iron. (Don't use non-stick spray with aerosol.) (Don't use non-stick spray with aerosol.) Pour 1 Cup of batter into the waffle iron (the exact quantity depends on the scale of the waffle iron) cover the iron and cook according to the manufacturer's instructions before is the waffle goldenbrown.
7. From the iron, cut the waffle, move to a baking tray and keep the oven warm when preparing the Residual waffles.
8. Split the squares into waffles. Stack 2 waffle squares on a plate for each serving.
9. Cover with 1/4 cup of the yogurt and 1/3 cup of the blueberries, then serve Instantly.

COOK BOOK

Banana-berries smoothie

Ready in10 Minutes|Servings 1 |Difficulty: Normal

Nutrition Info: (1 serving without sweetener) 180 calories, 8 g protein, 33 g carbohydrates, 2 gfat, 3 g fiber

INGREDIENTS

DIRECTIONS

1/2 mature banana, frozen ideally

1/2 cup of fresh blueberries or frozen ones

1/2 cup of low-fat (1/%) milk

1/2 cup low-fat plain yogurt

1/4 tsp extract of vanilla

1 tbsp of agave nectar from amber (optional)

1.Slice and cut the banana into pieces.

2. Purée all products, such as the Sweetener (if used), when creamy, in a processor.

3.Toss in a high glass and serve Instantly.

....

Smoothie of Chocolate-Peanut Butter

Ready in 15 MinutesServings 2 |Difficulty: Normal

Nutrition Info: (1 serving) 250 calories, 13 g protein, 31 g carbohydrates, 11 g fat, 5 g fiber.

INGREDIENTS

DIRECTIONS

One ripe banana, at least overnight, preserved

2/3cup of low-fat (1%) milk

2/3cup low-fat plain yogurt

Crunchy peanut butter 2 tbsp

Two teaspoons of cocoa powder unsweetened

One tablespoon of agave nectar from amber (optional)

Four cubes of ice

1.Slice and cut the banana into pieces.

2.Purée the bananas in a mixer with the milk, yogurt, peanut butter, sugar substitute (if used), cocoa powder, and ice cubes.

3.Load in two large glasses and serve right away.

....

Kale and Apple Smoothie

Ready in 8Minutes|Servings 1 |Difficulty: Easy

Nutrition Info: (1 serving) 171 calories, 5 g protein, 19 g carbohydrates, 10 g fat, 5 g fiber.

INGREDIENTS

DIRECTIONS

1 cup of kale leaves, stemmed and loosely packed, well washed

1/2 of Jonathan or Gala's sweet fruit, cored and coarsely chopped

1/3 cup vinegar apple

2 spoonsful of sunflower seeds

Six cubes of ice

Eight leaves of healthy mint

1.In a blender, puree all the ingredients until creamy.

2. Sprinkle in a high glass and serve Instantly.

Lassi mango

Ready in 10 Minutes|Servings 1 |Difficulty: Normal

Nutrition Info: (1 serving) 235 calories, 13 g protein, 47 g carbohydrates, 1 g fat, 3 g fiber

INGREDIENTS

DIRECTIONS

One ripe, pitted, sliced, coarsely chopped mango 1/2 cup

Non-fat plain yogurt

1/2 cup of milk free from fat

Three cubes of ice

Ground cardamom pinch (optional)

1. Purée the cubes of mango, yogurt, milk, and ice until soft.
2. Pour into a Long glass. Spray with the cardamom, if using. Serve Instantly.

Papaya and Coconut Breakfast Shake

Ready in 11 Minutes|Servings 2|Difficulty: Normal

Nutrition Info: 158 calories, 8 g protein, 26 g carbohydrates, 3 g fat, 2 g fiber, 7 mg.

INGREDIENTS

DIRECTIONS

One ripe, seeded, peeled papaya and cut into 1-inch chunks

One cup low-fat plain yogurt

One cup of water with coconut (not coconut milk)

Two spoonsful of wheat germ

1/2 teaspoon sweetener with zero calories (optional)

1. In a processor, purée all materials, such as the sweetener (if used).
2. Pour in 2 large glasses and serve them.

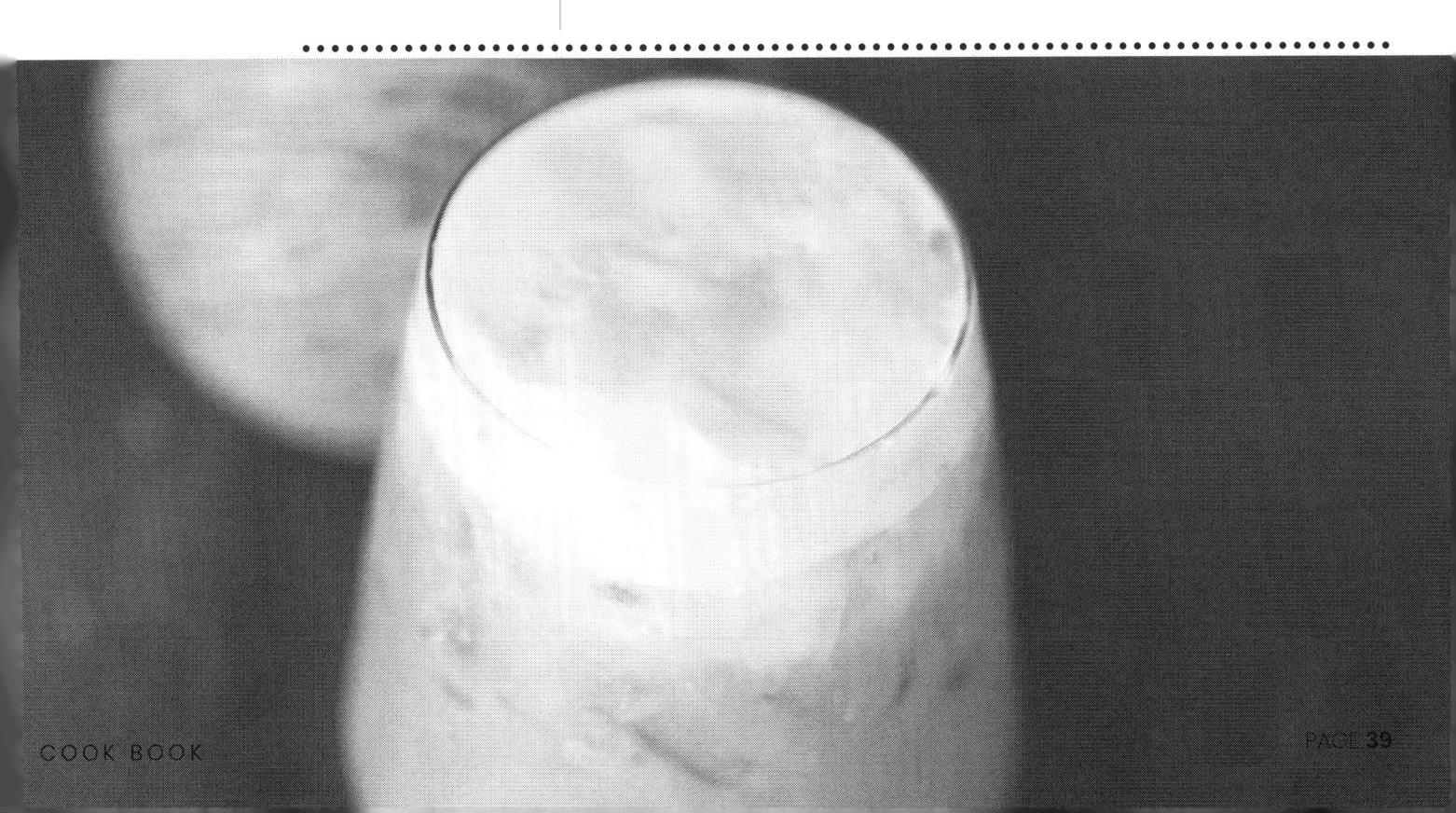

Cappuccino At-Home

Ready in 10 Minutes | Servings 2 | Difficulty: Hard

Nutrition Info: (1 serving) 135 calories, 10 g protein, 17 g carbohydrates, 2 g fat, 0 g fiber

INGREDIENTS

One cup of milk that is low-fat (1%) or fat-free
Three spoonfuls of ground espresso beans

DIRECTIONS

1. Heat the milk over moderate flame in a small saucepan until it steams. (Or warmth in a Microwave oven for approximately 1 min on elevated.)
2. In the meantime, bring cool water to the base of the coffeepot Up to the steam vent.
3. To the basket, transfer the coffee beans screw it to the peak. Take to a high-temperature boiling and cook till the coffee has quit sputtering underneath the cover via the longitudinal spout.
4. Remove that from the Temperature Heat.
5. In a blender, pour the hot milk and process once gooey.
6. Split the coffee into Two coffee cups. Spoon the same amount of milk from the blenderto Cap the coffee with the leftover milk, then pour it in. Serve it warm.

Green Tea Gingered

Ready in 12 Minutes | Servings 1 | Difficulty: Easy

Nutrition Info: (1 serving) 2 calories, 0 g protein, 1 g carbohydrates, 0 g fat, 0 g fiber

INGREDIENTS

One ripe banana, at least overnight, preserved
2/3 cup of low-fat (1%) milk
2/3 cup low-fat plain yogurt
Crunchy peanut butter 2 tbsp
Two teaspoons of cocoa powder unsweetened
One tablespoon of agave nectar from amber (optional)
Four cubes of ice

DIRECTIONS

Two strips of qtr.-size unpeeled fresh ginger
3/4 cup of water
One Green Teabag

Directions:
1. Inside a small pan, place the ginger and knock the pieces with the edge of a Spoon of wood.
2. Include the water and over high temperature, bring to a simmer.
3. To a cup, insert a teabag. With ginger, pour the hot water in. Let 2 to 3 minutes for steep.
4. Take away the ginger and the teabag, using only a spoon.
5. Drink it hot.

Crepes Buckwheat

Ready in 15 minutes | Servings 6 | Difficulty: Normal

Nutrition Info: Serving: 122 calories, 5.7g protein, 211.g carbohydrates, 2.2g fat, 2g fiber,

INGREDIENTS

One cup flour of buckwheat
1/3 cup of whole-grain flour
One beaten egg
One cup of skim Milk
One teaspoon of olive oil
1/2 tsp cinnamon ground

DIRECTIONS

1. Mix and match all the items in the blending bowl and whisk until Have a batter that's consistent.
2. Warm the non-stick pan for three minutes over high temperature.
3. Place a small amount of batter with the aid of the ladle. And straighten the skillet in the style of a crepe.
4. For 1 min, bake it and turn that on the other side. Just cook it for 30 Extra seconds.
5. With the leftover batter, repeat the previous procedure.

Muffins with Carrots

Ready in 10 minutes | Servings: 5 | Difficulty: Hard

Nutrition Info: Calories 212, fat 3, fiber 6, carbs 14, protein 6

INGREDIENTS

- One and 1/2 cups of whole wheat flour
- 1/2 a cup of stevia
- 1 tsp powder for baking
- 1/2 cinnamon teaspoon powder
- 1/2 tsp of soda for baking
- 1/4 cup of natural juice of apples
- Olive oil about 1/4 cup
- 1 single egg
- Fresh cranberries 1 cup
- Two carrots, grated
- Ginger 2 tsp, brushed
- 1/4 cup of chopped pecans
- Spray for cooking

DIRECTIONS

1. Combine the flour and the stevia in a big bowl, baking powder, baking soda, and Cinnamon and mix properly.
2. Include apple juice, oil, cranberries, carrots, cranberries, ginger, and pecans. But very well shake.
3. Gunk a cooking spray muffin pan, split the muffin mixture, put it in the oven, and bake it for thirty min at 375 ° Fahrenheit
4. Split among plates the muffins and serve for breakfast. Love!

Oatmeal Pineapple

Ready in 10 minutes |Cook time: 25 minutes| Servings: 4 |Difficulty: Normal

Nutrition Info: Calories 211, fat 2, fiber 4, carbs 14, protein 6

INGREDIENTS

- Old-fashioned oats with 2 cups
- 1 cup of sliced walnuts
- 2 cups of cut into cubes pineapple
- 1 tablespoon of grated ginger,
- Two cups of milk that is non-fat
- Two Eggs
- Stevia 2 teaspoons
- 2 tsp extracts of vanilla

DIRECTIONS

1. Integrate the oats with the pineapple, walnuts, and ginger in a dish. Mix and split into Four ramekins.
2. Integrate the Milk with the eggs, stevia, and vanilla in a mug, shake well and pour over the blend of oats.
3. Put it in the oven and bake it for 25 minutes at 400 ° Fahrenheit
4. For breakfast, serve. Love!

Muffins with Spinach

Ready in 10 minutes |Servings: 6 |Difficulty: Normal

Nutrition Info: Calories 155, fat 10, fiber 1, carbs 4, protein 10

INGREDIENTS

Six Eggs
1/2 cup milk that is non-fat
1 cup of low fat, collapsed cheese
Spinach 4 ounces
1/2 cup red pepper roast, minced
Prosciutto Two ounces, sliced
Spray cooking

DIRECTIONS

1. Integrate the eggs with the milk, cheese, spinach, and red spinach in a dish. Mix well with pepper and prosciutto.
2. Oil a cooking spray muffin tray, split the muffin mix, put them in the oven, and bake for thirty min at 350 ° Fahrenheit
3. Split the plates and serve them for breakfast. Enjoy!

....

Breakfast Blend for Chia Seeds

Ready in 8 hours | Servings: 4 |Difficulty: Normal

Nutrition Info: Calories 283, fat 12, fiber 3, carbs 13, protein 8

INGREDIENTS

Old-fashioned oats with 2 cups
Four tablespoons of Seeds of Chia
Four tablespoons of sugar from coconut
THREE cups of coconut milk
1 lemon zest tsp, grinded
Blueberries 1 cup

DIRECTIONS

1. Integrate the oats with the chia seeds, sugar, milk, lemon, and chia seeds in a cup. Mix the zest and blueberries, split them into cups, and keep them in the fridge. For eight hours.
2. For breakfast, serve. Enjoy!

....

Fruit Dishes for Breakfast

Ready in 10 minutes | Servings: 2 |Difficulty: Easy

Nutrition Info: Calories 182, fat 2, fiber 4, carbs 12, protein 6

INGREDIENTS

One mango cup, chopped
One sliced banana
Pineapple, 1 cup, chopped
One cup of milk with almonds

DIRECTIONS

1. Integrate the mango with almond milk banana, pineapple, and Stir, split into tiny bowls and offer for breakfast. Enjoy!

Pumpkin Cookies for Breakfast

Ready in 10 minutes |Servings: 6|Difficulty: Normal

Nutrition Info: Calories 281, fat 12, fiber 3, carbs 14, protein 6

INGREDIENTS

- Two cups of flour of whole wheat
- Old-fashioned oats for 1 cup
- One teaspoon of soda for baking
- One pumpkin pie spice teaspoon
- Pumpkin puree for 15 ounces
- One cup of melted coconut oil
- One cup of sugar from coconut
- One single egg
- 1/2 cup of roasted pepitas, roasted
- 1/2 cup of cherries, dried-up

DIRECTIONS

1. Combine the flour with the oats, baking soda, pumpkin Spices, pumpkin puree, eggs, pepitas and cherries, oil, sugar, blend Well, out of that whole combination, form moderate cookies, place them all on a lined sheet pan in the oven and bake at 350 Degrees F. For 25 minutes
2. For breakfast, offer the cookies. Enjoy!

Scramble Veggie Version

Ready in 10 |Servings: 1|Difficulty: Normal

Nutrition Info: Calories 211, fat 2, fiber 4, carbs 12, protein 6

INGREDIENTS

- One egg
- One spoonful of water
- 1/4 cup of chopped broccoli
- 1/4 cup, chopped mushrooms
- A squeeze of black pepper
- One tablespoon mozzarella, low-fat, shredded
- One tablespoon of chopped walnuts
- Cooking Spray

DIRECTIONS

1. Lubricate the cooking spray on a ramekin and insert the egg, water, pepper, Broccoli, and mushrooms and brush properly.
2. Place the microwave in the oven and cook for 2 minutes.
3. Put the walnuts and mozzarella on top and serve for breakfast. Fun!

Mushrooms and Tea with Turkey

Ready in 1 hour and 5 minutes| Servings 12 |Difficulty: Normal

Nutrition Info: Calories 221, fat 3, fiber 6, carbs 12, protein 6

INGREDIENTS

Whole wheat bread, 8 ounces, cubed
Twelve ounces of chopped turkey sausage
Two cups milk that is fat-free
Low-fat cheddar five ounces, sliced
Three Eggs
1/2 cup green, chopped onions
One cup of champignons, diced
1/2 of a teaspoon of warm paprika
A squeeze of black pepper
Two tablespoons low-fat, grated parmesan

DIRECTIONS

1. Place the cubes of bread on a rimmed baking sheet and put them in the oven, and cook for 8 minutes at 400 ° Fahrenheit.
2. In the meantime, over medium-high fire, heat up a skillet, introduce turkey, sausage, mix, and brown for 7 minutes.
3. In a cup, mix the cheddar milk, eggs, parmesan, Mix well with black pepper & paprika.
4. Add the mushrooms, sausage, green onions, and bread cubes, mix, pour into a large bowl, bring in the oven, and bake at 350 degrees F for 50 minutes.
5. Chunk, split between trays and serve for breakfast. Cherish!

Delicious Omelet

Ready in 10 minutes |Servings: 2|Difficulty: Normal

Nutrition Info: Nutrition: calories 221, fat 4, fiber 4, carbs 13, protein 7

INGREDIENTS

Two Eggs
Two spoonfuls of water
Olive oil, 1 teaspoon
1/4 cup Mexican low-fat cheese, shredded
1/4 cup of salsa chunky
A squeeze of black pepper

DIRECTIONS

1. Integrate the eggs with the water, cheese, salsa, and pepper in a dish. Whisk well.
2. On medium-high Heat, warm a pan with the oil and add the eggs. Comb, spread to the plate, bake for three minutes, flip, and cook for 3 minutes. Split into dishes and offer for breakfast. Fun!

Simple Waffles Omelet

Ready in 10 minutes | Servings 2 |Difficulty: Normal

Nutrition Info: Calories 211, fat 3, fiber 6, carbs 14, protein 8

INGREDIENTS

Four eggs

A squeeze of black pepper

Ham, 2 tablespoons, minced

1/4 cup cheddar, low-fat, sliced

Sawed 2 teaspoons of parsley

cooking Spray

DIRECTIONS

1. Integrate the eggs with pepper, ham, cheese, and parsley in a dish. Stir very good.
2. Oil the cooking spray on your waffle iron, apply the egg mixture, Heat for 4-5 minutes and break the waffles among plates and serve for breakfast.

Jared Omelets

Ready in 10 minutes |Servings: 2 |Difficulty: Hard

Nutrition Info: Calories 221, fat 3, fiber 3, carbs 14, protein 7

INGREDIENTS

Spray for cooking

Low-fat 2/3 cup cheddar, diced

Four eggs

1/2 onion purple, chopped

1/2 cup of ham, chopped

One bell pepper red, minced

A squeeze of black pepper

Chopped 1 tablespoon of chives,

DIRECTIONS

1. Integrate the eggs with the onion, ham, bell pepper, and pepper in a dish. Whisk and pepper well.

2. Gunk two cooking spray mason jars, divide the mixture of eggs, put them in the oven, and bake for 6 minutes at 350-degree Fahrenheit

3. Spray all over the cheese and eat it for breakfast. Love!

Mushrooms and Omelets Cheese

Ready in 10 minutes| Servings 4 |Difficulty: Normal

Nutrition Info: Calories 199, fat 3, fiber 4, carbs 14, protein 6

INGREDIENTS

Olive oil 2 tablespoons

A squeeze of black pepper

Mushrooms, three ounces, cut

One cup spinach baby, minced

Three eggs, shuffled

Low-fat cheese 2 teaspoons, grind

One thin, peeled, bruised, and cubed avocado

1 tbsp of chopped parsley

DIRECTIONS

1. On medium-high fire, burn up a pan with the oil, include mushrooms. Stir, cook them for five minutes, then move them to a pan.

2. At medium-hightemperature, Heat the same pot, add the eggs and Cover the black pepper in the skillet, cook for 7 minutes, and then cook for 7 minutes. To be moved to a tray.

3. Put on half the mushrooms, spinach, avocado, and cheese Omelet, flip over this mix with the other half, scatter parsley on top, and serve. Love!

Egg White Mix for Breakfast

Ready in 10 minutes | Servings: 4 | Difficulty: Normal

Nutrition Info: Calories 235, fat 4, fiber 7, carbs 14, protein 7

INGREDIENTS

One chopped yellow onion
Three tomatoes with plum, sliced
Spinach, 10 ounces, minced
A squeeze of black pepper
Two spoonfuls of water
Twelve Egg Whites
cooking Spray

DIRECTIONS

1. Integrate the whites of the eggs in a bowl with water and pepper and Stir thoroughly.
2. Oil a cooking spray tray, burn up over moderate flame, add to the pan, add 1/4 of the egg whites into the pan and cook for 2 minutes.
3. Put 1/4 of the spinach, tomatoes, and onion in a spoon, roll, and incorporate into the mixture Plate.
4. Repeat with the remainder of the vegetables and egg whites and serve for breakfast. Fun!

Omelet with Pistachio Pesto

Ready in 10 minutes | Servings: 2 | Difficulty: Normal

Nutrition Info: Calories 147, fat 5, fiber 5, carbs 11, protein 6

INGREDIENTS

Two olive oil tsp
A bunch of cherry tomatoes, sliced together
Pistachio pesto with 3 tablespoons
A squeeze of black pepper
Four eggs

DIRECTIONS

1. Integrate the eggs with the cherry tomatoes Pesto, pistachio, and black pepper in a container, and stir excellently.
2. Heat the pan with the oil over medium-high heat and add the mixture of eggs, Place into a saucepan, bake for three minutes, turn, and cook for three minutes. Additionally, split among Two plates and serve for breakfast.

Cashews and Salad with Blueberries

Ready in 10 minutes | Servings: 2 | Difficulty: Normal

Nutrition Info: Calories 179, fat 2, fiber 4, carbs, protein 7

INGREDIENTS

1/4 of a cup of cashews, raw
1/4 cup of blueberries
One banana, cut and peeled
1 tbsp of butter with almonds
1 cinnamon powder teaspoon

DIRECTIONS

1. Integrate the banana in a dish with the cashews, blueberries, simply throw and serve for breakfast with almond butter and Cinnamon.

Bowls of Quinoa

Ready in 10 minutes |Servings 2 |Difficulty: Normal

Nutrition Info: Calories 177, fat 2, fiber 4, carbs 9, protein 8

INGREDIENTS

peach, diced

1/3 cup, washed quinoa

2/3 cup milk that is low-fat

1/2 tsp concentrate of vanilla

Two brown sugar tsp

12 framboises

Fourteen blueberries

DIRECTIONS

1. Integrate the quinoa with the milk, sugar, and vanilla in a shallow saucepan. Whisk, put over moderate Heat to a boil, cover with a lid, Heat, and turn with a fork for 20 minutes.

2. Split this mixture into Two bowls with raspberries and cover each one with raspberries and Blueberries and serve for breakfast.

....

Sandwich with Strawberrys

Ready in 10 minutes | Servings 4 |Difficulty: Easy

Nutrition Info: Calories 211, fat 3, fiber 4, carbs 8, protein 4

INGREDIENTS

Eight ounces of cream cheese with low fat, soft cheese

Stevia for 1 tbsp

One lemon zest teaspoon, grind

Four English muffins with whole wheat, halved and toasted

Two cups of sliced strawberries

DIRECTIONS

1. Mix the cream cheese with the stevia in your mixing bowl. And zest of lemon and well pulse.

2. Distribute 1 tablespoon of this blend on one half of the muffin and top with 1 half of the muffin. The chopped strawberries,

3. Repeat with the rest of the muffin halves for breakfast and serve.

....

Quinoa Apple Muffins

Ready in 10 minutes | Servings 4 |Difficulty: Normal

Nutrition Info: Calories 200, fat 3, fiber 4, carbs 14, protein 7

INGREDIENTS

1/2 cup of non-sweetened, natural apple-sauce
1 cup banana, smashed and trimmed
1 cup of quinoa
Two and 1/2 cups of old-style oats
1/2 cup of milk with almonds
Stevia for 2 teaspoons
Extricate 1 teaspoon of vanilla
1 cup of water
Cooking spray
1 teaspoon cinnamon powder
One apple, cored, diced, and trimmed

DIRECTIONS

1. Put the water in a shallow saucepan, take to a moderate flame to boil. Heat, introduce quinoa, cook for fifteen min, fluff with a fork, and bake for 15 minutes. Move to a pan.

2. Include the banana, applesauce, oats, milk from the almonds, stevia, vanilla, etc. Whisk, separate the Cinnamon and apple into a muffin pan oil with the cooking spray in the oven and bake it at 375 degrees F. For twenty minutes.

3. Serve For breakfast.

....

Superb Quinoa Hash Browns

Ready in 10 minutes |Servings 2 |Difficulty: Normal

Nutrition Info: Calories 191, fat 3, fiber 8, carbs 14, protein 7

INGREDIENTS

Quinoa 1/3 cup
2/3 of a cup of water
One and 1/2 cups of peeled and grated potato
One portion of eggs
A squeeze of black pepper
Olive oil 1 tablespoon
Two green, chopped onions

DIRECTIONS

1. Put the water in a shallow pan, put to a moderate flame to simmer. Warm, incorporate quinoa, mix, wrap, cook, and fluff for fifteen minutes. With Fork.

2. Integrate the quinoa in a bowl with the potato, egg, green onions, and pepper, stir thoroughly.

3. Heat the oil in a pan over medium-high heat and incorporate the quinoa. Hash browns, bake on each side for five minutes, split between Two, And serve the dish for breakfast.

....

Quinoa Bars for Breakfast

Ready in 2 hours | Servings: 6 |Difficulty: Easy

Nutrition Info: Calories 182, fat 4, fiber 4, carbs 13, protein 11

INGREDIENTS

1/2 cup peanut butter without fat

Two teaspoons of sugar from coconut

Extract 1 teaspoon of vanilla

1/2 cinnamon teaspoon powder

1 cup quinoa Flakes

1/3 cup flaked coconut

Two tablespoons of chocolate chips unsweetened

DIRECTIONS

1. Integrate peanut butter and sugar, vanilla, in a big bucket, Chips of Cinnamon, quinoa, coconut, and chocolate, mix well and scatter well. Push well on the bottom of a rimmed baking sheet, chop into Six bars, Store for 2 hours in the refrigerator, split between trays, and start serving.

Quinoa Quiche

Ready in 45 minutes| Servings 4 |Difficulty: Easy

Nutrition Info: Calories 201, fat 2, fiber 4, carbs 12, protein 7

INGREDIENTS

- One Quinoa Cup, Fried
- Spinach, three ounces, minced
- 1 cup of ricotta cheese free from fat
- Three Eggs
- One and 1/2 teaspoons of powdered Garlic
- Low-fat 2/3 cup parmesan, grind

DIRECTIONS

1. Integrate the quinoa in a pan with the spinach, ricotta, eggs, etc. Parmesan and garlic powder, brush well, pour into a lined pie, Pan, put into the oven, and bake at 355 degrees F 45 Minutes.
2. Cool the quiche, chop it, and serve it for breakfast.

Egg Muffins and Quinoa

Ready in 30 minutes |Servings: 3 |Difficulty: Normal

Nutrition Info: Calories 221, fat 7, fiber 2, carbs 13, protein 14

INGREDIENTS

- Quinoa for 1/3 cup, cooked
- One chopped zucchini
- Two Eggs
- Four Egg Whites
- 1/2 cup feta cheese, low fat, diced
- A squeeze of black pepper
- A hot sauce spill
- Cooking spray

DIRECTIONS

1. Integrate the quinoa with the zucchini, eggs, and eggs Whites, cheese, hot sauce, and black pepper in a pot. Mix well and shake well, Split the cooking spray into Six muffin cups oiled with the spray.
2. Cook the muffins for thirty min at 350 degrees F in the oven.
3. Split between plates the muffins and serve for breakfast.

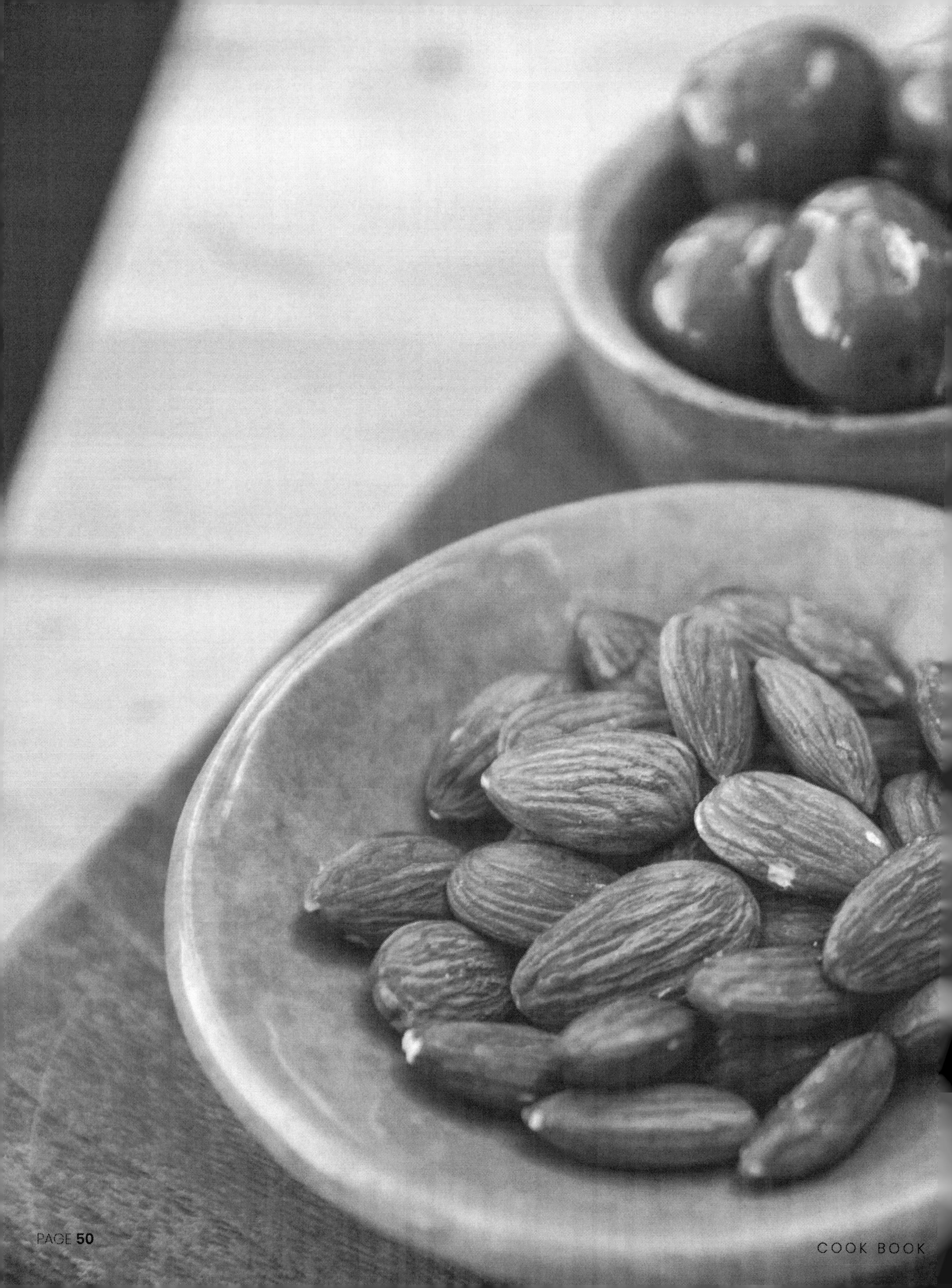

APPETIZERS

Spicy Hummus

Total Time: 10 minutes | Serves: 6

Nutrition Info:Per Serving: Calories 236, Fat 8.6g, Carbs 31.2g, Protein 10.4g

INGREDIENTS

½ tsp hot paprika

1 tsp hot pepper sauce

1 tsp ground cumin

3 garlic cloves, minced 1 (14-oz) can chickpeas, drained 2 tbsp tahini 2 tbsp chopped fresh parsley 2 tbsp olive oil 1 lemon, juiced and zested Salt to taste

DIRECTIONS

1. In a food processor, blend chickpeas, tahini, olive oil, garlic, lemon juice, lemon zest, salt, and hot pepper sauce for a minute until smooth. Serve decorated with parsley and hot paprika.

Almond & Parmesan Stuffed Cucumbers

Total Time: 10 minutes | Serves: 4

Nutrition Info: Per Serving: Calories 182, Fat 16g, Carbs 10g, Protein 4g

INGREDIENTS

3 cucumbers, julienned and deseeded ¼ tsp salt 1 garlic clove, minced 2 tbsp dill, chopped ¼ cup grate d Parmesan cheese ¼ cup almonds, chopped ¼ cup olive oil ½ tsp paprika

DIRECTIONS

1. Season cucumbers and arrange on a platter. Mix dill, almonds, garlic, Parmesan cheese, and olive oil in a food processor until smooth. Spoon the pesto sauce over the cucumbers and season with paprika to serve.

Jalapeno Poppers Stuffed with Hummus

Total Time: 1 hour + chilling time | Serves: 6

Nutrition Info: Per Serving: Calories 250, Fat 12.7g, Carbs 27.9g, Protein 8.9g

INGREDIENTS

½ lb chickpeas, soaked overnight 1 lb jalapeño peppers, seeded and halved 1 shallot 2 tbsp tahini 1 tbsp lemon juice 3 tbsp olive oil ½ tsp red pepper flakes 1 tsp cumin 1 tsp harissa seasoning 1 garlic clove, minced Salt to taste 1 tbsp paprika

DIRECTIONS

1. Preheat oven to 400 F. Pour the chickpeas in a pot over medium heat and cover with water by 1 inch. Bring to a boil, then lower the heat and simmer for 45-50 minutes. Remove 1 cup of the cooking liquid to a bowl and drain the chickpeas. Reserve some whole chickpeas for garnishing. Bake the jalapeño peppers in the preheated oven for 10 minutes. Remove to a serving platter. Pour the chickpeas in a food processor and half of the reserved cooking liquid and pulse until no large pieces remain. Add in the remaining cooking liquid, lemon juice, olive oil, red pepper flakes, cumin, harissa seasoning, garlic, tahini, shallot, and salt. Pulse until smooth. Spoon the hummus into each jalapeño pepper half and top with the whole chickpeas. Sprinkle with paprika and serve.

Sweet Curried Almonds

Total Time: 25 minutes | Serves: 4

Nutrition Info: Per Serving: Calories 134, Fat 8g, Carbs 18g, Protein 1g

INGREDIENTS

2 tbsp olive oil 3 cups almonds 1 tbsp curry powder ¼ cup honey 1 tsp salt

DIRECTIONS

1. Preheat oven to 260 F. Coat almonds with olive oil, curry powder, and salt in a bowl; mix well. Arrange on a lined with aluminum foil sheet, and bake for 15 minutes. Remove from the oven and let cool for 10 minutes. Drizzle with honey and let cool at room temperature.

Baileys Ice Coffee

Total Time: 5 minutes | Serves: 4

Nutrition Info: Per Serving: Calories 100, Fat 5g, Carbs 8g, Protein 4g

INGREDIENTS

2 cups milk 4 tbsp Baileys ½ tsp ground cinnamon 1 cup espresso, at room temperature ½ tsp vanilla extract Ice cubes

DIRECTIONS

1. Fill four glasses with ice cubes. Mix milk, cinnamon, and vanilla in a food processor until nice and frothy. Pour into the glasses. Combine the Baileys with the espresso and mix well. Pour ¼ of the espresso mixture over the milk and serve.

Truffle Popcorn

Total Time: 20 minutes | Serves: 6

Nutrition Info: Per Serving: Calories 80, Fat 5g, Carbs 8.4g, Protein 1.1g

INGREDIENTS

2 tbsp butter, melted 1 tbsp truffle oil 8 cups air-popped popcorn 2 tbsp packed brown sugar 2 tbsp Italian seasoning ¼ tsp sea salt

DIRECTIONS

1. Preheat oven to 350 F. Combine butter, Italian seasoning, brown sugar, and salt in a bowl. Pour over the popcorn and toss well to coat. Remove to a baking dish and bake for 15 minutes, stirring frequently. Drizzle with truffle oil and serve.

Eggplant Dip with Mayonnaise

Total Time: 25 minutes | Serves: 4

Nutrition Info: Per Serving: Calories 235, Fat 18.1g, Carbs 17.3g, Protein 4.1g

INGREDIENTS

1 lemon, juiced 1 pound eggplants, peeled and sliced 1 garlic clove, minced ¼ cup tahini ¼ tsp ground cumin Salt and black pepper to taste 2 tbsp fresh parsley, chopped ½ cup mayonnaise

DIRECTIONS

1. Preheat oven to 350 F. Arrange the eggplant slices on a baking sheet and bake for 15 minutes until tender. Let cool slightly before chopping. In a food processor, mix eggplants, salt, lemon juice, tahini, cumin, garlic, and pepper for 30 seconds. Remove to a bowl. Stir in mayonnaise. Serve topped with parsley.

Garlic Lentil-Walnut Spread with Cilantro

Total Time: 40 minutes | Serves: 6

Nutrition Info: Per Serving: Calories 234, Fat 12.78g, Carbs 21.7g, Protein 9.9g

INGREDIENTS

1 cup split red lentils ½ red onion 1 garlic bulb, top removed ½ tsp cumin seeds 1 tsp coriander seeds 1 roasted red bell pepper, chopped 4 tbsp olive oil ¼ cup walnuts 2 tbsp tomato paste ½ tsp Cayenne powder Salt and black pepper to taste 2 tbsp fresh cilantro, chopped

DIRECTIONS

1. Preheat the oven to 370 F. Drizzle the garlic with half of the olive oil and wrap it in a piece of aluminum foil. Roast for 35-40 minutes. Remove and allow to cool for a few minutes. Cover the lentils with salted water in a pot over medium heat and bring to a boil. Lower the heat and simmer for 15 minutes. Drain and set aside. Squeeze out the garlic cloves and place them in a food processor. Add in the cooled lentils, cumin seeds, coriander seeds, roasted red bell pepper, onion, walnuts, tomato paste, Cayenne powder, remaining olive oil, salt, and black pepper. Pulse until smooth. Top with cilantro and serve with crostini or crackers.

Cucumber Bites

Total Time: 5 minutes | Serves: 4

Nutrition Info: Per Serving: Calories 130, Fat 3g, Carbs 7g, Protein 3g

INGREDIENTS

2 tbsp olive oil 2 cucumbers, sliced into rounds 1 cup cherry tomatoes, halved Salt and black pepper to taste 1 red chili pepper, dried 8 oz cream cheese, softened 1 tbsp balsamic vinegar 1 tsp chives, chopped

DIRECTIONS

1. In a bowl, mix cream cheese, balsamic vinegar, olive oil, and chives. Spread the mixture over the cucumber rounds and top with the cherry tomato halves. Serve.

COOK BOOK

Curly Kale & Artichoke Flatbread

Total Time: 25 minutes | Serves: 4

Nutrition Info: Per Serving: Calories 230, Fat 12g, Carbs 16g, Protein 8g

INGREDIENTS

1 cup curly kale, chopped 3 tbsp olive oil 1 tbsp garlic powder 2 tbsp parsley, chopped 2 whole-wheat flatbread wraps 4 tbsp Parmesan cheese, grated ½ cup mozzarella cheese, grated 14 oz canned artichokes, drained ½ cup cherry tomatoes, halved Salt and black pepper to taste

DIRECTIONS

1. Preheat the oven to 390 F. Line a baking sheet with parchment paper. Brush the flatbread wrap with some olive oil and sprinkle with garlic, salt, and pepper. Top with half of the Parmesan and mozzarella cheeses. Combine artichokes, tomatoes, salt, pepper, and remaining olive oil in a bowl. Spread the mixture on the top of the wraps and top with the remaining Parmesan cheese. Transfer to the baking sheet and bake for 15 minutes. Top with curly kale and serve immediately.

Artichoke & Bean Spread

Total Time: 10 minutes | Serves: 4

Nutrition Info: Per Serving: Calories 280, Fat 12g, Carbs 19g, Protein 17g

INGREDIENTS

2 tbsp olive oil 15 oz canned Cannellini beans, drained 1 red onion, chopped 6 oz canned artichoke hearts, drained 4 garlic cloves, minced 1 tbsp thyme, chopped ½ lemon, juiced and zested Salt and black pepper to taste

DIRECTIONS

1. Warm olive oil in a skillet over medium heat and sauté onion and garlic for 4-5 minutes until translucent. Add in the artichoke hearts and cook for 2-3 more minutes. Set aside to cool slightly. Transfer the cooled mixture to a blender along with cannellini beans, thyme, lemon juice, lemon zest, salt, and pepper and blitz until it becomes smooth. Serve.

Garbanzo Patties with Yogurt Sauce

Total Time: 20 minutes | Serves: 4

Nutrition Info: Per Serving: Calories 120, Fat 7g, Carbs 13g, Protein 4g

INGREDIENTS

3 garlic cloves, minced 1 cup canned garbanzo beans, drained 2 tbsp parsley, chopped 1 onion, chopped 1 tsp ground coriander Salt and black pepper to taste ¼ tsp cayenne pepper ¼ tsp cumin powder 1 tsp lemon juice 3 tbsp flour ¼ cup olive oil ¼ cup Greek yogurt 2 tbsp chopped cilantro ½ tsp garlic powder

DIRECTIONS

1. In a blender, blitz garbanzo, parsley, onion, garlic, salt, pepper, cayenne pepper, cumin powder, and lemon juice until smooth. Remove to a bowl and mix in flour. Form 16 balls out of the mixture and flatten them into patties. Warm the olive oil in a skillet over medium heat and fry patties for 10 minutes on both sides. Remove to a place them a double sheet of kitchen paper to drain the excess fat. In a bowl, mix the Greek yogurt, cilantro, garlic powder, salt, and pepper. Serve the patties with yogurt sauce.

Cheesy Grilled Asparagus

Per Serving: Calories 105, Fat 8.6g, Carbs 4.7g, Protein 4.3g

Nutrition Info: (1 serving) 235 calories, 13 g protein, 47 g carbohydrates, 1 g fat, 3 g fiber

INGREDIENTS

2 tbsp olive oil 1 lb asparagus, trimmed 4 tbsp Grana Padano cheese, grated ½ tsp garlic powder Salt to taste 2 tbsp parsley, chopped

DIRECTIONS

1. Preheat the grill to high. Season the asparagus with salt and garlic powder and coat with olive oil. Grill the asparagus for 10 minutes, turning occasionally until lightly charred and tender. Remove to a serving platter and sprinkle with cheese and parsley.

Thyme Artichoke with Aioli

Total Time: 25 minutes | Serves: 4 Per Serving: Calories 120, Fat 8g, Carbs 7g, Protein 3g

Nutrition Info: Per Serving: **Calories 280, Fat 12g, Carbs 19g, Protein 17g**

INGREDIENTS

1 tbsp olive oil 1 red onion, chopped 2 garlic cloves, minced Salt and black pepper to taste 10 oz canned artichoke hearts, drained 1 tsp lemon juice 1 cup light mayonnaise 2 tbsp thyme, chopped

DIRECTIONS

1. Warm the olive oil in a skillet over medium heat and cook onion for 3 minutes. Stir in artichokes, salt, and pepper and stir-fry for 4-5 minutes; reserve. In a bowl, mix mayonnaise, lemon juice, and garlic. Sprinkle the artichokes with thyme and serve with aioli.

Anchovy & Pepper Tapenade

Total Time: 10 minutes | Serves: 4

Nutrition Info: Per Serving: Calories 210, Fat 6g, Carbs 13g, Protein 5g

INGREDIENTS

2 anchovy fillets, chopped 3 tbsp olive oil 1 cup roasted red peppers, chopped 2 tbsp parsley, chopped 14 oz canned artichokes, drained ¼ cup capers, drained 1 tbsp lemon juice 2 garlic cloves, minced

DIRECTIONS

1. In a food processor, blend roasted peppers, anchovies, parsley, artichokes, oil, capers, lemon juice, and garlic until smooth.

Roasted Carrot Ribbons with Mayo Sauce

Total Time: 50 minutes | Serves: 4

Nutrition Info: Per Serving: Calories 200, Fat 6g, Carbs 8g, Protein 6g

INGREDIENTS

1 lb carrots, shaved into ribbons 2 tbsp olive oil Salt and black pepper to taste ½ lemon, zested 1/3 cup light mayonnaise 1 garlic clove, minced 1 tsp cumin, ground 1 tbsp dill, chopped

DIRECTIONS

1. Preheat the oven to 380 F. Spread carrot ribbons on a paper-lined roasting tray. Drizzle with some olive oil and sprinkle with cumin, salt, and pepper. Roast for 20-25 minutes until crisp and golden. In a bowl, mix mayonnaise, lemon zest, garlic, dill, and remaining olive oil. Serve the roasted carrots with mayo sauce.

Roasted Pepper Hummus

Total Time: 10 minutes | Serves: 6

Nutrition Info: Per Serving: Calories 260, Fat 12g, Carbs 18g, Protein 7g

INGREDIENTS

4 tbsp olive oil 6 oz roasted red peppers, chopped 16 oz canned chickpeas, drained ¼ cup mayonnaise 3 tbsp tahini paste 1 lemon, juiced 3 garlic cloves, minced Salt and black pepper to taste 1 tbsp parsley, chopped

DIRECTIONS

1. In a blender, pulse red peppers, chickpeas, mayonnaise, tahini paste, lemon juice, garlic, salt, and pepper until you obtain a smooth mixture. Continue blending while gradually adding olive oil, until smooth. Serve sprinkled with parsley.

Spanish-Style Avocado Dip

Total Time: 5 minutes | Serves: 4

Nutrition Info: Per Serving: Calories 210, Fat 15g, Carbs 9g, Protein 8g

INGREDIENTS

2 avocados, chopped ½ cup heavy cream 1 serrano pepper, chopped Salt and black pepper the taste 2 tbsp cilantro, chopped ¼ cup lime juice

DIRECTIONS

1. In a food processor, blitz heavy cream, serrano pepper, salt, pepper, avocados, cilantro, and lime juice until smooth. Refrigerate before serving.

Parsley Lamb Tagliatelle

Total Time: 25 minutes | Serves: 4

Nutrition Info: Per Serving: Calories 140, Fat 10g, Carbs 7g, Protein 6g

INGREDIENTS

2 tbsp olive oil 16 oz tagliatelle 1 tsp paprika 1 tsp cumin Salt and black pepper to taste 1 lb ground lamb 1 cup onions, chopped ¼ cup parsley, chopped 2 garlic cloves, minced

DIRECTIONS

1. Boil the tagliatelle in a pot over medium heat for 9-11 minutes or until "al dente". Drain and set aside. Warm the olive oil in a skillet over medium heat and sauté lamb, onions, and garlic until the meat is browned, about 10-15 minutes. Stir in cumin, paprika, salt, and pepper for 1-2 minutes. Spoon tagliatelle on a platter and scatter lamb over. Top with parsley and serve.

Cheese & Cucumber Mini Sandwiches

Total Time: 5 minutes | Serves: 4

Nutrition Info: Per Serving: Calories 190, Fat 13g, Carbs 5g, Protein 9g

INGREDIENTS

4 bread slices 1 cucumber, sliced 2 tbsp cream cheese, soft 1 tbsp chives, chopped ¼ cup hummus Salt and black pepper to taste

DIRECTIONS

1. In a bowl, mix hummus, cream cheese, chives, salt, and pepper until well combined. Spread the mixture onto bread slices. Top with cucumber and cut each sandwich into three pieces. Serve immediately.

Almond Spinach with Chickpeas

Total Time: 5 minutes | Serves: 4

Nutrition Info: Per Serving: Calories 230, Fat 6g, Carbs 10g, Protein 16g

INGREDIENTS

2 tbsp olive oil 3 spring onions, chopped 1 cup baby spinach 15 oz canned chickpeas, drained Salt and black pepper to taste 2 tbsp lemon juice 1 tbsp cilantro, chopped 2 tbsp almonds flakes, toasted

DIRECTIONS

1. Toss chickpeas, spring onions, spinach, salt, pepper, olive oil, lemon juice, and cilantro in a bowl. Serve topped with almond flakes.

Italian Eggplant Balls

Total Time: 55 minutes | Serves: 4

Nutrition Info: Per Serving: Calories 230, Fat 11g, Carbs 6g, Protein 4g

INGREDIENTS

3 tbsp olive oil 2 cups eggplants, chopped 3 garlic cloves, minced 2 eggs, whisked Salt and black pepper to taste 2 tbsp parsley, chopped ½ cup Pecorino cheese, finely grated ¾ cups panko breadcrumbs

DIRECTIONS

1. Preheat the oven to 360 F. Line a baking sheet with parchment paper. Warm olive oil in a skillet over medium heat and sauté garlic and eggplants for 15 minutes. Mix cooked eggplants, eggs, salt, pepper, parsley, Pecorino cheese, and breadcrumbs in a bowl and form medium balls out of the mixture. Place balls on the sheet and bake for 30 minutes. Serve warm.

Cream Cheese & Tomato Toast

Total Time: 5 minutes | Serves: 4

Nutrition Info: Per Serving: Calories 210s, Fat 7g, Carbs 8g, Protein 5g

INGREDIENTS

1 tomato, cubed 12 ounces cream cheese, soft ¼ cup mayonnaise 2 garlic clove, minced 1 red onion, chopped 2 tbsp lime juice 4 slices whole-wheat toast

DIRECTIONS

1. In a bowl, blend cream cheese, mayonnaise, garlic, onion, and lime juice until smooth. Spread the mixture onto the bread slices and top with the tomato cubes to serve.

Chili Butternut Squash with Walnuts

Total Time: 50 minutes | Serves: 4

Nutrition Info: Per Serving: Calories 190, Fat 5g, Carbs 7g, Protein 2g

INGREDIENTS

1 lb butternut squash, peeled and cut into wedges 1 cup walnuts, chopped 1 tbsp chili paste 3 tbsp olive oil 1 tbsp balsamic vinegar 1 tbsp chives, chopped

DIRECTIONS

1. Preheat the oven to 380 F. Line a baking sheet with parchment paper. Combine squash wedges, chili paste, olive oil, vinegar, and chives in a bowl and arrange on the sheet. Bake for 40 minutes, turning often. Sprinkle with walnuts and serve.

Grilled Eggplant Rounds

Total Time: 25 minutes | Serves: 4

Nutrition Info: Per Serving: Calories 220, Fat 11g, Carbs 16g, Protein 6g

INGREDIENTS

4 tbsp olive oil 2 eggplants, cut into rounds 1 cup roasted peppers, chopped ½ cup Kalamata olives, chopped 1 tsp red chili flakes, crushed Salt and black pepper to taste 2 tbsp basil, chopped 2 tbsp Parmesan cheese, grated

DIRECTIONS

1. Combine roasted peppers, half of the olive oil, olives, red chili flakes, salt, and pepper in a bowl. Rub eac h eggplant slice with remaining olive oil and salt grill them on the preheated grill for 14 minutes on both sides. Remove to a platter. Distribute the pepper mixture across the eggplant rounds and top with basil and Parmesan cheese to serve.

Pepper & Tomato Dip

Total Time: 10 minutes | Serves: 4

Nutrition Info: Per Serving: Calories 130, Fat 5g, Carbs 4g, Protein 4g

INGREDIENTS

3 tbsp olive oil 1 cup roasted red peppers, chopped 1 lb tomatoes, peeled and chopped Salt and black pepper to taste 1 ½ tsp balsamic vinegar ½ tsp oregano, chopped 2 garlic cloves, minced 2 tbsp parsley, chopped

DIRECTIONS

1. In a food processor, blend tomatoes, red peppers, salt, pepper, vinegar, oregano, olive oil, garlic, and parsley until smooth.

Garlic Lentil Dip

Total Time: 10minutes | Serves: 6

Nutrition Info: Per Serving: Calories 295, Fat 10g, Carbs 16g, Protein 10g

INGREDIENTS

3 tbsp olive oil 1 garlic clove, minced 1 cup split red lentils, rinsed ½ tsp dried thyme 1 tbsp balsamic vinegar Salt and black pepper to taste

DIRECTIONS

1. Bring to a boil salted water in a pot over medium heat. Add in the lentils and cook for 15 minutes until cooked through. Drain and set aside to cool. In a food processor, place the lentils, garlic, thyme, vinegar, salt, and pepper. Gradually add olive oil wile blending until smooth. Serve with crackers.

Cucumber & Prawn Bites

Total Time: 5 minutes | Serves: 4

Nutrition Info: Per Serving: Calories 160, Fat 9g, Carbs 12g, Protein 18g

INGREDIENTS

1 lb prawns, cooked and chopped 1 cucumber, cubed 2 tbsp cream cheese Salt and black pepper to taste 12 whole grain crackers

DIRECTIONS

1. Combine cucumber, prawns, heavy cream, salt, and pepper in a bowl. Place crackers in a plate and top them with shrimp mixture. Serve right away.

Spicy Caper & Eggplant Spread

Total Time: 10 minutes | Serves: 4

Nutrition Info: Per Serving: Calories 364, Fat 38g, Carbs 9.3g, Protein 1.5g

INGREDIENTS

1 lemon, zested ¾ cup olive oil 1 lb eggplants, baked, peeled and chopped 1 red chili pepper, chopped 1 red bell pepper, roasted and chopped 1 ½ tsp capers, drained and chopped 1 garlic clove, minced Salt and black pepper to taste Baguette toast for serving

DIRECTIONS

1. In a food processor, place eggplants, lemon zest, red chili pepper, bell pepper, capers, garlic, salt, and pepper. Blend while gradually adding the olive oil until smooth. Serve the spread on toast.

Gluten-Free Pizza Caprese

Total Time: 40 minutes | Serves: 2

Nutrition Info: Per Serving: Calories 420, Fat 26g, Carbs 35g, Protein 14g

INGREDIENTS

2 tbsp olive oil 2 ¼ cups chickpea flour Salt and black pepper to taste 1 tsp onion powder 1 tomato, sliced ¼ tsp dried oregano 2 oz mozzarella cheese, sliced ¼ cup tomato sauce 2 tbsp fresh basil, chopped

DIRECTIONS

1. Preheat oven to 360 F. Combine the chickpea flour, salt, pepper, 1 ¼ cups of water, olive oil, and onion powder in a bowl. Mix well to form a soft dough, then knead a bit until elastic. Let sit covered in a greased bowl to rise, for 25 minutes in a warm place. Remove the dough to a floured surface and roll out it with a rolling pin into a thin circle. Transfer to a floured baking tray and bake in the oven for 10 minutes. Evenly spray the tomato sauce over the pizza base. Sprinkle with oregano and arrange the mozzarella cheese and tomato slices on top. Bake for 10 minutes. Top with basil and serve sliced.

Light & Creamy Garlic Hummus

Preparation Time: 10 minutes | Cooking Time: 40 minutes | Servings: 12

Nutrition Info: Calories 152 Fat 6.9 g Carbohydrates 17.6 g Sugar 2.8 g Protein 6.6 g Cholesterol 0 mg

INGREDIENTS

1 1/2 cups dry chickpeas, rinsed 2 1/2 tbsp fresh lemon juice 1 tbsp garlic, minced 1/2 cup tahini 6 cups of water Pepper Salt

DIRECTIONS

1. Add water and chickpeas into the instant pot. Seal pot with a lid and select manual and set timer for 40 minutes. Once done, allow to release pressure naturally. Remove lid. Drain chickpeas well and reserved 1/2 cup chickpeas liquid. Transfer chickpeas, reserved liquid, lemon juice, garlic, tahini, pepper, and salt into the food processor and process until smooth. Serve and enjoy.

Creamy Potato Spread

Preparation Time: 10 minutes | Cooking Time: 15 minutes | Servings: 6

Nutrition Info: Calories 108 Fat 0.3 g Carbohydrates 25.4 g Sugar 2.4 g Protein 2 g Cholesterol 0 mg

INGREDIENTS

1 lb sweet potatoes, peeled and chopped 3/4 tbsp fresh chives, chopped 1/2 tsp paprika 1 tbsp garlic, minced 1 cup tomato puree Pepper Salt

DIRECTIONS

1. Add all ingredients except chives into the inner pot of instant pot and stir well. Seal pot with lid and cook on high for 15 minutes. Once done, allow to release pressure naturally for 10 minutes then release remaining using quick release. Remove lid. Transfer instant pot sweet potato mixture into the food processor and process until smooth. Garnish with chives and serve.

Parmesan Potatoes

Preparation Time: 10 minutes | Cooking Time: 6 minutes | Servings: 4

Nutrition Info: Calories 237 Fat 8.3 g Carbohydrates 36.3 g Sugar 2.8 g Protein 5.9 g Cholesterol 2 mg

INGREDIENTS

2 lb potatoes, rinsed and cut into chunks 2 tbsp parmesan cheese, grated 2 tbsp olive oil 1/2 tsp parsley 1/2 tsp Italian seasoning 1 tsp garlic, minced 1 cup vegetable broth 1/2 tsp salt

DIRECTIONS

1. Add all ingredients except cheese into the instant pot and stir well. Seal pot with lid and cook on high for 6 minutes. Once done, release pressure using quick release. Remove lid. Add parmesan cheese and stir until cheese is melted. Serve and enjoy.

Homemade Salsa

Preparation Time: 10 minutes | Cooking Time: 5 minutes | Servings: 8

Nutrition Info: Calories 146 Fat 1.2 g Carbohydrates 33.2 g Sugar 4 g Protein 6.9 g Cholesterol 0 mg

INGREDIENTS

DIRECTIONS

12 oz grape tomatoes, halved 1/4 cup fresh cilantro, chopped 1 fresh lime juice 28 oz tomatoes, crushed 1 tbsp garlic, minced 1 green bell pepper, chopped 1 red bell pepper, chopped 2 onions, chopped 6 whole tomatoes Salt

1. Add whole tomatoes into the instant pot and gently smash the tomatoes. Add remaining ingredients except cilantro, lime juice, and salt and stir well. Seal pot with lid and cook on high for 5 minutes. Once done, allow to release pressure naturally for 10 minutes then release remaining using quick release. Remove lid. Add cilantro, lime juice, and salt and stir well. Serve and enjoy.

Flavorful Roasted Baby Potatoes

Preparation Time: 10 minutes | Cooking Time: 10 minutes | Servings: 4

Nutrition Info: Calories 175 Fat 4.5 g Carbohydrates 29.8 g Sugar 0.7 g Protein 6.1 g Cholesterol 2 mg

INGREDIENTS

DIRECTIONS

2 lbs baby potatoes, clean and cut in half 1/2 cup vegetable stock 1 tsp paprika 3/4 tsp garlic powder 1 tsp onion powder 2 tsp Italian seasoning 1 tbsp olive oil Pepper Salt

1. Add oil into the inner pot of instant pot and set the pot on sauté mode. Add potatoes and sauté for 5 minutes. Add remaining ingredients and stir well. Seal pot with lid and cook on high for 5 minutes. Once done, release pressure using quick release. Remove lid. Stir well and serve.

Garlic Pinto Bean Dip

Preparation Time: 10 minutes | Cooking Time: 43 minutes | Servings: 6

Nutrition Info: Calories 129 Fat 0.9 g Carbohydrates 23 g Sugar 1.9 g Protein 8 g Cholesterol 2 m g

INGREDIENTS

DIRECTIONS

1 cup dry pinto beans, rinsed 1/2 tsp cumin 1/2 cup salsa 2 garlic cloves 2 chipotle peppers in adobo sauce 5 cups vegetable stock Pepper Salt

1. Add beans, stock, garlic, and chipotle peppers into the instant pot. Seal pot with lid and cook on high for 43 minutes. Once done, release pressure using quick release. Remove lid. Drain beans well and reserve 1/2 cup of stock. Transfer beans, reserve stock, and remaining ingredients into the food processor and process until smooth. Serve and enjoy.

Jalapeno-Chickpea Hummus

Preparation Time: 10 minutes | Cooking Time: 25 minutes | Servings: 4

Nutrition Info: Calories 425 Fat 30.4 g Carbohydrates 31.8 g Sugar 5.6 g Protein 10.5 g Cholesterol 0 mg

INGREDIENTS

1 cup dry chickpeas, soaked overnight and drained 1 tsp ground cumin 1/4 cup jalapenos, diced 1/2 cup fresh cilantro 1 tbsp tahini 1/2 cup olive oil Pepper Salt

DIRECTIONS

1. Add chickpeas into the instant pot and cover with vegetable stock. Seal pot with lid and cook on high for 25 minutes. Once done, allow to release pressure naturally. Remove lid. Drain chickpeas well and transfer into the food processor along with remaining ingredients and process until smooth. Serve and enjoy.

Healthy Kidney Bean Dip

Preparation Time: 10 minutes | Cooking Time: 10 minutes | Servings: 6

Nutrition Info: Calories 136 Fat 3.2 g Carbohydrates 20 g Sugar 2.1 g Protein 7.7 g Cholesterol 0 mg

INGREDIENTS

1 cup dry white kidney beans, soaked overnight and drained 1 tbsp fresh lemon juice 2 tbsp water 1/2 cup coconut yogurt 1 roasted garlic clove 1 tbsp olive oil 1/4 tsp cayenne 1 tsp dried parsley Pepper Salt

DIRECTIONS

1. Add soaked beans and 1 3/4 cups of water into the instant pot. Seal pot with lid and cook on high for 10 minutes. Once done, allow to release pressure naturally. Remove lid. Drain beans well and transfer them into the food processor. Add remaining ingredients into the food processor and process until smooth. Serve and enjoy.

Healthy Spinach Dip

Preparation Time: 10 minutes | Cooking Time: 8 minutes | Servings: 4

Nutrition Info:: Calories 109 Fat 9.2 g Carbohydrates 6.6 g Sugar 1.1 g Protein 3.2 g Cholesterol 0 mg

INGREDIENTS

14 oz spinach 2 tbsp fresh lime juice 1 tbsp garlic, minced 2 tbsp olive oil 2 tbsp coconut cream Pepper Salt

DIRECTIONS

1. Add all ingredients except coconut cream into the instant pot and stir well. Seal pot with lid and cook on low pressure for 8 minutes. Once done, allow to release pressure naturally for 5 minutes then release remaining using quick release. Remove lid. Add coconut cream and stir well and blend spinach mixture using a blender until smooth. Serve and enjoy.

Tomato Cucumber Salsa

Preparation Time: 10 minutes | Cooking Time: 5 minutes | Servings: 4

Nutrition Info: Calories 129 Fat 7.5 g Carbohydrates 15 g Sugar 8.3 g Protein 2.7 g Cholesterol 0 mg

INGREDIENTS

1 cucumber, chopped 1 1/2 lbs grape tomatoes, chopped 1 tbsp fresh chives, chopped 1 tbsp fresh parsley, chopped 1 tbsp fresh basil, chopped 2 onion, chopped 1/4 cup vinegar 2 tbsp olive oil 1/4 cup vegetable stock 2 chili peppers, chopped Pepper Salt

DIRECTIONS

1. Add tomatoes, stock, and chili peppers into the instant pot and stir well. Seal pot with lid and cook on low pressure for 5 minutes. Once done, allow to release pressure naturally for 5 minutes then release remaining using quick release. Remove lid. Transfer tomato mixture into the mixing bowl. Add remaining ingredients into the bowl and mix well. Serve and enjoy.

Rosemary Cauliflower Dip

Preparation Time: 10 minutes | Cooking Time: 15 minutes | Servings: 4

Nutrition Info: Calories 128 Fat 9.4 g Carbohydrates 10.4 g Sugar 4 g Protein 3.1 g Cholesterol 21 mg

INGREDIENTS

1 lb cauliflower florets 1 tbsp fresh parsley, chopped 1/2 cup heavy cream 1/2 cup vegetable stock 1 tbsp garlic, minced 1 tbsp rosemary, chopped 1 tbsp olive oil 1 onion, chopped Pepper Salt

DIRECTIONS

1. Add oil into the inner pot of instant pot and set the pot on sauté mode. Add onion and sauté for 5 minutes. Add remaining ingredients except for parsley and heavy cream and stir well. Seal pot with lid and cook on high for 10 minutes. Once done, allow to release pressure naturally for 10 minutes then release remaining using quick release. Remove lid. Add cream and stir well. Blend cauliflower mixture using immersion blender until smooth. Garnish with parsley and serve.

Easy Tomato Dip

Preparation Time: 10 minutes | Cooking Time: 13 minutes | Servings: 4

Nutrition Info: Calories 94 Fat 3.9 g Carbohydrates 14.3 g Sugar 7.3 g Protein 2.5 g Cholesterol 0 mg

INGREDIENTS

2 cups tomato puree 1/2 tsp ground cumin 1 tsp garlic, minced 1/4 cup vinegar 1 onion, chopped 1 tbsp olive oil Pepper Salt

DIRECTIONS

1. Add oil into the inner pot of instant pot and set the pot on sauté mode. Add onion and sauté for 3 minutes. Add remaining ingredients and stir well. Seal pot with lid and cook on high for 10 minutes. Once done, allow to release pressure naturally for 10 minutes then release remaining using quick release. Remove lid. Blend tomato mixture using an immersion blender until smooth. Serve and enjoy.

....

Spicy Chicken Dip

Preparation Time: 10 minutes | Cooking Time: 15 minutes | Servings: 10

Nutrition Info: Calories 248 Fat 19 g Carbohydrates 1.6 g Sugar 0.3 g Protein 17.4 g Cholesterol 83 mg

INGREDIENTS

1 lb chicken breast, skinless and boneless 1/2 cup sour cream 8 oz cheddar cheese, shredded 1/2 cup chicken stock 2 jalapeno pepper, sliced 8 oz cream cheese Pepper Salt

DIRECTIONS

1. Add chicken, stock, jalapenos, and cream cheese into the instant pot. Seal pot with lid and cook on high for 12 minutes. Once done, release pressure using quick release. Remove lid. Shred chicken using a fork. Set pot on sauté mode. Add remaining ingredients and stir well and cook until cheese is melted. Serve and enjoy.

....

Olive Eggplant Spread

Preparation Time: 10 minutes | Cooking Time: 8 minutes | Servings: 12

Nutrition Info: Calories 65 Fat 5.3 g Carbohydrates 4.7 g Sugar 2 g Protein 0.9 g Cholesterol 0 mg

INGREDIENTS

1 3/4 lbs eggplant, chopped 1/2 tbsp dried oregano 1/4 cup olives, pitted and chopped 1 tbsp tahini 1/4 cup fresh lime juice 1/2 cup water 2 garlic cloves 1/4 cup olive oil Salt

DIRECTIONS

1. Add oil into the inner pot of instant pot and set the pot on sauté mode. Add eggplant and cook for 3-5 minutes. Turn off sauté mode. Add water and salt and stir well. Seal pot with lid and cook on high for 3 minutes. Once done, release pressure using quick release. Remove lid. Drain eggplant well and transfer into the food processor. Add remaining ingredients into the food processor and process until smooth. Serve and enjoy.

• •

Paprika Cauliflower

Steaks Total Time: 35 minutes | Serves: 4

Nutrition Info: Per Serving: Calories 78, Fat 7g, Carbs 4g, Protein 1g

INGREDIENTS

2 tbsp olive oil 1 head cauliflower, cut into steaks 1 tsp paprika Salt to taste

DIRECTIONS

1. Preheat oven to 240 F and line a baking sheet with aluminum foil. Rub each cauliflower steak with olive oil, salt, and paprika. Arrange on the baking sheet and bake for 20 minutes, flip, and bake for another 15-20 minutes until crispy. Serve.

• •

Crispy Potato Chips

Total Time: 40 minutes | Serves: 4

Nutrition Info: Per Serving: Calories 359, Fat 8g, Carbs 66g, Protein 9g

INGREDIENTS

4 large potatoes, cut into wedges 2 tbsp grated Parmesan cheese Salt and black pepper to taste 2 tbsp olive oil

DIRECTIONS

1. Preheat the oven to 340 F. In a bowl, combine the potatoes, olive oil, salt, and black pepper. Spread on a lined baking sheet and bake for 40 minutes until the edges are browned. Serve sprinkled with Parmesan cheese.

Healthy Trail Mix

Total Time: 30 minutes | Serves: 4

Nutrition Info: Per Serving: Calories 267, Fat 14g, Carbs 35g, Protein 7g

INGREDIENTS

1 cup pepitas 1 cup walnut halves 1 cup dried dates, chopped 1 cup dried apricots, cut into thin strips 1 cup golden raisins 1 cup raw almonds 2 tbsp olive oil 1 tsp salt

DIRECTIONS

1. Preheat the oven to 310 F. Combine almonds, pepitas, dates, walnuts, apricots, and raisins in a bowl. Mix in olive oil and salt and toss to coat. Spread the mixture on a lined with parchment paper sheet, and bake for 30 minutes or until the fruits are slightly browned. Let to cool and transfer to an airtight container

Citrusy Watermelon & Cantaloupe Balls

Total Time: 5 minutes + chilling time | Serves: 4

Nutrition Info: Per Serving: Calories 71, Fat 0g, Carbs 18g, Protein 1.5g

INGREDIENTS

2 cups watermelon balls 2 cups cantaloupe balls ½ cup orange juice ¼ cup lemon juice 1 tbsp orange zest

DIRECTIONS

1. Place the watermelon and cantaloupe in a bowl. In another bowl, mix the lime juice, orange juice and zest. Pour over the fruit. Transfer to the fridge covered for 5 hours. Serve.

Caper & Olive Snack

Total Time: 5 minutes + chilling time | Serves: 2

Nutrition Info: Per Serving: Calories 261, Fat 27.2g, Carbs 6.8g, Protei n 1.5g

INGREDIENTS

1 ½ cups green olives, drained ½ cup capers ½ red onion, sliced 3 garlic cloves, minced ¼ cup extra-virgin olive oil ¼ cup red wine vinegar 1 tbsp chopped fresh oregano 1 lemon, zested ½ tsp sea salt

DIRECTIONS

1. Combine olive oil, basil, vinegar, garlic, oregano, lemon zest, and salt in a bowl. Place red onion, olives, and capers in a bowl and pour over the marinade mixture. Serve chilled.

Party Nut Mix

Total Time: 20 minutes | Serves: 6

Nutrition Info: Per Serving: Calories 315, Fat 29.2g, Carbs 10.7g, Protein 7.5g

INGREDIENTS

1 tbsp olive oil 2 cups raw mixed nuts 1 tsp ground cumin ½ tsp garlic powder ½ tsp kosher salt 1/4 tsp chili powder 1/2 tsp ground coriander

DIRECTIONS

1. Place nuts in a skillet over medium heat and toast for 3 minutes, shaking the pan continuously. Remove to a bowl and reserve. Warm olive oil in the same skillet. Add in cumin, garlic powder, chili powder, and ground coriander and cook for about 20-30 seconds. Mix in nuts and cook for another 4 minutes. Serve chilled.

Greek-Style White Bean Spread

Total Time: 5 minutes | Serves: 6

Nutrition Info: Per Serving: Calories 222, Fat 6.8g, Carbs 30.4g, Protein 11.7g

INGREDIENTS

1 lemon, zested and juiced 1 (14-oz) can white beans, drained ¼ cup extra-virgin olive oil 2 garlic cloves, minced ¼ tsp ground cumin 2 tbsp chopped fresh Greek oregano 1 tsp stone-ground mustard Salt to taste

DIRECTIONS

1. In a food processor, blend beans, olive oil, garlic, mustard, lemon zest, lemon juice, cumin, and salt until smooth. Top with Greek oregano and serve.

Cucumber Tzatziki Dip with Walnuts

Total Time: 10 minutes + chilling time | Serves: 6

Nutrition Info: Per Serving: Calories 66, Fat 3.8g, Carbs 4g, Protein 5g

INGREDIENTS

1 large cucumber, grated 1 garlic clove, minced 1 cup Greek yogurt 1 tsp chopped fresh dill 1 tsp chopped fresh parsley Salt and black pepper to taste ¼ cup ground walnuts

DIRECTIONS

1. In a colander over the sink, squeeze the excess liquid out of the grated cucumber. Combine the yogurt, cucumber, garlic, salt, dill, and pepper in a bowl. Keep in the fridge covered for 2 hours. Serve topped with ground walnuts and parsley.

Greek-Style Potato Boats

Total Time: 1 hour 10 minutes | Serves: 4

Nutrition Info: Per Serving: Calories 294, Fat 18.6g, Carbs 21.6g, Protein 11.5g

INGREDIENTS

1 cup feta cheese, crumbled 1 lb potatoes ½ cup Greek yogurt 2 spring onions, chopped 3 sun-dried tomatoes, chopped ¼ cup Kalamata olives, pitted and chopped ½ tsp dried dill 1 tsp Greek oregano 2 tbsp halloumi cheese, grated 2 tbsp extra-virgin olive oil Salt and black pepper to taste

DIRECTIONS

1. Preheat oven to 400 F. Pierce the potatoes in several places with a fork. Wrap in aluminum foil and bake in the oven for 45-50 minutes until tender. Let cool. Split the cooled potatoes lengthwise and scoop out some of the flesh. Put the flesh in a bowl and mash with a fork. Add in the spring onions, sun-dried tomatoes, olives, dill, oregano, feta cheese, and yogurt and stir. Season with salt and pepper. Fill the potato shells with the feta mixture and Top with halloumi cheese. Transfer the boats to a baking sheet and place under the broiler for 5 minutes until the top is golden and crisp. Serve right away.

Herby Vegetable Medley with Marsala Sauce

Total Time: 30 minutes | Serves: 4

Nutrition Info: Per Serving: Calories 280, Fat 20.2g, Carbs 21.3g, Protein 4g

INGREDIENTS

Vegetables:
1 lb green beans, trimmed ½ lb carrots, trimmed 1 fennel bulb, sliced ¼ cup olive oil ¼ cup dry white wine ¼ tsp oregano ½ tsp thyme ½ tsp rosemary ¼ tsp coriander seeds ¼ tsp celery seeds ¼ tsp dried dill weed 1 head garlic, halved 1 red onion, sliced Salt and black pepper to taste

Sauce:
2 tbsp Marsala wine 2 tbsp plain yogurt 1 tbsp yellow mustard 1 tsp honey 1 tbsp lemon juice 1 yolk, from 1 hard-boiled egg 2 tbsp olive oil Salt to taste 1 tbsp paprika

DIRECTIONS

1. Preheat the oven to 380 F. In a bowl, combine the olive oil, white wine, oregano, thyme, rosemary, coriander seeds, celery seeds, dill weed, salt, and black pepper and mix well. Add in carrots, green beans, fennel, garlic, and onion and toss to coat. Spread the mixture on a baking dish and roast in the oven for 15-20 minutes until tender, checking occasionally. In the meantime, in a food processor, place the honey, yogurt, mustard, lemon juice, Marsala wine, yolk, olive oil, salt, and paprika, and blitz until smooth and uniform. Transfer to a bowl and place in the fridge until ready to use. When the veggies are ready, remove and serve with the prepared sauce on the side.

Lamb Arancini

Total Time: 25 minutes | Serves: 4

Nutrition Info: Per Serving: Calories 310, Fat 10g, Carbs 23g, Protein 7g

INGREDIENTS

1 lb ground lamb 1 cup Greek yogurt ½ tsp cumin, ground 1 garlic clove, minced Salt and black pepper to taste 1 cup rice 2 cups vegetable broth ¼ cup parsley, chopped ¼ cup shallots, chopped ½ tsp allspice 3 tbsp olive oil 2 eggs, lightly beaten 1 cup breadcrumbs

DIRECTIONS

1. Cook the rice in the vegetable broth for about 15 minutes. Remove from the heat and leave to cool uncovered. In a large bowl, mix the cooled rice, ground lamb, cumin, garlic, salt, pepper, parsley, shallots, and allspice until combined. Form medium balls out of the mixture. Dip the arancini in the beaten eggs and toss in the breadcrumbs. Warm the olive oil in a skillet over medium heat and fry meatballs for 14 minutes on all sides until golden brown. Remove to paper towels to absorb excess oil. Serve warm

---

Bell Pepper & Eggplant Dip

Total Time: 55 minutes | Serves: 4

Nutrition Info: Per Serving: Calories 220, Fat 14g, Carbs 25g, Protein 4g

INGREDIENTS

¼ cup olive oil 1 cup light mayonnaise 1 cup mushrooms, sliced 2 eggplants, sliced Salt and black pepper t o taste 4 garlic cloves, minced 1 tbsp chives, chopped

DIRECTIONS

1. Preheat the oven to 360 F. Arrange bell peppers and eggplants on a baking pan. Sprinkle with salt, pepper, and garlic and drizzle with some olive oil. Bake for 45 minutes. Transfer to a food processor and pulse until smooth a few times while gradually adding the remaining olive oil. Remove to a bowl and mix in mayonnaise. Top with chives to serve.

Cheesy Meatballs

Total Time: 25 minutes | Serves: 4

Nutrition Info: Per Serving: Calories 310, Fat 16g, Carbs 23g, Protein 36g

INGREDIENTS

1 lb ground beef ¼ cup panko breadcrumbs ¼ cup fresh mozzarella cheese, crumbled Salt and black pepper to taste 1 red onion, grated 2 tbsp parsley, chopped 2 garlic cloves, minced 1 lemon, juiced and zested 1 egg ½ tsp ground cumin ½ tsp ground coriander ¼ tsp cinnamon powder

DIRECTIONS

1. Preheat oven to 390 F. Line a baking sheet with parchment paper. Combine beef, breadcrumbs, salt, pepper, onion, parsley, garlic, lemon juice, lemon zest, egg, cumin, coriander, cinnamon powder, and fresh mozzarella cheese in a bowl and form balls out of the mixture. Place meatballs on the sheet and bake for 15 minutes. Serve warm.

Parmesan Trail Mix

Total Time: 10 minutes | Serves: 6

Nutrition Info: Per Serving: Calories 195, Fat 15.6g, Carbs 9.8g, Protein 7.3g

INGREDIENTS

¼ cup dried figs ½ cup almonds ¼ seed mix ¼ cup dried cranberries ½ cup walnut halves ½ cup hazelnuts ½ tsp paprika 1 tbsp Parmesan cheese, grated

DIRECTIONS

1. Spread almonds, walnuts, hazelnuts, and seeds on a greased baking dish. Bake in preheated oven for 10 minutes at 350 F. Remove and mix with figs and cranberries. Toss to combine. Sprinkle with Parmesan cheese and paprika and serve.

Za'atar Yogurt Spread

Total Time: 10 minutes | Serves: 6

Nutrition Info: Per Serving: Calories 300, Fat 19g, Carbs 22g, Protein 11g

INGREDIENTS

1/3 cup olive oil 2 cups Greek yogurt 2 tbsp pistachios, toasted and chopped Salt and white pepper to taste 2 tbsp mint, chopped 1 tbsp kalamata olives, chopped ¼ cup za'atar seasoning 3 pitta breads, cut into triangles

DIRECTIONS

1. Mix yogurt, pistachios, salt, pepper, mint, olives, za´atar spice, and olive oil in a bowl. Grill the pitta bread until golden, about 5-6 minutes. Serve with the yogurt spread.

Speedy Shallot & Kale Spread

Total Time: 10 minutes | Serves: 4

Nutrition Info: Per Serving: Calories 210, Fat 12g, Carbs 5g, Protein 6g

INGREDIENTS

2 shallots, chopped 1 lb kale, roughly chopped 2 tbsp mint, chopped ¾ cup cream cheese, soft Salt and black pepper to taste

DIRECTIONS

1. In a food processor, blend kale, shallots, mint, cream cheese, salt, and pepper until smooth. Serve.

Basil & Tomato Bruschetta

Total Time: 20 minutes | Serves: 4

Nutrition Info: Per Serving: Calories 170, Fat 5g, Carbs 30g, Protein 5g

INGREDIENTS

2 tbsp olive oil 1 ciabatta loaf, halved lengthwise 3 tbsp basil, chopped 4 tomatoes, cubed 1 shallot, sliced 2 garlic cloves, minced Salt and black pepper to taste 1 tbsp balsamic vinegar ½ tsp garlic powder

DIRECTIONS

1. Preheat the oven to 380 F. Line a baking sheet with parchment paper. Cut in half each half of the ciabatta loaf. Place them on the sheet and sprinkle with some olive oil. Bake for 10 minutes. Combine tomatoes, shallot, basil, garlic, salt, pepper, olive oil, vinegar, and garlic powder in a bowl and let sit for 10 minutes. Apportion the mixture among bread pieces. Serve.

Feta & Olive Stuffed Cherry Tomatoes

Total Time: 10 minutes | Serves: 4

Nutrition Info: Per Serving: Calories 140, Fat 9g, Carbs 6g, Protein 6g

INGREDIENTS

2 tbsp olive oil 16 cherry tomatoes 1 tbsp lemon zest ½ cup feta cheese, crumbled 2 tbsp olive tapenade ¼ cup parsley, torn

DIRECTIONS

1. Using a sharp knife, slice off the tops of the tomatoes and hollow out the insides. Combine olive oil, lemon zest, feta cheese, olive tapenade, and parsley in a bowl. Fill the cherry tomatoes with the feta cheese mixture and arrange them on a plate.

Scallion & Goat Cheese Dip

Total Time: 10 minutes | Serves: 4

Nutrition Info: Per Serving: Calories 230, Fat 12g, Carbs 9g, Protein 6g

INGREDIENTS

2 tbsp extra virgin olive oil 2 oz goat cheese, crumbled ¾ cup sour cream 2 tbsp scallions, chopped 1 tbsp lemon juice Salt and black pepper to taste

DIRECTIONS

1. Combine goat cheese, sour cream, scallions, lemon juice, salt, pepper, and olive oil in a bowl and transfer to the fridge for 10 minutes before serving.

Spicy Baba Ganoush

Total Time: 50 minutes | Serves: 4

Nutrition Info: Per Serving: Calories 130, Fat 5g, Carbs 2g, Protein 5g

INGREDIENTS

2 tbsp olive oil 2 eggplants, poked with a fork 2 tbsp tahini paste 1 tsp cayenne pepper 2 tbsp lemon juice 2 garlic cloves, minced Salt and black pepper to taste 1 tbsp parsley, chopped

DIRECTIONS

1. Preheat the oven to 380 F. Arrange eggplants on a roasting pan and bake for 40 minutes. Set aside to cool. Peel the cooled eggplants and place them in a blender along with the tahini paste, lemon juice, garlic, cayenne pepper, salt, and pepper. Puree these ingredients while gradually adding olive oil until smooth and homogeneous consistency. Serve with parsley.

Avocado Boats

Total Time: 10 minutes | Serves: 2

Nutrition Info: Per Serving: Calories 200, Fat 6g, Carbs 8g, Protein 6g

INGREDIENTS

4 anchovy fillets, chopped 1 avocado, halved and pitted 2 tbsp sun-dried tomatoes, chopped 1 tbsp basil pesto 2 tbsp black olives, pitted and chopped Salt and black pepper to taste 2 tsp pine nuts, toasted 1 tbsp basil, chopped

DIRECTIONS

1. Per Serving: Calories 240, Fat 10g, Carbs 12g, Protein 6g
2. Toss anchovies, sun-dried tomatoes, basil pesto, olives, salt, pepper, pine nuts, and basil in a bowl. Fill each avocado half with the mixture and serve immediately.

Tuna-Zucchini Rolls

Total Time: 5 minutes | Serves: 4

Nutrition Info: Per Serving: Calories 210, Fat 7g, Carbs 8g, Protein 4g

INGREDIENTS

2 tbsp olive oil ½ cup mayonnaise 2 tbsp capers 5 oz canned tuna, drained and mashed 2 zucchinis, sliced lengthwise 1 tbsp parsley, chopped Salt and black pepper to taste 1 tsp lime juice

DIRECTIONS

1. Heat a grill pan over medium heat. Drizzle the zucchini slices with olive oil and season with salt and pepper. Grill for 5-6 minutes on both sides. In a bowl, mix the tuna, capers, parsley, lime juice, mayonnaise, salt, and pepper until well combined. Spread the tuna mixture onto zucchini slices and roll them up. Transfer the rolls to a plate and serve.

Prosciutto Wrapped Pears

Total Time: 5 minutes | Serves: 4

Nutrition Info: Per Serving: Calories 35, Fat 2g, Carbs 5g, Protein 12g

INGREDIENTS

2 pears, cored and cut into wedges
4 oz prosciutto slices, halved lengthwise 1 tbsp chives, chopped 1 tsp red pepper flakes

DIRECTIONS

1. Wrap the pear wedges with a prosciutto and transfer to a platter. Garnish with chives and pepper flakes. Serve right away.

Yogurt & Walnut Dip

Total Time: 5 minutes | Serves: 8

Nutrition Info: Per Serving: Calories 210, Fat 7g, Carbs 16g, Protein 9g

INGREDIENTS

2 cups Greek yogurt 3 garlic cloves, minced ¼ cup dill, chopped 1 green onion, chopped ¼ cup walnuts, chopped Salt and black pepper to taste

DIRECTIONS

1. Combine garlic, yogurt, dill, walnuts, salt, and pepper in a bowl. Serve topped with green onion.

Parsley Ricotta Cheese Dip

Total Time: 5 minutes | Serves: 4

Nutrition Info: Per Serving: Calories 260, Fat 12g, Carbs 9g, Protein 12g

INGREDIENTS

8 oz ricotta cheese, crumbled 2 tbsp fresh parsley, chopped ¼ cup chives, chopped Salt and black pepper to taste 2 tbsp extra virgin olive oil

DIRECTIONS

1. In a blender, pulse ricotta cheese, parsley, chives, salt, pepper, and olive oil until smooth. Serve.

Vegetable Cakes

Total Time: 20 minutes | Serves: 4

Nutrition Info: Per Serving: Calories 220, Fat 12g, Carbs 5g, Protein 5g

INGREDIENTS

2 carrots, grated 2 zucchinis, grated and drained 2 garlic cloves, minced 2 spring onions, chopped 1 tsp cumin ½ tsp turmeric powder Salt and black pepper to taste ¼ tsp ground coriander 2 tbsp parsley, chopped ¼ tsp lemon juice ½ cup flour 1 egg, whisked ¼ cup breadcrumbs 3 tbsp olive oil

DIRECTIONS

1. Combine garlic, spring onions, carrot, cumin, turmeric, salt, pepper, coriander, parsley, lemon juice, almond flour, zucchinis, egg, and breadcrumbas in a bowl and mix well. Form balls out of the mixture and flatten them to form patties. Warm olive oil in a skillet over medium heat. Fry the cakes for 10 minutes on both sides. Remove to a paper-lined plate to drain the excessive grease. Serve warm.

Dilled Salmon Rolls

Total Time: 5 minutes | Serves: 4

Nutrition Info: Per Serving: Calories 250, Fat 16g, Carbs 17g, Protein 18g

INGREDIENTS

8 Kalalmata olives, pitted and chopped 4 oz smoked salmon, cut into strips 1 cucumber, thinly sliced lengthwise 2 tsp lime juice 4 oz cream cheese, soft 1 tsp lemon zest, grated Salt and black pepper to taste 2 tsp dill, chopped

DIRECTIONS

1. Place cucumber slices on a flat surface and top each with a salmon strip. Combine olives, lime juice, cream cheese, lemon zest, salt, pepper, and dill in a bowl. Smear cream mixture over salmon and roll them up. Serve immediately.

Eggplant Fries

Total Time: 35 minutes | Serves: 4

Nutrition Info: Per Serving: Calories 140, Fat 8g, Carbs 12g, Protein 3g

INGREDIENTS

2 eggplants, sliced 2 tbsp olive oil ½ tbsp smoked paprika Salt and black pepper to taste ½ tsp onion powder 2 tsp dried sage 1 cup fine breadcrumbs 1 large egg white, beaten

DIRECTIONS

1. Preheat the oven to 350 F. Line a baking sheet with parchment paper. In a bowl, mix olive oil, paprika, salt, pepper, onion powder, and sage. Dip the eggplant slices in the egg white then coat in the breadcrumb mixture. Arrange them on the sheet and roast in the oven for 25 minutes, flipping once. Serve cold.

Balsamic Beet Bites with Feta

Total Time: 40 minutes | Serves: 4

Nutrition Info: Per Serving: Calories 210, Fat 6g, Carbs 9g, Protein 4g

INGREDIENTS

1 cup feta cheese, crumbled 1 cup olive oil 2 beets, sliced Salt and black pepper to taste 1/3 cup balsamic vinegar

DIRECTIONS

1. Preheat the oven to 340 F. Line a baking sheet with parchment paper. Arrange beet slices, salt, pepper, vinegar, and olive oil on the sheet and toss to combine. Bake for 30 minutes. Serve topped with feta cheese.

Arugula & Pesto Dip

Total Time: 5 minutes | Serves: 4

Nutrition Info: Per Serving: Calories 240, Fat 15g, Carbs 7g, Protein 6g

INGREDIENTS

1 cup arugula, chopped 3 tbsp basil pesto 1 cup cream cheese, soft Salt and black pepper to taste 1 cup heavy cream 1 tbsp chives, chopped

DIRECTIONS

1. Combine arugula, basil pesto, salt, pepper, and heavy cream in a blender and pulse until smooth. Transfer to a bowl and mix in cream cheese. Serve topped with chives.

Olive & Cucumber "Pasta"

Total Time: 5 minutes | Serves: 4

Nutrition Info: Per Serving: Calories 150, Fat 15g, Carbs 4g, Protein 2g

INGREDIENTS

2 cucumbers, spiralized ½ cup black olives, pitted and sliced 1 cup cherry tomatoes, halved Salt and black pepper to taste 1 small red onion, chopped ½ cup goat cheese, crumbled ½ cup olive oil ¼ cup apple cider vinegar

DIRECTIONS

1. Combine olives, tomatoes, salt, pepper, onion, goat cheese, olive oil, and vinegar in a bowl and mix well. Place the cucumbers on a platter and top with the cheese mixture. Serve immediately.

Feta-Stuffed Zucchini

Total Time: 50 minutes | Serves: 4

Nutrition Info: Per Serving: Calories 200, Fat 16.5g, Carbs 7g, Protein 8.3g

INGREDIENTS

2 tbsp olive oil 1 egg 2 zucchinis, halved lengthwise 2 garlic cloves, minced 2 tbsp oregano, chopped 1 lemon, juiced Salt and black pepper to taste 1 cup feta cheese, crumbled

DIRECTIONS

1. Preheat the oven to 390 F. Line a baking sheet with parchment paper. Scoop the flesh from the zucchini halves to make shells and place them on the baking sheet. In a bowl, mix egg, feta cheese, garlic, oregano, salt, pepper, and olive oil and bake for 40 minutes. Remove to a plate and serve.

Ricotta Stuffed Potatoes

Total Time: 40 minutes | Serves: 4

Nutrition Info: Per Serving: Calories 310, Fat 10g, Carbs 23g, Protein 9g

INGREDIENTS

2 tbsp olive oil 1 lb red baby potatoes 1 cup ricotta cheese, crumbled 2 garlic cloves, minced 1 tbsp chives, chopped ½ tsp hot chili sauce Salt and black pepper to taste

DIRECTIONS

1. Place potatoes and enough water in a pot over medium heat and bring to a boil. Simmer for 15 minutes and drain. Let them cool. Cut them in halves and scoop out the pulp. Place the pulp in a bowl and mash it a bit with a fork. Add in the ricotta cheese, olive oil, garlic, chives, hot chili sauce, salt, and pepper and mix to combine. Fill potato skins with the mixture. Preheat the oven to 360 F. Line a baking sheet with parchment paper. Place filled skins on the sheet and bake for 10 minutes.

Baked Sweet Potatoes

Total Time: 1 hour 10 minutes | Serves: 4

Nutrition Info: Per Serving: Calories 220, Fat 6g, Carbs 7g, Protein 4g

INGREDIENTS

4 tbsp olive oil 1 cup arugula 1 garlic clove, minced 4 sweet potatoes, pricked with a fork 1 red onion, sliced 1 lemon, juiced and zested 2 tbsp dill, chopped 2 tbsp Greek yogurt 2 tbsp tahini paste Salt and black pepper to taste

DIRECTIONS

1. Boil the tagliatelle in a pot over medium heat for 9-11 minutes or until "al dente". Drain and set aside. Warm the olive oil in a skillet over medium heat and sauté lamb, onions, and garlic until the meat is browned, about 10-15 minutes. Stir in cumin, paprika, salt, and pepper for 1-2 minutes. Spoon tagliatelle on a platter and scatter lamb over. Top with parsley and serve.

Perfect Queso

Preparation Time: 10 minutes | Cooking Time: 15 minutes | Servings: 16

Nutrition Info: Calories 257 Fat 15.9 g Carbohydrates 10.2 g Sugar 4.9 g Protein 21 g Cholesterol 71 m g

INGREDIENTS

1 lb ground beef 32 oz Velveeta cheese, cut into cubes 10 oz can tomatoes, diced 1 1/2 tbsp taco seasoning 1 tsp chili powder 1 onion, diced Pepper Salt

DIRECTIONS

1. Set instant pot on sauté mode. Add meat, onion, taco seasoning, chili powder, pepper, and salt into the pot and cook until meat is no longer pink. Add tomatoes and stir well. Top with cheese and do not stir. Seal pot with lid and cook on high for 4 minutes. Once done, release pressure using quick release. Remove lid. Stir everything well and serve.

Cucumber Tomato Okra Salsa

Preparation Time: 10 minutes | Cooking Time: 5 minutes | Servings: 8

Nutrition Info: Calories 99 Fat 4.2 g Carbohydrates 14.3 g Sugar 6.4 g Protein 2.9 g Cholesterol 0 mg

INGREDIENTS

28 oz can artichoke hearts, drain and quartered 1 1/2 cups parmesan cheese, shredded 1 cup sour cream 1 cup mayonnaise 3.5 oz can green chilies 1 cup of water Pepper Salt

DIRECTIONS

1. Add artichokes, water, and green chilies into the instant pot. Seal pot with the lid and select manual and set timer for 1 minute. Once done, release pressure using quick release. Remove lid. Drain excess water. Set instant pot on sauté mode. Add remaining ingredients and stir well and cook until cheese is melted. Serve and enjoy.

Creamy Artichoke Dip

Total Time: 50 minutes | Serves: 4

Nutrition Info: Calories 262 Fat 7.6 g Carbohydrates 14.4 g Sugar 2.8 g Protein 8.4 g Cholesterol 32 mg

INGREDIENTS

2 tbsp olive oil 1 egg 2 zucchinis, halved lengthwise 2 garlic cloves, minced 2 tbsp oregano, chopped 1 lemon, juiced Salt and black pepper to taste 1 cup feta cheese, crumbled

DIRECTIONS

1. DIRECTION S
2. Preheat the oven to 390 F. Line a baking sheet with parchment paper. Scoop the flesh from the zucchini halves to make shells and place them on the baking sheet. In a bowl, mix egg, feta cheese, garlic, oregano, salt, pepper, and olive oil and bake for 40 minutes. Remove to a plate and serve.

Delicious Eggplant Caponata

Preparation Time: 10 minutes | Cooking Time: 5 minutes | Servings: 8

Nutrition Info: Calories 60 Fat 0.4 g Carbohydrates 14 g Sugar 8.8 g Protein 2.3 g Cholesterol 0.4 mg

INGREDIENTS

1 eggplant, cut into 1/2-inch chunks 1 lb tomatoes, diced 1/2 cup tomato puree 1/4 cup dates, chopped 2 tbsp vinegar 1/2 cup fresh parsley, chopped 2 celery stalks, chopped 1 small onion, chopped 2 zucchini, cut into 1/2-inch chunks Pepper Salt

DIRECTIONS

1. Add all ingredients into the inner pot of instant pot and stir well. Seal pot with lid and cook on high for 5 minutes. Once done, release pressure using quick release. Remove lid. Stir well and serve.

Perfect Italian Potatoes

Preparation Time: 10 minutes | Cooking Time: 7 minutes | Servings: 6

Nutrition Info: Calories 149 Fat 0.3 g Carbohydrates 41.6 g Sugar 11.4 g Protein 4.5 g Cholesterol 0 mg

INGREDIENTS

2 lbs baby potatoes, clean and cut in half 3/4 cup vegetable broth 6 oz Italian dry dressing mix

DIRECTIONS

1. Add all ingredients into the inner pot of instant pot and stir well. Seal pot with lid and cook on high for 7 minutes. Once done, allow to release pressure naturally for 3 minutes then release remaining using quick release. Remove lid. Stir well and serve.

Creamy Eggplant Dip

Preparation Time: 10 minutes | Cooking Time: 20 minutes | Servings: 4

Nutrition Info: Calories 108 Fat 7.8 g Carbohydrates 9.7 g Sugar 3.7 g Protein 2.5 g Cholesterol 0 mg

INGREDIENTS

1 eggplant 1/2 tsp paprika 1 tbsp olive oil 1 tbsp fresh lime juice 2 tbsp tahini 1 garlic clove 1 cup of water Pepper Salt

DIRECTIONS

1. Add water and eggplant into the instant pot. Seal pot with the lid and select manual and set timer for 20 minutes. Once done, release pressure using quick release. Remove lid. Drain eggplant and let it cool. Once the eggplant is cool then remove eggplant skin and transfer eggplant flesh into the food processor. Add remaining ingredients into the food processor and process until smooth. Serve and enjoy.

Tasty Black Bean Dip

Preparation Time: 10 minutes | Cooking Time: 18 minutes | Servings: 6

Nutrition Info: : Calories 402 Fat 15.3 g Carbohydrates 46.6 g Sugar 4.4 g Protein 22.2 g Cholesterol 30 mg

INGREDIENTS

2 cups dry black beans, soaked overnight and drained 1 1/2 cups cheese, shredded 1 tsp dried oregano 1 1/2 tsp chili powder 2 cups tomatoes, chopped 2 tbsp olive oil 1 1/2 tbsp garlic, minced 1 medium onion, sliced 4 cups vegetable stock Pepper Salt

DIRECTIONS

1. Add all ingredients except cheese into the instant pot. Seal pot with lid and cook on high for 18 minutes. Once done, allow to release pressure naturally. Remove lid. Drain excess water. Add cheese and stir until cheese is melted. Blend bean mixture using an immersion blender until smooth. Serve and enjoy.

Creamy Pepper Spread

Preparation Time: 10 minutes | Cooking Time: 15 minutes | Servings: 4

Nutrition Info: Calories 41 Fat 3.6 g Carbohydrates 3.5 g Sugar 1.7 g Protein 0.4 g Cholesterol 0 mg

INGREDIENTS

1 lb red bell peppers, chopped and remove seeds 1 1/2 tbsp fresh basil 1 tbsp olive oil 1 tbsp fresh lime juice 1 tsp garlic, minced Pepper Salt

DIRECTIONS

1. Add all ingredients into the inner pot of instant pot and stir well. Seal pot with lid and cook on high for 15 minutes. Once done, allow to release pressure naturally for 10 minutes then release remaining using quick release. Remove lid. Transfer bell pepper mixture into the food processor and process until smooth. Serve and enjoy.

Kidney Bean Spread with Lemon

Preparation Time: 10 minutes | Cooking Time: 18 minutes | Servings: 4

Nutrition Info: Calories 461 Fat 8.6 g Carbohydrates 73 g Sugar 4 g Protein 26.4 g Cholesterol 0 mg

INGREDIENTS

1 lb dry kidney beans, soaked overnight and drained 1 tsp garlic, minced 2 tbsp olive oil 1 tbsp fresh lemon juice 1 tbsp paprika 4 cups vegetable stock 1/2cup onion, chopped Pepper Salt

DIRECTIONS

1. Add beans and stock into the instant pot. Seal pot with lid and cook on high for 18 minutes. Once done, allow to release pressure naturally. Remove lid. Drain beans well and reserve 1/2 cup stock. Transfer beans, reserve stock, and remaining ingredients into the food processor and process until smooth. Serve and enjoy.

Spicy Berry Dip

Preparation Time: 10 minutes | Cooking Time: 15 minutes | Servings: 4

Nutrition Info: Calories 49 Fat 0.2 g Carbohydrates 8.6 g Sugar 4.1 g Protein 0.3 g Cholesterol 0 mg

INGREDIENTS

10 oz cranberries 1/4 cup fresh orange juice 3/4 tsp paprika 1/2 tsp chili powder 1 tsp lemon zest 1 tbsp lemon juice

DIRECTIONS

1. Add all ingredients into the inner pot of instant pot and stir well. Seal pot with lid and cook on high for 15 minutes. Once done, allow to release pressure naturally for 5 minutes then release remaining using quick release. Remove lid. Blend cranberry mixture using a blender until getting the desired consistency. Serve and enjoy.

Tomato Olive Salsa

Preparation Time: 10 minutes | Cooking Time: 5 minutes | Servings: 4

Nutrition Info: Calories 119 Fat 10.8 g Carbohydrates 6.5 g Sugar 1.3 g Protein 1.2 g Cholesterol 0 mg

INGREDIENTS

2 cups olives, pitted and chopped 1/4 cup fresh parsley, chopped 1/4 cup fresh basil, chopped 2 tbsp green onion, chopped 1 cup grape tomatoes, halved 1 tbsp olive oil 1 tbsp vinegar Pepper Salt

DIRECTIONS

1. Add all ingredients into the inner pot of instant pot and stir well. Seal pot with lid and cook on high for 5 minutes. Once done, allow to release pressure naturally for 5 minutes then release remaining using quick release. Remove lid. Stir well and serve.

Balsamic Bell Pepper Salsa

Preparation Time: 10 minutes | Cooking Time: 6 minutes | Servings: 2

Nutrition Info: Calories 235 Fat 14.2 g Carbohydrates 19.8 g Sugar 10.7 g Protein 9.2 g Cholesterol 25 mg

INGREDIENTS

2 red bell peppers, chopped and seeds removed 1 cup grape tomatoes, halved 1/2 tbsp cayenne 1 tbsp balsamic vinegar 2 cup vegetable broth 1/2 cup sour cream 1/2 tsp garlic powder 1/2 onion, chopped Salt

DIRECTIONS

1. Add all ingredients except cream into the instant pot and stir well. Seal pot with lid and cook on high for 6 minutes. Once done, release pressure using quick release. Remove lid. Add sour cream and stir well. Blend the salsa mixture using an immersion blender until smooth. Serve and enjoy.

Slow Cooked Cheesy Artichoke Dip

Preparation Time: 10 minutes | Cooking Time: 60 minutes | Servings: 6

Nutrition Info: Calories 226 Fat 19.3 g Carbohydrates 7.5 g Sugar 1.2 g Protein 6.8 g Cholesterol 51 mg

INGREDIENTS

DIRECTIONS

10 oz can artichoke hearts, drained and chopped 4 cups spinach, chopped 8 oz cream cheese 3 tbsp sour cream 1/4 cup mayonnaise 3/4 cup mozzarella cheese, shredded 1/4 cup parmesan cheese, grated 3 garlic cloves, minced 1/2 tsp dried parsley Pepper Salt

1. Add all ingredients into the inner pot of instant pot and stir well. Seal the pot with the lid and select slow cook mode and set the timer for 60 minutes. Stir once while cooking. Serve and enjoy.

Pepper Tomato Eggplant Spread

Preparation Time: 10 minutes | Cooking Time: 10 minutes | Servings: 3

Nutrition Info: Calories 178 Fat 14.4 g Carbohydrates 12.8 g Sugar 7 g Protein 2.4 g Cholesterol 0 mg

INGREDIENTS

DIRECTIONS

2 cups eggplant, chopped 1/4 cup vegetable broth 2 tbsp tomato paste 1/4 cup sun-dried tomatoes, minced 1 cup bell pepper, chopped 1 tsp garlic, minced 1 cup onion, chopped 3 tbsp olive oil Salt

1. Add oil into the inner pot of instant pot and set the pot on sauté mode. Add onion and sauté for 3 minutes. Add eggplant, bell pepper, and garlic and sauté for 2 minutes. Add remaining ingredients and stir well. Seal pot with lid and cook on high for 5 minutes. Once done, release pressure using quick release. Remove lid. Lightly mash the eggplant mixture using a potato masher. Stir well and serve.

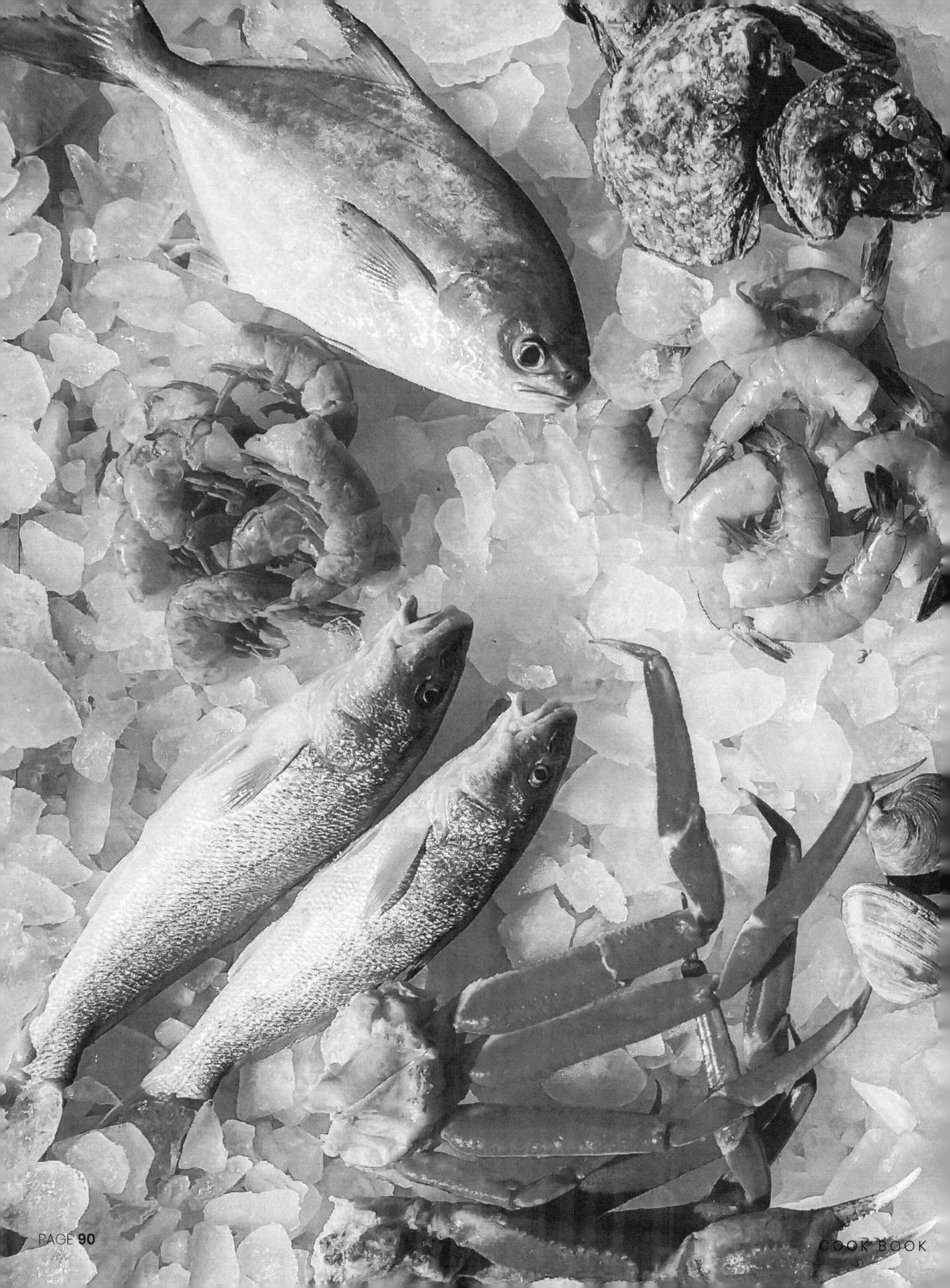

FISH & SEAFOODS

Roasted Salmon Parcels

Total Time : 20 minutes | Serves : 4

Nutrition Info: Per Serving : Calories 212, Fat 14g, Carbs 0.5g, Protein 22.1g

INGREDIENTS

- 1 pound salmon fillets
- ¼ fresh parsley, chopped
- 1 garlic clove, minced
- ¼ tsp dried dill
- ¼ tsp chili powder
- ¼ tsp garlic powder
- 1 lemon, grated
- 2 tbsp olive oil
- Salt and black pepper to taste

DIRECTIONS

1. Preheat oven to 350 F. Sprinkle the salmon with dill, chili powder, garlic powder, salt, and pepper.
2. Warm olive oil in a pan over medium heat and sear salmon skin-side down for 5 minutes. Transfer to the oven and bake for another 4-5 minutes. Combine parsley, lemon zest, garlic, and salt in a bowl. Serve the salmon topped with the mixture.

Salmon with Shrimp Tomato Sauce

Total Time : 30 minutes | Serves : 4

Nutrition Info: Per Serving : Calories 290, Fat 19g, Carbs 5g, Protein 26g

INGREDIENTS

- 4 oz smoked salmon, sliced
- 2 oz feta cheese, crumbled
- 4 oz cream cheese, softened
- 2 tbsp horseradish sauce
- 2 tsp orange zest
- 1 red onion, chopped
- 2 tbsp chives, chopped
- 1 thin baguette, sliced and toasted

DIRECTIONS

1. In a bowl, mix cream cheese, horseradish sauce, onion, feta cheese, and orange zest until smooth. Spread the mixture on the baguette slices. Top with salmon and sprinkle with chives to serve.

Roasted Salmon with Asparagus

Total Time : 20 minutes | Serves : 4

Nutrition Info: Per Serving : Calories 310, Fat 16g, Carbs 19g, Protein 21 g

INGREDIENTS

- 4 salmon fillets, skinless
- 2 tbsp balsamic vinegar
- 1 bunch of asparagus, trimmed
- 2 tbsp olive oil
- Salt and black pepper to taste

DIRECTIONS

1. Preheat the oven to 380F. In a roasting pan, arrange the salmon fillets and asparagus spears. Season with salt and pepper and drizzle with olive oil and balsamic vinegar; roast for 12-15 minutes. Serve warm.

Saucy Thyme Salmon

Total Time : 25 minutes | Serves : 4

Nutrition Info: Per Serving : Calories 300, Fat 18g, Carbs 27g, Protein 26g

INGREDIENTS

- 4 salmon fillets, boneless
- 1 tsp thyme, chopped
- 2 tbsp olive oil
- Salt and black pepper to taste
- 1 lb cherry tomatoes, halved

DIRECTIONS

1. Warm the olive oil in a skillet over medium heat and sear salmon for 6 minutes, turning once; set aside. In the same skillet, stir in cherry tomatoes for 3-4 minutes and sprinkle with thyme, salt, and pepper. Pour the sauce over the salmon and serve.

Fried Salmon with Escarole & Olives

Total Time : 25 minutes | Serves : 4

Nutrition Info: Per Serving : Calories 280, Fat 15g, Carbs 25g, Protein 19g

INGREDIENTS

- 1 head escarole, torn
- 4 salmon fillets, boneless
- 1 lime, juiced
- Salt and black pepper to taste
- ¼ cup fish stock
- ¼ cup green olives, pitted and chopped
- ¼ cup fresh chives, chopped
- 3 tbsp olive oil

DIRECTIONS

1. Warm half of oil in a skillet over medium heat and sauté escarole, lime juice, salt, pepper, fish stock, and olives for 6 minutes. Share into plates. Warm the remaining oil in the same skillet. Sprinkle salmon with salt and pepper and fry for 8 minutes on both sides until golden brown. Transfer to the escarole plates and serve warm.

Chili Salmon with Fennel & Peppers

Total Time : 30 minutes | Serves : 4

Nutrition Info: Per Serving : Calories 580, Fat 19g, Carbs 73g, Protein 35g

INGREDIENTS

- 2 tbsp olive oil
- 4 salmon fillets, boneless
- 1 fennel bulb, sliced
- Salt and black pepper to taste
- ½ tsp chili powder
- 1 yellow bell pepper, chopped
- 1 red bell pepper, chopped
- 1 green bell pepper, chopped

DIRECTIONS

1. Warm olive oil in a skillet over medium heat. Season the salmon with chili powder, salt, and pepper and cook for 6-8 minutes, turning once. Remove to a serving plate. Add fennel and peppers to the skillet and cook for another 10 minutes until tender. Top the salmon with the mixture and serve warm.

Mustard Salmon with Walnuts

Total Time : 25 minutes | Serves : 4

Nutrition Info: Per Serving : Calories 300, Fat 16g, Carbs 22g, Protein 17g

INGREDIENTS

- 4 salmon fillets, boneless
- 2 tbsp olive oil
- 2 tbsp mustard
- 5 tsp honey
- 1 cup walnuts, chopped
- 1 tbsp lemon juice
- 2 tsp parsley, chopped
- Salt and pepper to the taste

DIRECTIONS

1. Preheat the oven to 380F. Line a baking tray with parchment paper. In a bowl, whisk the olive oil, mustard, and honey. In a separate bowl, combine walnuts and parsley. Sprinkle salmon with salt and pepper and place them on the tray. Rub each fillet with mustard mixture and scatter with walnut mixture; bake for 15 minutes. Drizzle with lemon juice and serve.

Paprika Cod with Cabbage

Total Time : 30 minutes | Serves : 4

Nutrition Info: Per Serving : Calories 200, Fat 14g, Carbs 24g, Protein 18 g

INGREDIENTS

- 1 head white cabbage, shredded
- 1 tsp garlic powder
- 1 tsp smoked paprika
- 2 tbsp olive oil
- 4 cod fillets, boneless
- ½ cup tomato sauce
- 1 tsp Italian seasoning
- 1 tbsp chives, chopped

DIRECTIONS

1. Preheat the oven to 390F. Mix cabbage, garlic powder, paprika, olive oil, tomato sauce, Italian seasoning, and chives in a roasting pan. Top with cod fillets and bake covered with foil for 20 minutes. Serve immediately.

Balsamic Salmon with Haricots Vert

Total Time : 25 minutes | Serves : 4

Nutrition Info: Per Serving : Calories 230, Fat 16g, Carbs 23g, Protein 17g

INGREDIENTS

- 2 tbsp olive oil
- 3 tbsp balsamic vinegar
- 1 garlic clove, minced
- ½ tsp red pepper flakes, crushed
- ½ tsp lime zest
- 1 ½ lb haricots vert, chopped
- Salt and black pepper to taste
- 1 red onion, sliced
- 4 salmon fillets, boneless

DIRECTIONS

1. Warm half of oil in a skillet over medium heat and sauté vinegar, onion, garlic, red pepper flakes, lime zest, haricots vert, salt, and pepper for 6 minutes. Share into plates. Warm the remaining oil. Sprinkle salmon with salt and pepper and sear for 8 minutes on all sides. Serve with haricots vert.

Avocado Salmon Tartare

Total Time : 10 minutes + chilling time | Serves : 4

Nutrition Info: Per Serving : Calories 230, Fat 15g, Carbs 13g, Protein 6g

INGREDIENTS

- 1 tbsp olive oil
- 4 tbsp scallions, chopped
- 2 tsp lemon juice
- 1 avocado, chopped
- 1 lb salmon, skinless, boneless and cubed
- Salt and black pepper to taste
- 1 tbsp parsley, chopped

DIRECTIONS

1. Mix scallions, lemon juice, olive oil, salmon, salt, pepper, and parsley in a bowl. Place in the fridge for 1 hour. Place a baking ring on a serving plate and pour in the salmon mixture. Top with avocado and gently press down. Serve.

Eggplant & Salmon Rolls

Total Time : 20 minutes | Serves : 4

Nutrition Info: Per Serving : Calories 310, Fat 25g, Carbs 16g, Protein 12g

INGREDIENTS

2 tbsp olive oil
1 cup ricotta cheese, soft
4 oz smoked salmon, chopped
2 eggplants, lengthwise cut into thin slices
2 tsp lemon zest, grated
1 tbsp dill, chopped
1 small red onion, sliced
Salt and pepper to the taste

DIRECTIONS

1. Combine ricotta cheese, lemon zest, dill, onion, salt, and pepper in a bowl. Grease the eggplant slices with olive oil and grill them on a preheated grill pan for 3-4 minutes per side. Set aside to cool. Spread the cooled eggplant slices with the salmon mixture. Gently roll out and secure with toothpicks and serve cold.

Smoked Trout Dip

Total Time : 5 minutes | Serves : 4

Nutrition Info: Per Serving : Calories 270, Fat 5g, Carbs 6g, Protein 8g

INGREDIENTS

1 cup Greek yogurt
2 oz smoked trout, flaked
1 tbsp lemon juice
2 tbsp chives, chopped
Salt and black pepper to taste
2 tbsp olive oil

DIRECTIONS

1. Place trout, lemon juice, yogurt, chives, salt, pepper, and olive oil in a bowl and toss to combine. Serve with crackers.

Rosemary Trout with Roasted Beets

Total Time : 45 minutes | Serves : 4

Nutrition Info: Per Serving : Calories 240, Fat 6g, Carbs 22g, Protein 18 g

INGREDIENTS

3 tbsp olive oil
4 trout fillets, boneless
1 lb medium beets, peeled and sliced
Salt and black pepper to taste
1 tbsp rosemary, chopped
2 spring onions, chopped
2 tbsp lemon juice
½ cup vegetable stock

DIRECTIONS

1. Preheat the oven to 390F. Line a baking sheet with parchment paper. Arrange the beets on the sheet, season with salt and pepper, and drizzle with some olive oil. Roast for 20 minutes.

2. Warm the remaining oil in a skillet over medium heat. Cook trout fillets for 8 minutes on all sides; reserve. Add spring onions to the skillet and sauté for 2 minutes. Stir in lemon juice and vegetable stock and cook for 5-6 minutes until the sauce thickens. Remove the beets to a plate and top with trout fillets. Pour the sauce all over and sprinkle with rosemary to serve.

Trout & Farro Bowls

Total Time : 50 minutes | Serves : 4

Nutrition Info: Per Serving : Calories 290, Fat 13g, Carbs 6g, Protein 37g

INGREDIENTS

- 8 trout fillets, boneless
- 1 cup farro
- Juice of 2 lemons
- 4 tbsp olive oil
- Salt and black pepper to taste
- 1 avocado, chopped
- ¼ cup balsamic vinegar
- 1 garlic cloves, minced
- ¼ cup parsley, chopped
- ¼ cup mint, chopped
- 2 tbsp yellow mustard

DIRECTIONS

1. Boil salted water in a pot over medium heat and stir in farro. Simmer for 30 minutes and drain. Remove to a bowl and combine with lemon juice, mustard, garlic, salt, pepper, and half olive oil. Set aside. Mash the avocado with a fork in a bowl and mix with vinegar, salt, pepper, parsley, dill, and mint.
2. Warm the remaining oil in a skillet over medium heat and brown trout fillets skin-side down for 10 minutes on both sides. Let cool and cut into pieces. Put over farro and stir in avocado dressing. Serve immediately.

Pan-Seared Trout with Tzatziki

Total Time : 20 minutes | Serves : 4

Nutrition Info: Per Serving : Calories 400, Fat 19g, Carbs 19g, Protein 41g

INGREDIENTS

- 4 trout fillets, boneless
- ½ lime, juiced
- Salt and black pepper to taste
- 1 garlic clove, minced
- 1 tsp sweet paprika
- 3 tbsp olive oil
- 1 cucumber, grated and squeezed
- 4 garlic cloves, minced
- 2 cups Greek yogurt
- 1 tbsp dill, chopped

DIRECTIONS

1. Warm 2 tbsp of the olive oil in a skillet over medium heat. Sprinkle the trout with salt, pepper, lime juice, garlic, and paprika and sear for 8 minutes on all sides. Remove to a paper towel–lined plate. Combine cucumber, garlic, remaining olive oil, yogurt, salt, and dill in a bowl. Share trout into plates and serve with tzatziki.

Oven-Baked Rainbow Trout

Total Time : 35 minutes | Serves : 4

Nutrition Info: Per Serving : Calories 310, Fat 10g, Carbs 25g, Protein 16g

INGREDIENTS

- 3 tbsp olive oil
- 2 tbsp horseradish sauce
- 1 onion, sliced
- 2 tsp Italian seasoning
- 4 trout fillets, boneless
- ¼ cup panko breadcrumbs
- ½ cup green olives, pitted and chopped
- 1 lemon, juiced

DIRECTIONS

1. Preheat the oven to 380F. Line a baking sheet with parchment paper. Sprinkle trout fillets with salt and pepper and dip in breadcrumbs. Arrange them along with the onion on the sheet. Sprinkle with olive oil, Italian seasoning, and lemon juice and bake for 15-18 minutes. Transfer to a serving plate and top with horseradish sauce and olives. Serve right away.

Roasted Cod with Mozzarella & Tomatoes

Total Time : 35 minutes | Serves : 4

Nutrition Info: Per Serving : Calories 270, Fat 11g, Carbs 25g, Protein 21 g

INGREDIENTS

- 2 tbsp olive oil
- 4 cod fillets, boneless
- Salt and black pepper to taste
- 12 cherry tomatoes, halved
- 1 red chili pepper, chopped
- 1 tbsp cilantro, chopped
- 2 tbsp balsamic vinegar
- 1 oz fresh mozzarella cheese, torn

DIRECTIONS

1. Preheat the oven to 380F.
2. Drizzle the cod fillets with some olive oil and season with salt and pepper. Place them on a roasting tray, top with mozzarella cheese, and bake for 15 minutes until golden and crispy.
3. In the meantime, warm the remaining oil in a skillet over medium heat and cook the cherry tomatoes for 5 minutes. Stir in red chili pepper, cilantro, and balsamic vinegar for another 1-2 minutes. Serve the fish with sautéed veggies on the side.

Turmeric Cod

Total Time : 35 minutes | Serves : 2

Nutrition Info: Per Serving : Calories 300, Fat 15g, Carbs 28g, Protein 33g

INGREDIENTS

- 1 tbsp olive oil
- 2 cod fillets
- 1 tbsp basil, chopped
- Salt and black pepper to taste
- 2 potatoes, peeled and sliced
- 2 tsp turmeric powder
- 1 garlic clove, minced

DIRECTIONS

1. Preheat the oven to 360F. Spread the potatoes on a greased baking dish and season with salt and pepper. Bake for 10 minutes. Arrange the cod fillets on top of the potatoes, sprinkle with salt and pepper, and drizzle with some olive oil. Bake for 10-12 more minutes until the fish flakes easily.
2. Warm the remaining olive oil in a skillet over medium heat and sauté garlic for 1 minute. Stir in basil, salt, pepper, turmeric powder, and 3-4 tbsp of water; cook for another 2-3 minutes. Pour the sauce over the cod fillets and serve warm.

Lemon Cod with Rice

Total Time : 45 minutes | Serves : 4

Nutrition Info: Per Serving : Calories 410, Fat 22g, Carbs 22g, Protein 32g

INGREDIENTS

1 cup rice
1 garlic clove, minced
1 tsp red pepper, crushed
2 shallots, chopped
2 tbsp olive oil
1 tsp anchovy paste
1 tbsp oregano, chopped
2 tbsp black olives, pitted and chopped
2 tbsp capers, drained
1 tsp paprika
15 oz canned tomatoes, crushed
Salt and black pepper to taste
4 cod fillets, boneless
1 oz feta cheese, crumbled
1 tbsp parsley, chopped
2 cups chicken stock
1 lemon, zested

DIRECTIONS

1. Preheat the oven to 360F.
2. Warm the olive oil in a skillet over medium heat and sauté garlic, red pepper, and shallot for 5 minutes. Stir in anchovy paste, paprika, oregano, olives, capers, tomatoes, salt, and pepper and cook for another 5 minutes. Put in cod fillets and top with the feta cheese and parsley. Bake for 15 minutes.
3. In the meantime, boil chicken stock in a pot over medium heat. Add in pasta and lemon zest and bring to a simmer and cook for 15-18 minutes; fluff with a fork. Share the rice into plates and top with cod mixture. Serve warm.

Cod Fillets with Cherry Tomatoes

Total Time : 35 minutes | Serves : 4

Nutrition Info: Per Serving : Calories 240, Fat 17g, Carbs 26g, Protein 17

INGREDIENTS

2 tbsp olive oil
1 tsp lime juice
Salt and black pepper to taste
1 tsp sweet paprika
1 tsp chili powder
1 onion, chopped
2 garlic cloves, minced
4 cod fillets, boneless
1 tsp ground coriander
½ cup fish stock
½ lb cherry tomatoes, cube d

DIRECTIONS

1. Warm olive oil in a skillet over medium heat. Season the cod with salt, pepper, and chili powder and cook in the skillet for 8 minutes on all sides; set aside. In the same skillet, cook onion and garlic for 3 minutes. Stir in lime juice, paprika, coriander, fish stock, and cherry tomatoes and bring to a boil. Simmer for 10 minutes. Serve topped with cod fillets.

Cod with Paprika and Mushroom Sauce

Total Time : 45 minutes | Serves : 4

Nutrition Info: Per Serving : Calories 317, Fat 13.7g, Carbs 26g, Protein 25g

INGREDIENTS

2 cups Cremini mushrooms, sliced
4 cod fillets
½ cup shallots, chopped
2 garlic cloves, minced
2 cups canned crushed tomatoes
½ cup clam juice
¼ tsp chili flakes
¼ tsp sweet paprika
1 tbsp capers
¼ cup olive oil
¼ cup raisins, soaked
1 lemon, cut into wedges
Salt to taste

DIRECTIONS

1. Heat the oil in a skillet over medium heat. Sauté shallots and garlic for 2-3 minutes. Add in mushrooms and cook for another 4 minutes. Stir in tomatoes, clam juice, chili flakes, paprika, capers, and salt. Bring to a boil and simmer for 15 minutes.

2. Preheat oven to 380 F. Arrange the cod fillets on a greased baking pan. Cover with the mushroom mixture and top with the soaked raisins. Bake for 18-20 minutes. Serve garnished with lemon wedges.

Herby Cod Skewers

Total Time : 30 minutes | Serves : 4

Nutrition Info: Per Serving : Calories 244, Fat 8.4g, Carbs 15.5g, Protein 27.5g

INGREDIENTS

1 pound cod fillets, cut into chunks
2 sweet peppers, cut into chunks
2 oranges, juiced
1 tbsp Dijon mustard
1 tsp dried dill
1 tsp dried parsley
2 tbsp olive oil
Salt and black pepper to taste

DIRECTIONS

1. Mix olive oil, orange juice, dill, parsley, mustard, salt, and pepper in a bowl. Stir in cod to coat. Allow sitti for 10 minutes. Heat the grill over medium heat and grease with cooking spray. Thread the cod and peppers onto skewers. Grill for 7-8 minutes, turning regularly until the fish is cooked through.

Cod & Calamari with Mango Sauce

Total Time : 20 minutes | Serves : 4

Nutrition Info: Per Serving : Calories 290, Fat 13g, Carbs 12g, Protein 16

INGREDIENTS

1 mango, peeled and cubed
1 lb cod, skinless, boneless and cubed
½ lb calamari rings
1 tbsp garlic chili sauce
2 tbsp olive oil, ¼ cup lime juice
½ tsp smoked paprika
½ tsp cumin, ground
2 garlic cloves, minced
Salt and black pepper to taste

DIRECTIONS

1. Warm the olive oil in a skillet over medium heat and cook chili sauce, lime juice, paprika, cumin, garlic, salt, pepper, and mango for 3 minutes. Stir in cod and calamari and cook for another 7 minutes. Serve warm.g
2. 362.Haddock Fillets with Caper s

Haddock Fillets with Capers

Total Time : 25 minutes | Serves : 4

Nutrition Info: Per Serving : Calories 170, Fat 10g, Carbs 13g, Protein 18g

INGREDIENTS

2 tbsp olive oil
4 haddock fillets, boneless
¼ cup capers, drained
1 tbsp tarragon, chopped
Salt and black pepper to taste
2 tbsp parsley, chopped
1 tbsp olive oil
1 tbsp lemon juice

DIRECTIONS

1. Warm the olive oil in a skillet over medium heat and sear cod for 6 minutes on both sides. Stir in capers, tarragon, salt, pepper, parsley, and lemon juice and cook for another 6-8 minutes. Serve right away.

Haddock in Tomato Sauce

Total Time : 20 minutes | Serves : 4

Nutrition Info:Per Serving : Calories 170, Fat 10g, Carbs 13g, Protein 18g

INGREDIENTS

- 2 tbsp olive oil
- 4 haddock fillets, boneless
- ¼ cup tomatoes, drained
- 3 Fresh Tomatoes
- 1 tbsp oregano, chopped
- Salt and black pepper to taste
- 2 tbsp parsley, chopped
- 1 tbsp olive oil
- 1 tbsp white wine

DIRECTIONS

1. Warm the olive oil in a skillet over medium heat and sear cod for 6 minutes on both sides. Stir in white wine and leave it cook.
2. Add the fresh and dried tomatoes.
3. Add salt, pepper, parsley and cook for another 6-8 minutes. Serve right away.

Wine Poached Haddock

Total Time : 40 minutes | Serves : 4

Nutrition Info: Per Serving : Calories 215, Fat 4g, Carbs 3g, Protein 35 g

INGREDIENTS

- 4 haddock fillets
- Salt and black pepper to taste
- 2 garlic cloves, minced
- ½ cup dry white wine
- ½ cup seafood stock
- 4 rosemary sprigs for garnish

DIRECTIONS

1. Preheat oven to 380 F. Sprinkle haddock fillets with salt and black pepper, and arrange them on a baking dish. Pour in the wine, garlic, and stock. Bake covered for 20 minutes until the fish is tender; remove to a serving plate. Pour the cooking liquid to a pot over high heat. Cook for 10 minutes until reduced by half. Place on serving dishes and top with the reduced poaching liquid. Serve garnished with rosemary.

Tomato Tilapia with Parsley

Total Time : 20 minutes | Serves : 4

Nutrition Info: Per Serving : Calories 308, Fat 17g, Carbs 3g, Protein 16g

INGREDIENTS

- 2 tbsp olive oil
- 4 tilapia fillets, boneless
- ½ cup tomato sauce
- 2 tbsp parsley, chopped
- Salt and black pepper to taste

DIRECTIONS

1. Warm olive oil in a skillet over medium heat. Sprinkle tilapia with salt and pepper and cook until golden brown, flipping once, about 6 minutes. Pour in the tomato sauce and parsley and cook for an additional 4 minutes. Serve immediately.

Tilapia & Brown Rice Pilaf

Total Time : 45 minutes | Serves : 2

Nutrition Info: Per Serving : Calories 270, Fat 18g, Carbs 26g, Protein 13g

INGREDIENTS

- 3 tbsp olive oil
- 2 tilapia fillets, boneless
- ½ tsp Italian seasoning
- ½ cup brown rice
- ½ cup green bell pepper, chopped
- ½ cup white onions, chopped
- ½ tsp garlic powder
- Salt and black pepper to taste

DIRECTIONS

1. Warm 1 tbsp of olive oil in a saucepan over medium heat and cook onions, bell pepper, garlic powder, Italian seasoning, salt, and pepper for 3 minutes. Stir in brown rice and 2 cups of water and bring to a simmer. Cook for 18 minutes.
2. Warm the remaining oil in a skillet over medium heat. Season the tilapia with salt and pepper and fry for 10 minutes on both sides. Share the rice among plates and top with the tilapia fillets. Serve warm.

Garlic & Lemon Sea Bass

Total Time : 25 minutes | Serves : 2

Nutrition Info: Per Serving : Calories 530, Fat 30g, Carbs 15g, Protein 54g

INGREDIENTS

2 tbsp olive oil
2 sea bass fillets
1 lemon, juiced
4 garlic cloves, minced
Salt and black pepper to taste

DIRECTIONS

1. Combine arugula, basil pesto, salt, pepper, and heavy cream in a blender and pulse until smooth. Transfer to a bowl and mix in cream cheese. Serve topped with chives.

Tuna Burgers with Green Olives

Total Time : 20 minutes | Serves : 4

Nutrition Info: Per Serving : Calories 423, Fat 24.4g, Carbs 35.2g, Protein 16.5 g

INGREDIENTS

2 (5-oz) cans tuna, flaked
4 hamburger buns
3 green onions, finely chopped
¼ cup breadcrumbs
1 egg, beaten
2 tbsp chopped fresh parsley
1 tbsp Italian seasoning
1 lemon, zested
½ cup mayonnaise
2 tbsp olive oil
1 tbsp chopped fresh dill
1 tbsp green olives, chopped
Sea salt to taste

DIRECTIONS

1. Combine salmon, breadcrumbs, green onions, eggs, Italian seasoning, parsley, and lemon zest in a bowl. Shape the mixture into 6 patties. Warm olive oil in a skillet over medium heat and brown patties for 8 minutes on both sides. Mix mayonnaise, green olives, dill, and salt in a bowl. Spoon the mixture on the buns and top with the patties. Serve immediately.

Tzatziki Tuna Gyros

Total Time : 15 minutes | Serves : 4

Nutrition Info: Per Serving : Calories 334, Fat 24.6g, Carbs 9g, Protein 21.3g

INGREDIENTS

4 oz tzatziki
½ lb canned tuna, drained
½ cup tahini
4 sundried tomatoes in oil, chopped
2 tbsp warm water
2 garlic cloves, minced
1 tbsp lemon juice
4 pita wraps
1 tbsp black olives, pitted and chopped
Salt and black pepper to taste

DIRECTIONS

1. In a bowl, combine the tahini, water, garlic, lemon juice, salt, and black pepper. Warm the pita wraps in a grilled pan for a few minutes, turning once. Spread the tahini and tzatziki sauces over the warmed pitas and top with tuna, sundried tomatoes, and olives. Fold in half and serve immediately.

Basil Tuna Skillet

Total Time : 25 minutes | Serves : 4

Nutrition Info: Per Serving : Calories 260, Fat 9g, Carbs 6g, Protein 29

INGREDIENTS

- 2 tbsp olive oil
- 4 tuna fillets, boneless
- 1 red bell pepper, chopped
- 1 onion, chopped
- 4 garlic cloves, minced
- ½ cup fish stock
- 1 tsp basil, dried
- ½ cup cherry tomatoes, halved
- ½ cup black olives, pitted and halved
- Salt and black pepper to taste

DIRECTIONS

1. Warm the olive oil in a skillet over medium heat and fry tuna for 10 minutes on both sides. Divide the fish among plates. In the same skillet, cook onion, bell pepper, garlic, and cherry tomatoes for 3 minutes. Stir in salt, pepper, fish stock, basil, and olives and cook for another 3 minutes. Top the tuna with the mixture and serve immediately.

Herby Flounder

Total Time : 25 minutes | Serves : 4

Nutrition Info: Per Serving : Calories 370, Fat 16g, Carbs 57g, Protein 26g

INGREDIENTS

- 2 tbsp olive oil
- 4 flounder fillets, boneless
- 1 tsp rosemary, dried
- 2 tsp cumin, ground
- 1 tbsp coriander, ground
- 2 tsp cinnamon powder
- 2 tsp oregano, dried
- Salt and black pepper to taste
- 2 cups macaroni, cooked
- 1 cup cherry tomatoes, halved
- 1 avocado, peeled, pitted and sliced
- 1 cucumber, cubed
- ½ cup black olives, pitted and sliced
- 1 lemon, juiced

DIRECTIONS

1. Preheat the oven to 390F. Combine rosemary, cumin, coriander, cinnamon, oregano, salt, and pepper in a bowl. Add in the flounder and toss to coat.
2. Warm olive oil in a skillet over medium heat. Brown the fish fillets for 4 minutes on both sides. Transfer to a baking tray and bake in the oven for 7-10 minutes. Combine macaroni, tomatoes, avocado, cucumber, olives, and lemon juice in a bowl. Share macaroni into plates and top with the to serve.

Halibut Cream Soup

Total Time : 25 minutes | Serves : 6

Nutrition Info:Per Serving : Calories 215, Fat 17g, Carbs 7g, Protein 12g

INGREDIENTS

- 2 carrots, chopped
- 2 tbsp olive oil
- 1 red onion, chopped
- Salt and white pepper to the taste
- 3 gold potatoes, peeled and cubed
- 4 cups fish stock
- 4 oz halibut fillets, boneless and cubed
- ½ cup heavy cream
- 1 tbsp dill, chopped

DIRECTIONS

1. Warm the olive oil in a skillet over medium heat and cook the onion for 3 minutes. Put in potatoes, salt, pepper, carrots, and stock and bring to a boil. Cook for an additional 5-6 minutes. Stir in halibut, cream, and dill and simmer for another 5 minutes. Serve right away.

Barramundi with Dates & Hazelnuts

Total Time : 25 minutes | Serves : 2

Nutrition Info: Per Serving : Calories 240, Fat 17g, Carbs 26g, Protein 7g

INGREDIENTS

- 2 tbsp olive oil
- 2 barramundi fillets, boneless
- 1 shallot, sliced
- 4 lemon slices
- ½ lemon, zested and juiced
- 1 cup baby spinach
- ¼ cup hazelnuts, chopped
- 4 dates, pitted and chopped
- 2 tbsp parsley, chopped

DIRECTIONS

1. Preheat the oven to 380F. Sprinkle barramundi with salt and pepper and place on 2 parchment paper pieces. Top each fillet with lemon slices, lemon juice, shallot, lemon zest, spinach, hazelnuts, dates, and parsley. Sprinkle each fillet with 1 tbsp of oil and fold the paper around it. Place them on a baking sheet and bake for 12 minutes. Let cool a bit and serve.

Mackerel Fillets in Hot Tomato Sauce

Total Time : 15 minutes | Serves : 2

Nutrition Info: Per Serving : Calories 334, Fat 22g, Carbs 7.4g, Protein 23.8 g

INGREDIENTS

1 tbsp butter
2 mackerel fillets
¼ cup white wine
½ cup spring onions, sliced
2 garlic cloves, minced
½ tsp dried thyme
1 tsp dried parsley
Salt and black pepper to taste
½ cup vegetable broth
½ cup tomato sauce
½ tsp hot sauce
1 tbsp fresh mint, chopped

DIRECTIONS

1. In a pot over medium heat, melt the butter. Add in fish and cook for 6 minutes in total; set aside. Pour in the wine and scrape off any bits from the bottom. Add in spring onions and garlic; cook until fragrant. Sprinkle with thyme, parsley, salt, and pepper. Stir in broth, tomato sauce, and add back the fillets. Cook for 3-4 minutes. Pour in hot sauce and top with mint.

Sardine Patties

Total Time : 20 minutes | Serves : 4

Nutrition Info: Per Serving : Calories 300, Fat 14g, Carbs 23g, Protein 7g

INGREDIENTS

1 tsp mustard powder
1 tsp chili powder
20 oz canned sardines, mashed
3 tbsp olive oil
2 garlic cloves, minced
2 tbsp dill, chopped
1 onion, chopped
1 cup panko breadcrumbs
1 egg, whisked
Salt and black pepper to taste
2 tbsp lemon juice

DIRECTIONS

1. Combine sardines, garlic, dill, onion, breadcrumbs, egg, mustard powder, chili powder, salt, pepper, and lemon juice in a bowl and form medium patties out of the mixture. Warm the olive oil in a skillet over medium heat and fry the cakes for 10 minutes on both sides. Serve with aioli.

Quick Shrimp Rice

Total Time : 40 minutes | Serves : 4

Nutrition Info: Per Serving : Calories 342, Fat 12g, Carbs 33.4g, Protein 24.4g

INGREDIENTS

- 1 lb shrimp, peeled, deveined, and tails removed
- 1 cup white rice
- 4 garlic cloves, sliced
- ¼ tsp hot paprika
- 1 cup mushrooms, sliced
- ¼ cup green peas
- Juice of 1 lime
- 2 tbsp olive oil
- Sea salt to taste
- ¼ cup chopped fresh chives

DIRECTIONS

1. Bring a pot of salted water to a boil. Cook the rice for 15-18 minutes, stirring occasionally. Drain and place in a bowl. Add in the raisins and green peas and mix to combine well. Taste and adjust the seasoning. Remove to a serving plate.
2. Heat the olive oil in a saucepan over medium heat and sauté garlic and hot paprika for 30-40 seconds until garlic is light golden brown. Remove the garlic with a slotted spoon. Add the mushrooms to the saucepan and sauté them for 5 minutes, stirring often until tender. Put in the shrimp, lime juice, and salt and stir for 4 minutes. Turn the heat off.
3. Add the chives and reserved garlic to the cooked shrimp and pour over the rice. Enjoy!

Anchovy & Avocado Dip

Total Time : 5 minutes | Serves : 2

Nutrition Info:Per Serving : Calories 271, Fat 20g, Carbs 12g, Protein 15g

INGREDIENTS

- 1 ripe avocado, peeled and pitted
- 1 tsp lemon juice
- ¼ celery stalk, chopped
- ¼ cup chopped shallots
- 2 anchovy fillets in olive oil
- Salt and black pepper to taste

DIRECTIONS

1. Combine lemon juice, avocado, and anchovy fillets (with some olive oil) in a food processor. Blitz until smooth. Remove

Crispy Baked Pollock

Total Time : 25 minutes | Serves : 4

Nutrition Info: Per Serving : Calories 240, Fat 9g, Carbs 10g, Protein 26g

INGREDIENTS

- 4 pollock fillets, boneless
- 2 cups potato chips, crushed
- 2 tbsp mayonnaise

DIRECTIONS

1. Preheat the oven to 380F. Line a baking sheet with parchment paper. Sprinkle the pollock fillets with salt, pepper. Rub each fillet with mayonnaise and dip them in the potato chips. Place fillets on the sheet and bake for 12 minutes. Serve with salad.

Chili Anchovies

Total Time : 10 minutes | Serves : 2

Nutrition Info: Per Serving : Calories 103, Fat 3g, Carbs 5g, Protein 11 g

INGREDIENTS

- ½ tsp red pepper flakes
- 16 canned anchovies in olive oil
- 4 garlic cloves, minced
- Salt and black pepper to taste

DIRECTIONS

1. Preheat the broiler. Arrange the anchovies on a lined with aluminum foil baking dish. In a bowl, mix anchovy olive oil, garlic, salt, red flakes, and pepper and pour over anchovies. Broil for 3-4 minutes. Divide between 4 plates and drizzle with the remaining mixture from the dish. Serve.

Roasted Shrimp with Veggies

Total Time : 30 minutes | Serves : 4

Nutrition Info:Per Serving : Calories 350, Fat 20g, Carbs 35g, Protein 11g

INGREDIENTS

4 tbsp olive oil
2 bell peppers, cut into chunks
2 fennel bulbs, cut into wedges
2 red onions, cut into wedges
4 garlic cloves, unpeeled
½ cup Kalamata olives, halved
2 lb shrimp, peeled and deveined
1 tsp lemon zest, grated
2 tsp oregano, dried
2 tbsp parsley, chopped
Salt and black pepper to taste

DIRECTIONS

1. Preheat the oven to 390 F.
2. Place bell peppers, garlic, fennel, red onions, and olives in a roasting tray. Add in the lemon zest, oregano, half of the olive oil, salt, and pepper and toss to coat; roast for 15 minutes. Coat the shrimp with the remaining olive oil and pour over the veggies; roast for another 7 minutes. Serve topped with parsley.

Rosemary Shrimp in Lemon Sauce

Total Time : 25 minutes | Serves : 4

Nutrition Info:Per Serving : Calories 240, Fat 16g, Carbs 16g, Protein 9g

INGREDIENTS

3 tbsp olive oil
1 lb shrimp, peeled and deveined
1 lemon, juiced
1 tbsp flour
1 cup fish stock
Salt and black pepper to taste
1 cup black olives, pitted and halved
1 tbsp rosemary, chopped

DIRECTIONS

1. Whisk lemon juice and egg yolks in a bowl. Warm the olive oil in a skillet over medium heat and sear shrimp for 4 minutes on both sides; set aside. In the same skillet over low heat, stir in the flour for 2-3 minutes.
2. Gradually pour in the fish stock and lemon juice while stirring and simmer for 3-4 minutes until the sauce thickens. Adjust the seasoning with salt and pepper and mix in shrimp, olives, and rosemary. Serve immediately.

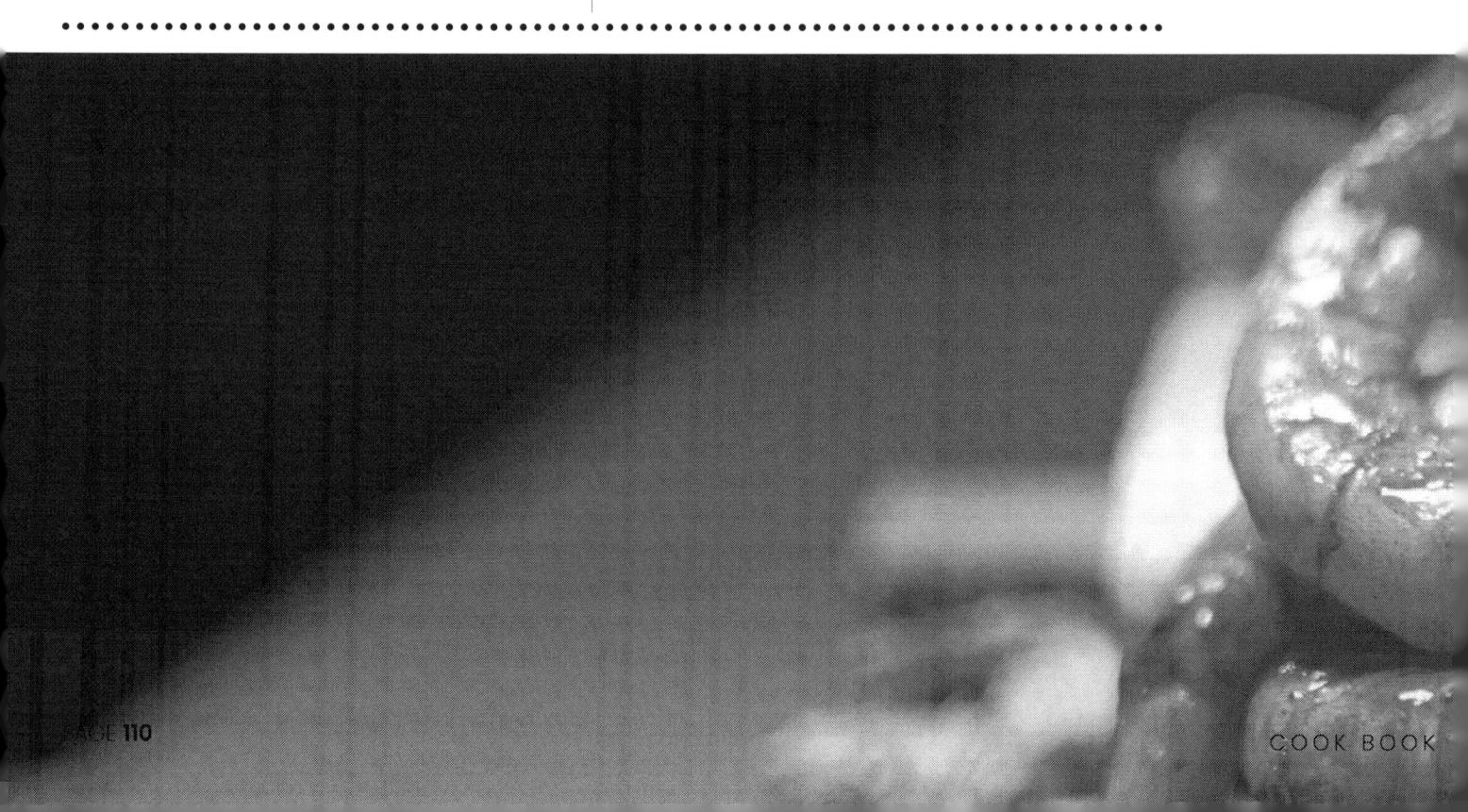

Butter & Garlic Squid & Shrimp

Total Time : 25 minutes | Serves : 4

Nutrition Info: Per Serving : Calories 300, Fat 14g, Carbs 23g, Protein 7 g

INGREDIENTS

½ lb squid rings
1 lb shrimp, peeled and deveined
Salt and black pepper to taste
2 garlic cloves, minced
2 tbsp butter
1 tsp rosemary, dried
1 red onion, chopped
1 cup vegetable stock1 lemon, juiced
1 tbsp parsley, chopped

DIRECTIONS

1. Melt butter in a skillet over medium heat and cook onion and garlic for 4 minutes. Stir in shrimp, salt, pepper, squid rings, rosemary, vegetable stock, and lemon juice and bring to a boil. Simmer for 8 minutes. Put in parsley and serve.

Tiger Prawns with Mushrooms

Total Time : 25 minutes | Serves : 4

Nutrition Info: Per Serving : Calories 260, Fat 9g, Carbs 13g, Protein 19g

INGREDIENTS

3 tbsp olive oil
1 lb tiger prawns, peeled and deveined
2 green onions, sliced
½ lb white mushrooms, sliced
2 tbsp balsamic vinegar
2 tsp garlic, minced

DIRECTIONS

1. Warm the olive oil in a skillet over medium heat and cook green onions and garlic for 2 minutes. Stir in mushrooms and balsamic vinegar and cook for an additional 6 minutes. Put in prawns and cook for 4 minutes. Serve right away.

Sicilian Prawns with Capers & Lemon

Total Time : 25 minutes | Serves : 2

Nutrition Info: Per Serving : Calories 230, Fat 14g, Carbs 23g, Protein 6g

INGREDIENTS

2 tbsp olive oil
1 lb prawns, peeled and deveined
1 lemon, zested and juiced
2 tomatoes, chopped
1 cup spring onions, chopped
2 tbsp capers, chopped
2 tbsp dill, chopped
Salt and black pepper to taste

DIRECTIONS

1. Warm the olive oil in a skillet over medium heat and cook onions and capers for 2-3 minutes. Stir in prawns, lemon zest, tomatoes, dill, salt, and pepper and cook for another 6 minutes. Serve drizzled with lemon juice.

Sour & Tasty Prawn

Total Time : 25 minutes | Serves : 4

Nutrition Info: Per Serving : Calories 388, Fat 9.5g, Carbs 38.2g, Protein 32g

INGREDIENTS

1 lb prawns, peeled and deveined
1 onion, chopped
6 garlic cloves, minced
1 lemon, juiced and zested
½ cup dry white wine
Sea salt and black pepper to taste
2 cups fusilli, cooked
2 tbsp olive oil
½ tsp red pepper flakes

DIRECTIONS

1. Warm olive oil in a pan over medium heat and sauté onion and garlic for 3 minutes, stirring often, until fragrant. Stir in prawns and cook for 3-4 minutes. Mix in lemon juice, lemon zest, salt, pepper, wine, and red flakes. Bring to a boil, then decrease the heat, and simmer for 2 minutes until the liquid is reduced by half. Turn the heat off. Stir in pasta and serve.

Awesome Calamari in Cilantro Sauce

Total Time : 25 minutes | Serves : 4

Nutrition Info: Per Serving : Calories 290, Fat 19g, Carbs 10g, Protein 19g

INGREDIENTS

2 tbsp olive oil
2 lb calamari, sliced into rings
4 garlic cloves, minced
1 lime, juiced
2 tbsp balsamic vinegar
3 tbsp cilantro, chopped

DIRECTIONS

1. Warm the olive oil in a skillet over medium heat and sauté garlic, lime juice, balsamic vinegar, and cilantro for 5 minutes. Stir in calamari rings and cook for another 10 minutes. Serve warm.

Chili Squid Stew with Capers

Total Time : 35 minutes | Serves : 4

Nutrition Info: Per Serving : Calories 280, Fat 12g, Carbs 14g, Protein 16g

INGREDIENTS

- 2 tbsp olive oil
- 1 onion, chopped
- 1 celery stalk, chopped
- 1 lb calamari rings
- 2 red chili peppers, chopped
- 2 garlic cloves, minced
- 14 oz canned tomatoes, chopped
- 2 tbsp tomato paste
- 1 tbsp thyme, chopped
- Salt and black pepper to taste
- 2 tbsp capers, drained
- 12 black olives, pitted and halved

DIRECTIONS

1. Warm the olive oil in a skillet over medium heat and cook onion, celery, garlic, and chili peppers for 2 minutes. Stir in calamari rings, tomatoes, tomato paste, salt, and pepper and bring to a simmer. Cook for 20 minutes. Put in olives and capers and cook for another 5 minutes. Serve right away.

Andalusian Squid with Zucchini

Total Time : 25 minutes | Serves : 4

Nutrition Info: Per Serving : Calories 240, Fat 16g, Carbs 24g, Protein 12g

INGREDIENTS

- 2 tbsp olive oil
- 10 oz squid, cut into medium pieces
- 2 zucchinis, chopped
- 2 tbsp cilantro, chopped
- 1 jalapeno pepper, chopped
- 3 tbsp balsamic vinegar
- Salt and black pepper to taste
- 1 tbsp dill, chopped

DIRECTIONS

1. Warm the olive oil in a skillet over medium heat and sauté squid for 5 minutes. Stir in zucchini, cilantro, jalapeño pepper, vinegar, salt, pepper, and dill and cook for another 10 minutes. Serve right away.

Citrus Squid with Olives

Total Time : 30 minutes | Serves : 4

Nutrition Info: Per Serving : Calories 310, Fat 10g, Carbs 23g, Protein 12g

INGREDIENTS

- 1 lb baby squid, cleaned, body and tentacles chopped
- ½ cup green olives, pitted and chopped
- ½ tsp lime zest, grated
- 1 tbsp lime juice
- ½ tsp orange zest, grated
- 3 tbsp olive oil
- 1 tsp red pepper flakes, crushed
- 1 tbsp parsley, chopped
- 4 garlic cloves, minced
- 1 shallot, chopped
- 1 cup vegetable stock
- 2 tbsp red wine vinegar
- Salt and black pepper to taste

DIRECTIONS

1. Warm the olive oil in a skillet over medium heat and stir in lime zest, lime juice, orange zest, red pepper flakes, garlic, shallot, olives, stock, vinegar, salt, and pepper. Bring to a boil and simmer for 10 minutes. Mix in squid and parsley and cook for another 10 minutes. Serve hot.

Creamy Basil Scallops

Total Time : 20 minutes | Serves : 4

Nutrition Info: Per Serving : Calories 270, Fat 12g, Carbs 17g, Protein 11g

INGREDIENTS

- 1 tbsp basil, chopped
- 1 lb scallops, scrubbed
- 1 tbsp garlic, minced
- 1 onion, chopped
- 6 tomatoes, cubed
- 1 cup heavy cream
- 2 tbsp olive oil
- 1 tbsp parsley, chopped

DIRECTIONS

1. Warm the olive oil in a skillet over medium heat and cook garlic and onion for 2 minutes. Stir in scallops, basil, tomatoes, heavy cream, and parsley and cook for an additional 7 minutes. Serve immediately.

Tuscan-Style Scallops with Kale

Total Time : 25 minutes | Serves : 4

Nutrition Info: Per Serving : Calories 214, Fat 7.9g, Carbs 15.2g, Protein 21.5g

INGREDIENTS

- 1 pound sea scallops, rinsed and drained
- 4 cups Tuscan kale
- 1 orange, juiced
- 2 tbsp olive oil
- Salt and black pepper to taste
- ¼ tsp red pepper flake s

DIRECTIONS

1. Sprinkle scallops with salt and pepper.
2. Warm olive oil in a skillet over medium heat and brown scallops for 6-8 minutes on all sides. Remove to a plate and keep warm covering with foil. In the same skillet, add the kale, red pepper flakes, orange juice, salt, and pepper and cook until the kale wilts, about 4-5 minutes. Share the kale mixture into 4 plates and top with the scallops. Serve warm.

Mayo Scallop & Veggie Mix

Total Time : 25 minutes | Serves : 4

Nutrition Info: Per Serving : Calories 310, Fat 16g, Carbs 33g, Protein 9g

INGREDIENTS

2 celery stalks, sliced
2 lb sea scallops, halved
3 tbsp olive oil
3 garlic cloves, minced
Salt and black pepper to taste
Juice of 1 lime
1 red bell pepper, chopped
1 tbsp capers, chopped
1 tbsp mayonnaise
1 tbsp rosemary, chopped
1 cup chicken stock

DIRECTIONS

1. Warm olive oil in a skillet over medium heat and cook celery and garlic for 2 minutes. Stir in bell pepper, lime juice, capers, rosemary, and stock and bring to a boil. Simmer for 8 minutes. Mix in scallops and mayonnaise and cook for 5 minutes.

Pancetta-Wrapped Scallops

Total Time : 20 minutes | Serves : 12

Nutrition Info: Per Serving : Calories 310, Fat 25g, Carbs 24g, Protein 19g

INGREDIENTS

12 thin pancetta slices
12 medium scallops
2 tsp lemon juice
2 tsp olive oil
1 tsp chili powder

DIRECTIONS

1. Wrap pancetta around scallops and secure with toothpicks. Warm the olive oil in a skillet over medium heat and cook scallops for 6 minutes on all sides. Serve sprinkled with chili powder and lemon juice.

Crab Patties with Radicchio Salad

Total Time : 30 minutes | Serves : 4

Nutrition Info: Per Serving : Calories 238, Fat 14.3g, Carbs 8g, Protein

INGREDIENTS

1 pound lump crabmeat
4 scallions, sliced
1 garlic clove, minced
¼ cup cooked shrimp
2 tbsp heavy cream
2 tbsp butter
¼ head radicchio, very thinly sliced
1 green apple, shredded
2 tbsp lemon juice
2 tbsp extra-virgin olive oil
Salt and black pepper to taste

DIRECTIONS

1. In a food processor, place the shrimp, heavy cream, salt, and pepper. Blend until smooth.
2. Mix crab meat and scallions in a bowl. Add in shrimp mixture and toss to combine. Make 4 patties out of the mixture. Transfer to the fridge for 10 minutes. Warm butter in a skillet over medium heat and brown patties for 8 minutes on all sides. Remove to a serving plate. Mix radicchio and apple in a bowl. Combine olive oil, lemon juice, garlic, and salt in a small bowl and stir well. Pour over the salad and toss to combine. Serve crab patties with the salad.

Drunken Mussels with Lemon-Butter Sauce

Total Time : 15 minutes | Serves : 4

Nutrition Info: Per Serving : Calories 487, Fat 18g, Carbs 26g, Protein 37g

INGREDIENTS

½ cup chopped parsley
1 chopped white onion
2 cups dry white wine
½ tsp sea salt
4 lb mussels
6 garlic cloves, minced
4 tbsp butter
Juice of ½ lemon

DIRECTIONS

1. Add wine, garlic, salt, shallots, and ¼ cup of parsley in a pot over medium heat and let simmer. Put in mussels and simmer covered for 7-8 minutes. Divide mussels between four bowls. Stir butter and lemon juice into the pot and drizzle over the mussels. Top with parsley and serve. to a bowl. Add in onion, salt, celery, and pepper and whisk using a fork. Serve.

White Wine Mussels

Total Time : 20 minutes | Serves : 4

Nutrition Info: Per Serving : Calories 280, Fat 10g, Carbs 7g, Protein 21 g

INGREDIENTS

3 tbsp olive oil
2 shallots, sliced
2 tsp coriander seeds
4 garlic cloves, minced
1 tsp red pepper flakes
Salt and black pepper to taste
1 cup white wine
1 tbsp lemon juice
2 ½ lb mussels, scrubbed
½ cup parsley, chopped
½ cup tomatoes, cubed

DIRECTIONS

1. Warm the olive oil in a skillet over medium heat and cook shallots and garlic for 2 minutes, stirring occasionally until tender. Add in coriander seeds, red pepper flakes, salt, pepper, white wine, lemon juice, tomatoes, and ½ cup of water and cook for another 3 minutes. Put in mussels and cook for an additional 6 minutes. Sprinkle with parsley and serve right away.

Mussels with Leeks

Total Time : 25 minutes | Serves : 6

Nutrition Info:Per Serving : Calories 250, Fat 10g, Carbs 16g, Protein 9g

INGREDIENTS

- 2 lb mussels, cleaned and de-bearded
- 2 tbsp olive oil
- 2 leeks, chopped
- 1 red onion, chopped
- Salt and black pepper to taste
- 1 tbsp parsley, chopped
- 1 tbsp chives, chopped
- ½ cup tomato sauce

DIRECTIONS

1. Warm the olive oil in a skillet over medium heat and cook leeks and onion for 5 minutes. Stir in mussels, salt, pepper, parsley, chives, and tomato sauce and cook for 10 minutes. Discard any unopened mussels. Serve right away.

Basil Clams with Snow Peas

Total Time : 30 minutes | Serves : 4

Nutrition Info: Per Serving : Calories 310, Fat 13g, Carbs 27g, Protein 22g

INGREDIENTS

- 1 tbsp basil, chopped
- 2 lb clams
- 2 tbsp olive oil
- 1 onion, chopped, 4 garlic cloves, minced
- Salt and black pepper to taste
- ½ cup vegetable stock
- 1 cup snow peas, sliced
- ½ tbsp balsamic vinegar
- 1 cup scallions, sliced

DIRECTIONS

1. Warm the olive oil in a skillet over medium heat. Sauté onion and garlic for 2 to 3 minutes until tender and fragrant, stirring often. Add in the clams, salt, pepper, vegetable stock, snow peas, balsamic vinegar, and basil and bring to a boil. Lower the heat and simmer for 10 minutes. Remove from the heat. Discard any unopened clams. Scatter with scallions and serve.

Clam & Chickpea Stew

Total Time : 40 minutes | Serves : 4

Nutrition Info: Per Serving : Calories 460, Fat 13g, Carbs 48g, Protein 35g

INGREDIENTS

- 2 tbsp olive oil
- 1 yellow onion, chopped
- 1 fennel bulb, chopped
- 1 carrot, chopped
- 1 red bell pepper, chopped
- 2 garlic cloves, minced
- 3 tbsp tomato paste
- 16 oz canned chickpeas, drained
- 1 tsp dried thyme
- ¼ tsp smoked paprika
- Salt and black pepper to taste
- 1 lb clams, scrubbed

DIRECTIONS

1. Warm the olive oil in a pot over medium heat and sauté fennel, onion, bell pepper, and carrot for 5 minutes until they're tender. Stir in garlic and tomato paste and cook for another minute. Mix in the chickpeas, thyme, paprika, salt, pepper, and 2 cups of water and bring to a boil; cook for 20 minutes.
2. Rinse the clams under cold, running water. Discard any clams that remain open when tapped with your fingers. Put the unopened clams into the pot and cook everything for 4-5 minutes until the shells have opened.
3. When finished, discard any clams that haven't opened fully during the cooking process. Taste and adjust the seasoning with salt and black pepper. Ladle the stew into serving bowls, drizzle with a little olive oil, and serve.

Italian Seafood Stew

Total Time : 25 minutes | Serves : 4

Nutrition Info: Per Serving : Calories 372, Fat 14.7g, Carbs 25.3g, Protein 34 g

INGREDIENTS

- ½ pound trout, skin removed, cubed
- ½ pound clams
- ½ pound cod, cubed
- 1 onion, chopped
- ½ fennel bulb, chopped
- 2 garlic cloves, minced
- ¼ cup dry white wine
- 2 tbsp chopped fresh parsley
- 1 (32-oz) can tomato sauce
- 1 cup fish broth
- 1 tbsp Italian seasoning
- ½ tsp red pepper flakes
- 2 tbsp olive oil
- Salt and black pepper to taste

DIRECTIONS

1. Warm olive oil in a pot over medium heat and sauté onion and fennel for 5 minutes. Add in garlic and cook for 30 seconds. Pour in the wine and cook for 1 minute. Stir in tomato sauce, clams, broth, cod, trout, salt, Italian seasoning, red pepper flakes, and pepper. Bring just a boil, then lower the heat and simmer for 5 minutes, stirring periodically. Discard any unopened clams. Sprinkle with parsley and serve.

Fish & Vegetable Stew

Total Time : 35 minutes | Serves : 4

Nutrition Info: Per Serving : Calories 280, Fat 16g, Carbs 15g, Protein 3g

INGREDIENTS

- 2 tbsp olive oil
- 2 tbsp parsley, chopped
- 2 tomatoes, peeled and chopped
- 2 tbsp cilantro, chopped
- 2 garlic cloves, minced
- ½ tsp paprika
- 2 cups chicken stock
- Salt and black pepper to taste
- 4 cod fillets, boneless, skinless, cubed
- 1 carrot, sliced
- 1 red bell pepper, chopped
- 1 ¼ lb potatoes, cubed
- ½ cup black olives, pitted and halved
- 1 red onion, sliced

DIRECTIONS

1. Warm olive oil in a saucepan over medium heat and cook garlic, cumin, carrot, bell pepper, and onion for 5 minutes. Stir in cod fillets, parsley, tomatoes, and paprika for 3-4 minutes. Pour in chicken stock and olives and bring to a boil. Cook for 15 minutes. Adjust the seasoning and sprinkle with cilantro. Serve immediately.

Seafood Soup

Total Time : 30 minutes | Serves : 4

Nutrition Info: Pe r Serving : Calories 200, Fat 9g, Carbs 5g, Protein 27g

INGREDIENTS

- ½ lb shrimp, deveined
- 2 tbsp olive oil
- 1 yellow onion, chopped
- 1 carrot, finely chopped
- 1 celery stalk, finely chopped
- 1 small pepper, deseeded and chopped
- 1 garlic clove, minced
- ½ cup tomatoes, crushed
- 4 cups fish stock
- ½ lb cod, skinless, boneless and cubed
- ¼ tsp rosemary, dried
- Salt and black pepper to taste

DIRECTIONS

1. Warm the olive oil in a pot over medium heat and cook onion, garlic, carrot, celery, and pepper for 5 minutes until soft, stirring occasionally. Stir in the tomatoes, fish stock, cod, shrimp, rosemary, salt, and pepper and simmer for 15 minutes.

....

Seafood Special Spaghetti

Total Time : 35 minutes | Serves : 4

Nutrition Info: Pe r Serving : Calories 200, Fat 9g, Carbs 5g, Protein 27g

INGREDIENTS

- ½ lb shrimp, deveined
- 2 tbsp olive oil
- 1 yellow onion, chopped
- 1 small pepper, deseeded and chopped
- 1 garlic clove, minced
- ½ cup tomatoes, crushed
- 2 cups fish stock
- ½ lb cod, skinless, boneless and cubed
- 2 lb clams
- ¼ tsp rosemary, dried
- Salt and black pepper to taste
- Spaghetti

DIRECTIONS

1. Warm the olive oil in a pot over medium heat and cook onion, garlic, rosemary and tomatoes for 5 minutes until soft, stirring occasionally.
2. Add clams and fish stock
3. Put some salted hot water on fire and add the spaghetti when the boil start.
4. When Spaghetti are cooked rinse and add to the sauce.
5. Stir in the shrimps, salt, and pepper and mix with the pasta.

COOK BOOK

SOUPS

Cheesy Keto Zucchini Soup

Preparation and Cooking Time: 20 minutes | Servings: 2

Nutrition Info: Calories: 154 Carbs: 8.9g Fats: 8.1g Proteins: 13.4g Sodium: 93mg Sugar: 3.9 g

INGREDIENTS

½ medium onion, peeled and chopped 1 cup bone broth 1 tablespoon coconut oil 1½ zucchinis, cut into chunks ½ tablespoon nutrition al yeast

Dash of black pepper ½ tablespoon parsley, chopped, for garnish ½ tablespoon coconut cream, for garnish

DIRECTIONS

1. Melt the coconut oil in a large pan over medium heat and add onions. Sauté for about 3 minutes and add zucchinis and bone broth. Reduce the heat to simmer for about 15 minutes and cover the pan. Add nutrition al yeast and transfer to an immersion blender. Blend until smooth and season with black pepper. Top with coconut cream and parsley to serve.

Mint Avocado Chilled Soup

Preparation and Cooking Time: 15 minutes | Servings: 2

Nutrition Info: Calories: 432 Carbs: 16.1g Fats: 42.2g Proteins: 5.2g Sodium: 33mg Sugar: 4.5g

INGREDIENTS

2 romaine lettuce leaves 1 Tablespoon lime juice 1 medium ripe avocado 1 cup coconut milk, chilled 20 fresh mint leaves Salt to taste

DIRECTIONS

1. Put all the ingredients in a blender and blend until smooth. Refrigerate for about 10 minutes and serve chilled.

Spring Soup Recipe with Poached Egg

Preparation and Cooking Time: 20 minutes | Servings: 2

Nutrition Info: Calories: 264 Carbs: 7g Fats: 18.9g Proteins: 16.1g Sodium: 1679mg Sugar: 3.4g

INGREDIENTS

2 eggs 2 tablespoons butter 4 cups chicken broth 1 head of romaine lettuce, chopped Salt, to taste

DIRECTIONS

1. Boil the chicken broth and lower heat. Poach the eggs in the broth for about 5 minutes and remove the eggs. Place each egg into a bowl and add chopped romaine lettuce into the broth. Cook for about 10 minutes and ladle the broth with the lettuce into the bowls.

Swiss Chard Egg Drop Soup

Preparation and Cooking time: 20 minutes | Servings: 4

Nutrition Info: Calories: 185 Carbs: 2.9g Fats: 11g Proteins: 18.3g Sodium: 252mg Sugar: 0.4g

INGREDIENTS

3 cups bone broth 2 eggs, whisked 1 teaspoon ground oregano 3 tablespoons butter 2 cups Swiss chard, chopped 2 tablespoons coconut aminos 1 teaspoon ginger, grated Salt and black pepper, to taste

DIRECTIONS

1. Heat the bone broth in a saucepan and add whisked eggs while stirring slowly. Add the swiss chard, butter, coconut aminos, ginger, oregano and salt and black pepper. Cook for about 10 minutes and serve hot.

Delicata Squash Soup

Preparation and Cooking time: 45 minutes | Servings: 5

Nutrition Info: Calories: 109 Carbs: 4.9g Fats: 8.5g Proteins: 3g Sodium: 279mg Sugar: 2.4g

INGREDIENTS

1½ cups beef bone broth 1small onion, peeled and grated. ½ teaspoon sea salt ¼ teaspoon poultry seasoning 2small Delicata Squash, chopped 2 garlic cloves, minced 2tablespoons olive oil ¼ teaspoon black pepper 1 small lemon, juiced 5 tablespoons sour cream

DIRECTIONS

1. Put Delicata Squash and water in a medium pan and bring to a boil. Reduce the heat and cook for about 20 minutes. Drain and set aside. Put olive oil, onions, garlic and poultry seasoning in a small sauce pan. Cook for about 2 minutes and add broth. Allow it to simmer for 5 minutes and remove from heat. Whisk in the lemon juice and transfer the mixture in a blender. Pulse until smooth and top with sour cream.

Apple Pumpkin Soup

Preparation and Cooking time: 10 minutes | Servings: 8

Nutrition Info: Calories: 186 Carbs: 10.4g Fats: 14.9g Proteins: 3.7g Sodium: 7mg Sugar: 5.4g

INGREDIENTS

1 apple, chopped 1 whole kabocha pumpkin, peeled, seeded and cubed 1 cup almond flour ¼ cup ghee 1 pinch cardamom powder 2 quarts water ¼ cup coconut cream 1 pinch ground black peppe r

DIRECTIONS

1. Heat ghee in the bottom of a heavy pot and add apples. Cook for about 5 minutes on a medium flame and add pumpkin. Sauté for about 3 minutes and add almond flour. Sauté for about 1 minute and add water. Lower the flame and cook for about 30 minutes. Transfer the soup into an immersion blender and blend until smooth. Top with coconut cream and serve.

Cauliflower and Thyme Soup

Preparation and Cooking time: 30 minutes | Servings: 6

Nutrition Info: Per Serving : Calories 334, Fat 24.6g, Carbs 9g, Protein 21.3g

INGREDIENTS

2 teaspoonsthyme powder 1head cauliflower 3cupsvegetable stock ½ teaspoon matcha green tea powder 3tablespoonsolive oil Salt and black pepper, to taste 5garlic cloves, chopped

DIRECTIONS

1. Put the vegetable stock, thyme and matcha powder to a large pot over medium-high heat and bring to a boil. Add cauliflower and cook for about 10 minutes. Meanwhile, put the olive oil and garlic in a small sauce pan and cook for about 1 minute. Add the garlic, salt and black pepper and cook for about 2 minutes. Transfer into an immersion blender and blend until smooth. Dish out and serve immediately.

Chicken Kale Soup

Preparation and Cooking time: 6 hours 10 minutes | Servings: 6

Nutrition Info: Calories: 79 Carbs: 3.8g Fats: 7.1g Proteins: 1.3g Sodium: 39mg Sugar: 1.5g

INGREDIENTS

2 teaspoonsthyme powder 1head cauliflower 3cupsvegetable stock ½ teaspoon matcha green tea powder 3tablespoonsolive oil Salt and black pepper, to taste 5garlic cloves, chopped

DIRECTIONS

1. Put the vegetable stock, thyme and matcha powder to a large pot over medium-high heat and bring to a boil. Add cauliflower and cook for about 10 minutes. Meanwhile, put the olive oil and garlic in a small sauce pan and cook for about 1 minute. Add the garlic, salt and black pepper and cook for about 2 minutes. Transfer into an immersion blender and blend until smooth. Dish out and serve immediately.

Chicken Mulligatawny Soup

Preparation and Cooking time: 30 minutes | Servings: 10

Nutrition Info: Calories: 215 Carbs: 7.1g Fats: 8.5g Proteins: 26.4g Sodium: 878mg Sugar: 2.2g

INGREDIENTS

1½ tablespoons curry powder 3 cups celery root, diced 2 tablespoons Swerve 10 cups chicken broth 5 cups chicken, chopped and cooked ¼ cup apple cider ½ cup sour cream ¼ cup fresh parsley, chopped 2 tablespoons butter Salt and black pepper, to taste

DIRECTIONS

1. Combine the broth, butter, chicken, curry powder, celery root and apple cider in a large soup pot. Bring to a boil and simmer for about 30 minutes. Stir in Swerve, sour cream, fresh parsley, salt and black pepper. Dish out and serve hot.

Traditional Chicken Soup

Preparation and Cooking time: 1 hours 45 minutes | Servings: 6

Nutrition Info: Calories: 357 Carbs: 3.3g Fats: 7g Proteins: 66.2g Sodium: 175mg Sugar: 1.1g

INGREDIENTS

3 pounds chicken 4 quarts water 4 stalks celery 1/3 large red onion 1 large carrot 3 garlic cloves 2 thyme sprigs 2 rosemary sprigs Salt and black pepper, to taste

DIRECTIONS

1. Put water and chicken in the stock pot on medium high heat. Bring to a boil and allow it to simmer for about 10 minutes. Add onion, garlic, celery, salt and pepper and simmer on medium low heat for 30 minutes. Add thyme and carrots and simmer on low for another 30 minutes. Dish out the chicken and shred the pieces, removing the bones. Return the chicken pieces to the pot and add rosemary sprigs. Simmer for about 20 minutes at low heat and dish out to serve.

Chicken Cabbage Soup

Preparation time: 35 minutes | Servings: 8

Nutrition Info: Calories: 184 Carbs: 4.2g Fats: 13.1g Proteins: 12.6g Sodium: 1244mg Sugar: 2.1g

INGREDIENTS

2celery stalks 2garlic cloves, minced 4 oz.butter 6 oz. mushrooms, sliced 2 tablespoons onions, dried and minced 1 teaspoon salt 8 cups chicken broth 1medium carrot 2 cups green cabbage, sliced into strips 2 teaspoons dried parsley ¼ teaspoon black pepper 1½ rotisserie chickens, shredded

DIRECTIONS

1. Melt butter in a large pot and add celery, mushrooms, onions and garlic into the pot. Cook for about 4 minutes and add broth, parsley, carrot, salt and black pepper. Simmer for about 10 minutes and add cooked chicken and cabbage. Simmer for an additional 12 minutes until the cabbage is tender. Dish out and serve hot.

Keto BBQ Chicken Pizza Soup

Preparation time: 1 hours 30 minutes | Servings: 6

Nutrition Info: Calories: 449 Carbs: 7.1g Fats: 32.5g Proteins: 30.8g Sodium: 252mg Sugar: 4.7g

INGREDIENTS

6 chicken legs 1 medium red onion, diced 4 garlic cloves 1 large tomato, unsweetened 4 cups green beans ¾ cup BBQ Sauce 1½ cups mozzarella cheese, shredded ¼ cup ghee 2 quarts water 2 quarts chicken stock Salt and black pepper, to taste Fresh cilantro, for garnishing

DIRECTIONS

1. Put chicken, water and salt in a large pot and bring to a boil. Reduce the heat to medium-low and cook for about 75 minutes. Shred the meat off the bones using a fork and keep aside. Put ghee, red onions and garlic in a large soup and cook over a medium heat. Add chicken stock and bring to a boil over a high heat. Add green beans and tomato to the pot and cook for about 15 minutes. Add BBQ Sauce, shredded chicken, salt and black pepper to the pot. Ladle the soup into serving bowls and top with shredded mozzarella cheese and cilantro to serve.

Spicy Halibut Tomato Soup

Preparation time: 1 hours 5minutes | Servings: 8

Nutrition Info: Per Serving : Calories 260, Fat 9g, Carbs 6g, Protein 29

INGREDIENTS

2 garlic cloves, minced 1 tablespoon olive oil ¼ cup fresh parsley, chopped 10 anchovies canned in oil, minced 6 cups vegetable broth 1 teaspoon black pepper 1 pound halibut fillets, chopped 3 tomatoes, peeled and diced 1 teaspoon salt 1 teaspoon red chili flakes

DIRECTIONS

1. Heat olive oil in a large stockpot over medium heat and add garlic and half of the parsley. Add anchovies, tomatoes, vegetable broth, red chili flakes, salt and black pepper and bring to a boil. Reduce the heat to medium-low and simmer for about 20 minutes. Add halibut fillets and cook for about 10 minutes. Dish out the halibut and shred into small pieces. Mix back with the soup and garnish with the remaining fresh parsley to serve.

Fall Soup

Total Time: 40 minutes | Serves: 4

Nutrition Info: Per Serving: Calories 200, Fat 8.7g, Carbs 25.8g, Protein 7.2g

INGREDIENTS

1 carrot, chopped 1 leek, chopped 2 garlic cloves, minced 1 celery stalk, chopped 1 parsnip, chopped 1 potato, chopped 4 cups vegetable broth 3 cups chopped butternut squash 1 tsp dried thyme 2 tbsp olive oil Salt and black pepper to taste

DIRECTIONS

1. Warm olive oil in a pot over medium heat and sauté leek, garlic, parsnip, carrot, and celery for 5-6 minute s until the veggies start to brown. Throw in squash, potato, broth, thyme, salt, and pepper. Bring to a boil, then decrease the heat and simmer for 20-30 minutes until the veggies soften. Transfer to a food processor and blend until you get a smooth and homogeneous consistency.

Sausage & Spinach Chickpea Soup

Total Time: 35 minutes | Serves: 6

Nutrition Info: Per Serving: Calories 473, Fat 21g, Carbs 46.7g, Protein 26.2g

INGREDIENTS

DIRECTIONS

8 oz Italian sausage, sliced 1 (14-oz) can chickpeas, drained 4 cups chopped spinach 1 onion, chopped 1 carrot, chopped 1 red bell pepper, seeded and chopped 3 garlic cloves, minced 6 cups chicken broth 1 tsp dried oregano Salt and black pepper to taste 2 tbsp olive oil ½ tsp red pepper flakes

1. Warm olive oil in a pot over medium heat. Sear the sausage for 5 minutes until browned. Set aside. Add carrot, onion, garlic, and bell pepper to the pot and sauté for 5 minutes until soft. Pour in broth, chickpeas, spinach, oregano, salt, pepper, and red flakes; let simmer for 5 minutes until the spinach softens. Bring the sausage back to the pot and cook for another minute. Serve warm.

Veggie & Chicken Soup

Total Time: 35 minutes | Serves: 4

Nutrition Info: Per Serving: Calories 335, Fat 9g, Carbs 28g, Protein 33g

INGREDIENTS

DIRECTIONS

1 cup mushrooms, chopped 2 tsp olive oil 1 large carrot, chopped 1 yellow onion, chopped 1 celery stalk, chopped 2 yellow squash, chopped 2 chicken breasts, cubed ½ cup chopped fresh parsley 4 cups chicken stock Salt and black pepper to taste

1. Warm the oil in a skillet over medium heat. Place in carrot, onion, mushrooms, and celery and cook for 5 minutes. Stir in chicken and cook for 10 more minutes. Mix in squash, salt, and black pepper. Cook for 5 minutes, then lower the heat and pour in the stock. Cook covered for 10 more minutes. Divide between bowls and scatter with parsley. Serve immediately.

Chicken Soup with Green Beans & Rice

Total Time: 45 minutes | Serves: 4

Nutrition Info: Per Serving: Calories 270, Fat 19g, Carbs 20g, Protein 15g

INGREDIENTS

DIRECTIONS

4 cups chicken stock 2 tbsp olive oil ½ lb chicken breasts, cut into strips 1 celery stalk, chopped 2 garlic cloves, minced 1 yellow onion, chopped ½ cup white rice 1 egg, whisked ½ lemon, juiced 1 cup green beans, trimmed and chopped 1 cup carrots, chopped ½ cup dill, chopped Salt and black pepper to taste

1. Warm the olive oil in a pot over medium heat and sauté onion, garlic, celery, carrots, and chicken for 6-7 minutes. Pour in stock and rice. Bring to a boil and simmer for 10 minutes. Stir in green beans, salt, and pepper and cook for another 15 minutes. Whisk the egg and lemon juice and pour into the pot. Stir and cook for 2 minutes. Serve warm.

Turkey & Rice Egg Soup

Total Time: 40 minutes | Serves: 4

Nutrition Info: Per Serving: Calories 303, Fat 10.6g, Carbs 28.6g, Protein 23.3g

INGREDIENTS

1 lb turkey breasts, cubed ½ cup Arborio rice 1 onion, chopped 2 tbsp olive oil 1 celery stalk, chopped 1 carrot, sliced 1 egg 2 tbsp yogurt 1 tsp dried tarragon 1 tsp lemon zest 2 tbsp fresh parsley, chopped Salt and black pepper to taste

DIRECTIONS

1. Heat olive oil in a pot over medium heat and sauté the onion, celery, turkey, and carrot for 6-7 minutes, stirring occasionally. Stir in the rice for 1-2 minutes, pour in 4 cups of water, and season with salt and pepper. Bring the soup to a boil. Lower the heat and simmer for 20 minutes until thoroughly cooked. In a bowl, beat the egg with yogurt until well combined. Remove 1 cup of the hot soup broth with a spoon and add slowly to the egg mixture, stirring constantly. Pour the whisked mixture into the pot and stir in salt, black pepper, tarragon, and lemon zest. Garnish with parsley and serve.

Oregano Chicken & Barley Soup

Total Time: 40 minutes | Serves: 4

Nutrition Info: Per Serving: Calories 373, Fat 17g, Carbs 14.2g, Protein 39.4g

INGREDIENTS

1 lb boneless chicken thighs ¼ cup pearl barley 2 tbsp olive oil 1 red onion, chopped 2 cloves garlic, minced 4 cups chicken broth ¼ tsp oregano ½ lemon, juiced ¼ tsp parsley ¼ cup fresh scallions, chopped Salt and black pepper to taste

DIRECTIONS

1. Heat the olive oil in a pot over medium heat and sweat the onion and garlic for 2-3 minutes until tender. Place in chicken thighs and cook for 5-6 minutes, stirring often. Pour in chicken broth and barley and bring to a boil. Then lower the heat and simmer for 5 minutes. Remove the chicken and shred it with two forks. Return to the pot and add in barley, lemon, oregano, and parsley. Simmer for 20-22 more minutes. Stir in shredded chicken and adjust the seasoning. Divide between 4 bowls and top with chopped scallions. Serve hot.

Slow Cooked Hot Lentil Soup

Total Time: 8 hours and 10 minutes | Serves: 6

Nutrition Info: Per Serving: Calories 280, Fat 2g, Carbs 49g, Protein 18g

INGREDIENTS

1 cup dry lentils 2 carrots, sliced 1 yellow onion, chopped 2 celery stalks, chopped 2 garlic cloves, minced 14 oz canned tomatoes, chopped 1 tbsp red pepper flakes 6 cups vegetable stock ½ tsp cumin Salt and black pepper to taste ¼ cup oregano, chopped 2 tbsp lime juice

DIRECTIONS

1. Place lentils, tomatoes, onion, celery, carrots, garlic, vegetable stock, cumin, red pepper flakes, salt, and pepper in your slow cooker. Place the lid cook on Low for 8 hours. Stir in oregano and lime juice and serve right away.

Italian Cavolo Nero Soup

Total Time: 35 minutes | Serves: 4

Nutrition Info: Per Serving: Calories 200, Fat 9g, Carbs 13g, Protein 5g

INGREDIENTS

2 tbsp olive oil 1 lb cavolo nero, torn 1 cup canned chickpeas, drained Salt and black pepper to taste 1 celery stalk, chopped 1 onion, chopped 1 carrot, chopped 14 oz canned tomatoes, chopped 2 tbsp rosemary, chopped 4 cups vegetable stock

DIRECTIONS

1. Warm the olive oil in a pot over medium heat and cook onion, celery, and carrot for 5 minutes. Stir in cavolo nero, salt, pepper, tomatoes, rosemary, chickpeas, and vegetable stock and simmer for 20 minutes. Serve warm.

Vegetable Soup

Total Time: 55 minutes | Serves: 4

Nutrition Info: Per Serving: Calories 310, Fat 12g, Carbs 18g, Protein 11g

INGREDIENTS

2 tbsp olive oil 1 yellow onion, chopped 2 garlic cloves, minced 1 carrot, chopped 1 zucchini, chopped 1 yellow squash, peeled and cubed 2 tbsp parsley, chopped ¼ fennel bulb, chopped 30 oz canned cannellini beans, drained 2 cups veggie stock ¼ tsp dried thyme Salt and black pepper to taste 1 cup green beans ¼ cup Parmesan cheese, grated

DIRECTIONS

1. Warm the olive oil in a pot over medium heat and cook onion, garlic, carrot, squash, zucchini, and fennel for 5 minutes. Stir in cannellini beans, veggie stock, 4 cups of water, thyme, salt, and pepper and bring to a boil; cook for 10 minutes. Put in broccoli and cook for another 10 minutes. Serve sprinkled with Parmesan cheese and parsley.

Tasty Zuppa Toscana

Total Time: 25 minutes | Serves: 6

Nutrition Info: Per Serving: Calories 480, Fat 9g, Carbs 77g, Protein 28g

INGREDIENTS

2 tbsp olive oil 1 yellow onion, chopped 4 garlic cloves, minced 1 celery stalk, chopped 1 carrot, chopped 15 oz canned tomatoes, chopped 1 zucchini, chopped 6 cups vegetable stock 2 tbsp tomato paste 15 oz canned white beans, drained and rinsed 5 oz Tuscan kale 1 tbsp basil, chopped Salt and black pepper to taste

DIRECTIONS

1. Warm the olive oil in a pot over medium heat and cook garlic and onion for 3 minutes. Stir in celery, carrot, tomatoes, zucchini, stock, tomato paste, white beans, kale, salt, and pepper and bring to a simmer. Cook for 10 minutes. Serve topped with basil

Spinach & Lentil Soup

Total Time: 55 minutes | Serves: 4

Nutrition Info: Per Serving: Calories 250, Fat 8g, Carbs 33g, Protein 15g

INGREDIENTS

2 tbsp olive oil 1 yellow onion, chopped 2 celery stalks, chopped 1 carrot, sliced 2 tbsp parsley, chopped 2 garlic cloves, minced 2 tbsp ginger, grated 1 tsp turmeric powder 2 tsp sweet paprika 1 tsp cinnamon powder ½ cup red lentils 1 cup spinach, torn 14 oz canned tomatoes, crushed 4 cups chicken stock Salt and black pepper to taste

DIRECTIONS

1. Warm the olive oil in a pot over medium heat and sauté onion, ginger, garlic, celery, and carrot for 5 minutes. Stir in turmeric powder, sweet paprika, cinnamon powder, red lentils, tomatoes, chicken stock, salt, and pepper and bring to a boil. Simmer for 15 minutes. Stir in spinach for 5 minutes until the spinach is wilted. Sprinkle with parsley and serve.

Super Bean & Celery Soup

Soup Total Time: 50 minutes | Serves: 4

Nutrition Info: Per Serving: Calories 280, Fat 17g, Carbs 16g, Protein 8g

INGREDIENTS

DIRECTIONS

2 tbsp olive oil 2 shallots, chopped 1 potato, chopped 5 celery sticks, chopped 1 carrot, chopped ½ tsp dried oregano 1 bay leaf 30 oz canned white beans, drained 2 tbsp tomato paste 4 cups chicken stock

1. Warm the olive oil in a pot over medium heat and cook shallots, celery, carrot, bay leaf, and oregano for 5 minutes. Stir in white beans, tomato paste, potato, and chicken stock and bring to a boil. Cook for 20 minutes. Remove the bay leaf. Serve.

Power Green Soup

Soup Total Time: 20 minutes | Serves: 4

Nutrition Info: Per Serving: Calories 300, Fat 12g, Carbs 28g, Protein 5g

INGREDIENTS

DIRECTIONS

1 tbsp olive oil 1 white onion, chopped ½ cup Greek yogurt 1 celery stalk, chopped 4 cups vegetable stock 2 cups green peas 2 tbsp mint leaves, chopped 1 cup spinach Salt and black pepper to taste

1. Warm the olive oil in a pot over medium heat and cook onion and celery for 4 minutes. Add in vegetable stock, green peas, spinach, salt, and pepper and bring to a boil. Simmer for 4 minutes. Take off the heat and let cool the soup for a few minutes. Blend the soup with an immersion blender until smooth. Apportion the soup among bowls and garnish with a swirl of Greek yogurt. Sprinkle with chopped mint and serve.

Tomato Beef Soup

Total Time: 1 hour | Serves: 4

Nutrition Info: Per Serving: Calories 350, Fat 16g, Carbs 16g, Protein 38g

INGREDIENTS

DIRECTIONS

2 tbsp olive oil ½ lb beef stew meat, cubed 1 celery stalk, chopped 1 tsp fennel seeds 1 tsp hot paprika 1 carrot, chopped 1 onion, chopped Salt and black pepper to taste 2 garlic cloves, chopped 4 cups beef stock ½ tsp dried cilantro 1 tsp dried oregano 14 oz canned tomatoes, chopped 2 tbsp parsley, chopped

1. Warm the olive oil in a pot over medium heat and cook beef meat, onion, and garlic for 10 minutes, stirring occasionally. Stir in celery, carrots, fennel seeds, paprika, salt, pepper, cilantro, and oregano for 3 minutes. Pour in beef stock and tomatoes and bring to a boil. Cook for 40 minutes. Sprinkle with parsley. Serve immediately.

Easy Vegetable Soup

Soup Total Time: 40 minutes | Serves: 4

Nutrition Info: Per Serving: Calories 260, Fat 12g, Carbs 18g, Protein 13g

INGREDIENTS

2 tbsp olive oil 2 potatoes, peeled and cubed 1 celery stalk, chopped 1 zucchini, chopped 1 small head broccoli, chopped 1 onion, chopped 1 carrot, cubed 1 tsp dried rosemary ½ tsp cayenne pepper 4 cups vegetable stock Salt and black pepper to taste 1 tbsp chives, chopped

DIRECTIONS

1. Warm the olive oil in a pot over medium heat and sauté onion, celery, and carrot for 5 minutes. Add in rosemary, cayenne pepper, potatoes, and zucchini and sauté for another 5 minutes. Pour in the vegetable stock and bring to a simmer. Cook for 20 minutes. Adjust the seasoning and add in the broccoli; cook for 5-8 minutes. Sprinkle with chives. Serve immediately.

Chicken & Eggplant Soup

Soup Total Time: 40 minutes | Serves: 4

Nutrition Info: Per Serving: Calories 320, Fat 18g, Carbs 21g, Protein 16g

INGREDIENTS

2 tbsp butter ¼ tsp celery seeds 2 cups eggplants, cubed Salt and black pepper to taste 1 red onion, chopped 2 garlic cloves, minced 1 red bell pepper, chopped 1 red chili pepper 2 tbsp parsley, chopped 2 tbsp oregano, chopped 4 cups chicken stock 1 lb chicken breasts, cubed 1 cup half and half 1 egg yolk

DIRECTIONS

1. Melt butter in a pot over medium heat and sauté chicken, garlic, and onion for 10 minutes. Put in bell pepper, eggplant, salt, pepper, red chili pepper, celery seeds, oregano, and chicken stock and bring to a simmer. Cook for 20 minutes. Whisk egg yolk, half and half, and 1 cup of the soup in a bowl and pour gradually into the pot. Stir and sprinkle with parsley. Serve immediately.

Cold Prawn Soup

Soup Total Time: 15 minutes | Serves: 6

Nutrition Info: Per Serving: Calories 270, Fat 12g, Carbs 13g, Protein 7g

INGREDIENTS

3 tbsp olive oil 1 cucumber, chopped 3 cups tomato juice 3 roasted red peppers, chopped 2 tbsp balsamic vinegar 1 garlic clove, minced Salt and black pepper to taste ½ tsp cumin 1 lb prawns, peeled and deveined 1 tsp thyme, chopped

DIRECTIONS

1. In a food processor, blitz tomato juice, cucumber, red peppers, 2 tbsp of olive oil, vinegar, cumin, salt, pepper, and garlic until smooth. Remove to a bowl and transfer to the fridge for 10 minutes. Warm the remaining oil in a pot over medium heat and sauté prawns, salt, pepper, and thyme for 4 minutes on all sides. Let cool. Ladle the soup into individual bowls and serve topped with prawns.

Soup with Spinach & Orzo

Soup Total Time: 20 minutes | Serves: 4

Nutrition Info: Per Serving: Calories 370, Fat 11g, Carbs 44g, Protein 23g

INGREDIENTS

2 tbsp butter 3 cups spinach ½ cup orzo 4 cups chicken broth 1 cup feta cheese, crumbled Salt and black pepper to taste ½ tsp dried oregano 1 onion, chopped 2 garlic cloves, minced 1 cup mushrooms, sliced

DIRECTIONS

1. Melt butter in a pot over medium heat and sauté onion, garlic, and mushrooms for 5 minutes until tender. Add in chicken broth, orzo, salt, pepper, and oregano. Bring to a boil and reduce the heat to a low. Continue simmering for 10 minutes, partially covered. Stir in spinach and continue to cook until the spinach wilts, about 3-4 minutes. Ladle into individual bowls and serve garnished with feta cheese. Enjoy!

Spicy Chicken Soup with Beans

Total Time: 40 minutes | Serves: 6

Nutrition Info: Per Serving: Calories 670, Fat 18g, Carbs 74g, Protein 56g

INGREDIENTS

3 tbsp olive oil 3 garlic cloves, minced 1 onion, chopped 3 tomatoes, chopped 4 cups chicken stock 1 lb chicken breasts, cubed 1 red chili pepper, chopped 1 tbsp fennel seeds, crushed 14 oz canned white beans, drained 1 lime, zested and juiced Salt and black pepper to taste 1 tbsp parsley, chopped

DIRECTIONS

1. Warm the olive oil in a pot over medium heat. Cook the onion and garlic, adding a splash of water, for 10 minutes until aromatic. Add in the chicken and chili pepper and sit-fry for another 6-8 minutes. Put in tomatoes, chicken stock, beans, lime zest, lime juice, salt, pepper, and fennel seeds and bring to a boil; cook for 30 minutes. Serve warm.

Leftover Lamb & Mushroom Soup

Total Time: 40 minutes | Serves: 4

Nutrition Info: Per Serving: Calories 300, Fat 12g, Carbs 23g, Protein 15g

INGREDIENTS

2 carrots, chopped 1 red onion, chopped 2 tbsp olive oil 2 celery stalks, chopped 2 garlic cloves, minced Salt and black pepper to taste 1 tbsp thyme, chopped 4 cups vegetable stock 1 cup white mushrooms, sliced 8 oz leftover lamb, shredded 14 oz canned chickpeas, drained 2 tbsp cilantro, chopped

DIRECTIONS

1. Warm the olive oil in a pot over medium heat and cook onion, celery, mushrooms, carrots, and thyme for 5 minutes until tender. Stir in vegetable stock and lamb and bring to a boil. Reduce the heat to low and simmer for 20 minutes. Mix in chickpeas and cook for an additional 5 minutes. Ladle your soup into individual bowls. Top with cilantro and serve hot.

Spring Soup with Poached Egg

Preparation and Cooking Time: 20 minutes | Servings: 2

Nutrition Info: Calories: 158 Carbs: 6.9g Fats: 7.3g Proteins: 15.4g Sodium: 1513mg Sugar: 3.3g

INGREDIENTS

32 oz vegetable broth 2 eggs 1 head romaine lettuce, chopped Salt, to taste

DIRECTIONS

1. Bring the vegetable broth to a boil and reduce the heat. Poach the eggs for 5 minutes in the broth and remove them into 2 bowls. Stir in romaine lettuce into the broth and cook for 4 minutes. Dish out in a bowl and serve hot.

Easy Butternut Squash Soup

Preparation and Cooking Time: 1 hour 45 minutes | Servings: 4

Nutrition Info: Calories: 149 Carbs: 6.6g Fats: 11.6g Proteins: 5.4g Sodium: 765mg Sugar: 2.2g

INGREDIENTS

1 small onion, chopped 4 cups chicken broth 1 butternut squash 3 tablespoons coconut oil Salt, to taste Nutmeg and pepper, to taste

DIRECTIONS

1. Put oil and onions in a large pot and add onions. Sauté for about 3 minutes and add chicken broth and butternut squash. Simmer for about 1 hour on medium heat and transfer into an immersion blender. Pulse until smooth and season with salt, pepper and nutmeg. Return to the pot and cook for about 30 minutes. Dish out and serve hot.

Cauliflower, leek & bacon soup

Preparation and Cooking time: 10 minutes | Servings: 4

Nutrition Info: Calories: 185 Carbs: 5.8g Fats: 12.7g Proteins: 10.8g Sodium: 1153mg Sugar: 2.4g

INGREDIENTS

4 cups chicken broth ½ cauliflower head, chopped 1 leek, chopped Salt and black pepper, to taste 5 bacon strips

DIRECTIONS

1. Put the cauliflower, leek and chicken broth into the pot and cook for about 1 hour on medium heat. Transfer into an immersion blender and pulse until smooth. Return the soup into the pot and microwave the bacon strips for 1 minute. Cut the bacon into small pieces and put into the soup. Cook on for about 30 minutes on low heat. Season with salt and pepper and serve.

Mushroom Spinach Soup

Preparation and Cooking time: 25 minutes | Servings: 4

Nutrition Info: Calories: 160 Carbs: 7g Fats: 13.3g Proteins: 4.7g Sodium: 462mg Sugar: 2.7g

INGREDIENTS

1cupspinach,cleaned and chopped 100 g mushrooms,chopped 1 onion 6 garlic cloves ½ teaspoon red chili powder Salt and black pepper, to taste 3 tablespoons buttermilk 1 teaspoon almond flour 2 cups chicken broth 3 tablespoons butter ¼ cup fresh cream for garnish

DIRECTIONS

1. Heat butter in a pan and add onions and garlic. Sauté for about 3 minutes and add spinach, salt and red chili powder. Sauté for about 4 minutes and add mushrooms. Transfer into a blender and blend to make a puree. Return to the pan and add buttermilk and almond flour for creamy texture. Mix well and simmer for about 2 minutes. Garnish with fresh cream and serve hot.

Broccoli Soup

Preparation and Cooking time: 10 minutes | Servings: 6

Nutrition Info: Calories: 183 Carbs: 5.2g Fats: 15.6g Proteins: 6.1g Sodium: 829mg Sugar: 1.8g

INGREDIENTS

3 tablespoons ghee 5 garlic cloves 1 teaspoon sage ¼ teaspoon ginger 2 cups broccoli 1 small onion 1 teaspoon oregano ½ teaspoon parsley Salt and black pepper, to taste 6 cups vegetable broth 4 tablespoons butter

DIRECTIONS

1. Put ghee, onions, spices and garlic in a pot and cook for 3 minutes. Add broccoli and cook for about 4 minutes. Add vegetable broth, cover and allow it to simmer for about 30 minutes. Transfer into a blender and blend until smooth. Add the butter to give it a creamy delicious texture and flavor

Keto French Onion Soup

Preparation and Cooking time: 40 minutes | Servings: 6

Nutrition Info: Calories: 198 Carbs: 6g Fats: 20.6g Proteins: 2.9g Sodium: 883mg Sugar: 1.7 g

INGREDIENTS

5 tablespoons butter 500 g brown onion medium 4 drops liquid stevia 4 tablespoons olive oil 3 cups beef stock

DIRECTIONS

1. Put the butter and olive oil in a large pot over medium low heat and add onions and salt. Cook for about 5 minutes and stir in stevia. Cook for another 5 minutes and add beef stock. Reduce the heat to low and simmer for about 25 minutes. Dish out into soup bowls and serve hot.

Homemade Spicy Chicken Soup

Preparation and Cooking time: 8 hours 25 minutes | Servings: 12

Nutrition Info: Calories: 255 Carbs: 1.2g Fats: 17.6g Proteins: 25.2g Sodium: 582mg Sugar: 0.1g

INGREDIENTS

1 lemongrass stalk, cut into large chunks 5 thick slices of fresh ginger 1 whole chicken 20 fresh basil leaves 1 lime, juiced 1 tablespoon salt

DIRECTIONS

1. Place the chicken, 10 basil leaves, lemongrass, ginger, salt and water into the slow cooker. Cook for about 8 hours on low and dish out into a bowl. Stir in fresh lime juice and basil leaves to serve.

Chicken Veggie Soup

Preparation and Cooking time: 20 minutes | Servings: 6

Nutrition Info: Calories: 250 Carbs: 6.4g Fats: 8.9g Proteins: 35.1g Sodium: 852mg Sugar: 2.5g

INGREDIENTS

5 chicken thighs 12 cups water 1 tablespoon adobo seasoning 4 celery ribs 1 yellow onion 1½ teaspoons whole black peppercorns 6 sprigs fresh parsley 2 teaspoons coarse sea salt 2 carrots 6 mushrooms, sliced 2 garlic cloves 1 bay leaf 3 sprigs fresh thyme

DIRECTIONS

1. Put water, chicken thighs, carrots, celery ribs, onion, garlic cloves and herbs in a large pot. Bring to a boil and reduce the heat to low. Cover the pot and simmer for about 30 minutes. Dish out the chicken and shred it, removing the bones. Put the bones back into the pot and simmer for about 20 minutes. Strain the broth, discarding the chunks and put the liquid back into the pot. Bring it to a boil and simmer for about 30 minutes. Put the mushrooms in the broth and simmer for about 10 minutes. Dish out to serve hot.

Buffalo Ranch Chicken Soup

Preparation and Cooking time: 40 minutes | Servings: 4

Nutrition Info: Calories: 444 Carbs: 4g Fats: 34g Proteins: 28g Sodium: 1572mg Sugar: 2 g

INGREDIENTS

2 tablespoons parsley 2 celery stalks, chopped 6 tablespoons butter 1 cup heavy whipping cream 4 cups chicken, cooked and shredded 4 tablespoons ranch dressing ¼ cup yellow onions, chopped 8 oz cream cheese 8 cups chicken broth 7 hearty bacon slices, crumbled

DIRECTIONS

1. Heat butter in a pan and add chicken. Cook for about 5 minutes and add 1½ cups water. Cover and cook for about 10 minutes. Put the chicken and rest of the ingredients into the saucepan except parsley and cook for about 10 minutes. Top with parsley and serve hot.

Chicken and Egg Soup

Preparation and Cooking time: 30 minutes | Servings: 6

Nutrition Info: Calories: 226 Carbs: 3.5g Fats: 8.9g Proteins: 31.8g Sodium: 152mg Sugar: 1.6g

INGREDIENTS

1 onion, minced 1 rib celery, sliced 3 cups chicken, shredded 3 eggs, lightly beaten 1 green onion, for garnish 2 tablespoons olive oil 1 carrot, peeled and thinly sliced 2 teaspoons dried thyme 2½ quarts homemade bone broth ¼ cup fresh parsley, minced Salt and black pepper, to taste

DIRECTIONS

1. Heat oil over medium-high heat in a large pot and add onions, carrots, and celery. Cook for about 4 minutes and stir in the bone broth, thyme and chicken. Simmer for about 15 minutes and stir in parsley. Pour beaten eggs into the soup in a slow steady stream. Remove soup from heat and let it stand for about 2 minutes. Season with salt and black pepper and dish out to serve.

Green Chicken Enchilada Soup

Preparation time: 20 minutes | Servings: 5

Nutrition Info: Calories: 265 Carbs: 2.2g Fats: 17.4g Proteins: 24.2g Sodium: 686mg Sugar: 0.8g

INGREDIENTS

4 oz. cream cheese, softened ½ cup salsa verde 1 cup cheddar cheese, shredded 2 cups cooked chicken, shredded 2 cups chicken stock

DIRECTIONS

1. Put salsa verde, cheddar cheese, cream cheese and chicken stock in an immersion blender and blend until smooth. Pour this mixture into a medium saucepan and cook for about 5 minutes on medium heat. Add the shredded chicken and cook for about 5 minutes. Garnish with additional shredded cheddar and serve hot.

Salmon Stew Soup

Preparation time: 25 minutes | Servings: 5

Nutrition Info: Calories: 262 Carbs: 7.8g Fats: 14g Proteins: 27.5g Sodium: 1021mg Sugar: 1.2g

INGREDIENTS

4 cups chicken broth 3 salmon fillets, chunked 2 tablespoons butter 1 cup parsley, chopped 3 cups Swiss chard, roughly chopped 2 Italian squash, chopped 1 garlic clove, crushed ½ lemon, juiced Salt and black pepper, to taste 2 eggs

DIRECTIONS

1. Put the chicken broth and garlic into a pot and bring to a boil. Add salmon, lemon juice and butter in the pot and cook for about 10 minutes on medium heat. Add Swiss chard, Italian squash, salt and pepper and cook for about 10 minutes. Whisk eggs and add to the pot, stirring continuously. Garnish with parsley and serve.

Italian Chicken & Veggie Soup

Total Time: 30 minutes | Serves: 4

Nutrition Info: Per Serving: Calories 293, Fat 14.2g, Carbs 18.5g, Protein 24.4g

INGREDIENTS

1 (14-oz) can diced tomatoes ½ pound chicken breasts, cubed 4 cups chicken broth 2 carrots, chopped 1 onion, chopped 1 red bell pepper, seeded and chopped 1 fennel bulb, chopped 2 garlic cloves, minced ½ tsp paprika 1 cup mushrooms, sliced 1 tbsp Italian seasoning 2 tbsp olive oil Salt and black pepper to taste

DIRECTIONS

1. Warm olive oil in a pot over medium heat. Place in chicken and brown for 5 minutes. Set aside. Add in onion, carrots, bell pepper, and fennel, sauté for 5 minutes until softened. Throw in garlic and paprika and cook for 30 seconds. Mix in tomatoes, mushrooms, Italian seasoning, broth, chicken, salt, and pepper. Bring to a boil, then decrease the heat and simmer for 20 minutes. Serve warm.

Rosemary Soup with Roasted Vegetables

Total Time: 45 minutes | Serves: 4

Nutrition Info: Per Serving: Calories 203, Fat 10g, Carbs 23g, Protein 2g

INGREDIENTS

2 carrots, sliced 3 tbsp olive oil 3 sweet potatoes, sliced 1 celery stalk, sliced 1 tsp chopped rosemary 4 cups vegetable broth Salt and black pepper to taste Grated Parmesan cheese

DIRECTIONS

1. Preheat oven to 400ºF. Mix carrots, sweet potatoes, and celery in a bowl. Drizzle with olive oil and toss. Sprinkle with rosemary, salt, and pepper. Arrange on a lined with parchment paper sheet and bake for 30 minutes or until the veggies are tender and golden brown. Remove from the oven and let cool slightly. Place the veggies and some broth in a food processor and pulse until smooth; work in batches. Transfer to a pot over low heat and add in the remaining broth. Cook just until heated through. Serve topped with Parmesan cheese.

Spicy Lentil Soup

Total Time: 30 minutes | Serves: 4

Nutrition Info: Per Serving: Calories 331, Fat 9g, Carbs 44.3g, Protein 19g

INGREDIENTS

1 cup lentils, rinsed 1 onion, chopped 2 carrots, chopped 1 potato, cubed 1 tomato, chopped 4 garlic cloves, minced 4 cups vegetable broth 2 tbsp olive oil ½ tsp chili powder Salt and black pepper to taste 2 tbsp fresh parsley, chopped

DIRECTIONS

1. Warm olive oil in a pot over medium heat. Add in onion, garlic, and carrots and sauté for 5-6 minutes until tender. Mix in lentils, broth, salt, pepper, chili powder, potato, and tomato. Bring to a boil, lower the heat and simmer for 15-18 minutes, stirring often. Top with parsley and serve.

Basil Meatball Soup

Total Time: 35 minutes | Serves: 6

Nutrition Info: Per Serving: Calories 265, Fat 9.8g, Carbs 18.8g, Protein 24.2g

INGREDIENTS

1 (14-oz) can chopped tomatoes, drained ½ cup rice, rinsed 12 oz ground beef 2 shallots, chopped 1 tbsp dried thyme 1 carrot, chopped 1 tsp garlic powder 2 tbsp olive oil 5 garlic cloves, minced 6 cups chicken broth ¼ cup chopped fresh basil leaves Salt and black pepper to taste

DIRECTIONS

1. Combine ground beef, shallots, garlic powder, thyme, salt, and pepper in a bowl. Make balls out of the mixture and reserve. Warm the olive oil in a pot over medium heat and sauté the garlic and carrot for 2 minutes. Mix in meatballs, rice, tomatoes, broth, salt, and pepper and bring to a boil. Lower the heat and simmer for 18 minutes. Top with basil before serving.

Basil Tomato & Roasted Pepper Soup

Total Time: 30 minutes | Serves: 4

Nutrition Info: Per Serving: Calories 164, Fat 11.6g, Carbs 9.8g, Protein 6.5g

INGREDIENTS

1 cup roasted bell peppers, chopped
3 tomatoes, cored and halved 2 cloves garlic, whole 1 yellow onion, quartered 1 celery stalk, chopped 1 carrot, shredded ½ tsp ground cumin 1 chili pepper, seeded 2 tbsp olive oil 4 cups vegetable broth ½ tsp red pepper flakes, crushed 2 tbsp fresh basil, chopped Salt and black pepper to taste ¼ cup crème fraîche

DIRECTIONS

1. Arrange the Roma tomatoes, garlic, onion, and peppers on a roasting pan. Drizzle olive oil over your vegetables. Heat olive oil in a pot over medium heat and sauté onion, garlic, celery, and carrots for 3-5 minutes until tender. Stir in chili pepper and cumin for 1-2 minutes. Pour in roasted bell peppers and tomatoes, stir, then add in the vegetable broth. Season with salt and pepper. Bring to a boil and reduce the heat; simmer for 10 minutes. Using an immersion blender, purée the soup until smooth. Sprinkle with red pepper flakes and basil. Serve topped with crème fraîche.

Pork & Vegetable Soup

Total Time: 40 minutes | Serves: 4

Nutrition Info: Per Serving: Calories 240, Fat 6g, Carbs 22g, Protein 7g

INGREDIENTS

2 tbsp olive oil 1 onion, chopped 2 garlic cloves, minced 1 pork loin, chopped 1 cup mushrooms, chopped 1 carrot, chopped 1 celery stalk, chopped Salt and black pepper to taste 14 oz canned tomatoes, drained 4 cups vegetable stock ½ tsp nutmeg, ground 2 tsp parsley, chopped

DIRECTIONS

1. Warm the olive oil in a pot over medium heat and cook pork meat, onion, and garlic for 5 minutes. Put in mushrooms, carrots, salt, pepper, tomatoes, vegetable stock, and nutmeg and bring to a boil. Cook for 25 minutes. Sprinkle with parsley.

Herbed Bean Soup

Total Time: 50 minutes | Serves: 6

Nutrition Info: Per Serving: Calories 270, Fat 18g, Carbs 24g, Protein 12g

INGREDIENTS

2 tbsp olive oil 6 cups veggie stock 1 cup celery, chopped 1 cup carrots, chopped 1 yellow onion, chopped 2 garlic cloves, minced ½ cup navy beans, soaked ½ tsp chopped parsley ½ tsp paprika 1 tsp thyme Salt and black pepper to taste

DIRECTIONS

1. Warm olive oil in a saucepan and sauté onion, garlic, carrots, and celery for 5 minutes, stirring occasionally. Stir in paprika, thyme, salt, and pepper for 1 minute. Pour in chicken broth and navy beans. Bring to a boil, then reduce the heat and simmer for 40 minutes covered. Sprinkle with basil and serve hot.

Quick Chicken & Vermicelli Soup

Total Time: 25 minutes | Serves: 4

Nutrition Info: Per Serving: Calories 310, Fat 13g, Carbs 17g, Protein 13g

INGREDIENTS

2 tbsp olive oil 1 carrot, chopped 1 leek, chopped ½ cup vermicelli 4 cups chicken stock 2 cups kale, chopped 2 chicken breasts, cubed 1 cup orzo ¼ cup lemon juice 2 tbsp parsley, chopped Salt and black pepper to taste

DIRECTIONS

1. Warm the olive oil in a pot over medium heat and sauté leek and chicken for 6 minutes. Stir in carrot and chicken stock and bring to a boil. Cook for 10 minutes. Add in vermicelli, kale, orzo, and lemon juice and continue cooking for another 5 minutes. Adjust the seasoning with salt and pepper and sprinkle with parsley. Ladle into soup bowls and serve.

Cannellini Bean & Feta Cheese Soup

Total Time: 30 minutes | Serves: 4

Nutrition Info: Per Serving: Calories 519, Fat 15.4g, Carbs 64.6g, Protein 32.3g

INGREDIENTS

4 oz feta cheese, crumbled 1 cup collard greens, torn into pieces 2 cups canned cannellini beans, rinsed 2 tbsp olive oil 1 fennel bulb, chopped 1 carrot, chopped ½ cup spring onions, chopped ½ tsp dried rosemary ½ tsp dried basil 1 garlic clove, minced 4 cups vegetable broth 2 tbsp tomato paste Salt and black pepper to taste

DIRECTIONS

1. In a pot over medium heat, warm the olive oil. Add in fennel, garlic, carrot, and spring onions and sauté until tender, about 2-3 minutes. Stir in tomato paste, rosemary, and basil and cook for 2 more minutes. Pour in vegetable broth and cannellini beans. Bring to a boil, then lower the heat, and simmer for 15 minutes. Add in collard greens and cook for another 2-3 minutes until wilted. Adjust the seasoning with salt and pepper. Top with feta cheese and serve.

Italian Sausage & Seafood Soup

Total Time: 30 minutes | Serves: 4

Nutrition Info: Per Serving: Calories 619, Fat 42.6g, Carbs 26.6g, Protein 32.5g

INGREDIENTS

½ lb shrimp, raw and deveined 2 tbsp butter 3 Italian sausages, sliced 1 red onion, chopped 1 ½ cups clams 1 carrot, chopped 1 celery stalk, chopped 2 garlic cloves, minced 1 (14.5-oz) canned tomatoes 1 tsp dried basil 1 tsp dried dill 4 cups chicken broth 2 tbsp olive oil 4 tbsp cornflour 2 tbsp lemon juice 2 tbsp fresh cilantro, chopped Salt and black pepper to taste

DIRECTIONS

1. Melt the butter in a pot over medium heat and brown the sausage; set aside. Heat the olive oil in the same pot and add in cornflour; cook for 4 minutes. Add in the onion, garlic, carrot, and celery and stir-fry them for 3 minutes. Stir in tomatoes, basil, dill, and chicken broth. Bring to a boil. Lower the heat and simmer for 5 minutes. Mix in the reserved sausages, salt, black pepper, clams, and shrimp and simmer for 10 minutes. Discard any unopened clams. Share into bowls and sprinkle with lemon juice. Serve warm garnished with fresh cilantro.

Cauliflower Soup with Pancetta Croutons

Total Time: 50 minutes | Serves: 4

Nutrition Info: Per Serving: Calories 250, Fat 18g, Carbs 42g, Protein 14g

INGREDIENTS

4 oz pancetta, cubed 2 tbsp olive oil 1 cauliflower head, cut into florets 1 yellow onion, chopped Salt and black pepper to taste 4 cups chicken stock 1 tsp mustard powder 2 garlic cloves, minced ½ cup mozzarella cheese, shredded

DIRECTIONS

1. Place a saucepan over medium heat and add in the pancetta. Cook it until crispy, about 4 minutes, and set aside. Add olive oil, onion, and garlic to the pot and cook for 3 minutes. Pour in chicken stock, cauliflower, mustard powder, salt, and pepper and cook for 20 minutes. Using an immersion blender, purée the soup and stir in the mozzarella cheese. Serve immediately topped with pancetta croutons.

Cheesy Tomato Soup

Total Time: 45 minutes | Serves: 4

Nutrition Info: Per Serving: Calories 240, Fat 11g, Carbs 16g, Protein 8g

INGREDIENTS

2 tbsp olive oil 2 lb tomatoes, halved 2 garlic cloves, minced 1 onion, chopped Salt and black pepper to taste 4 cups chicken stock ½ tsp red pepper flakes ½ cup basil, chopped ½ cup Pecorino cheese, grated

DIRECTIONS

1. Preheat the oven to 380ºF. Place the tomatoes in a baking tray, drizzle with olive oil, and season with salt and pepper. Roast in the oven for 20 minutes. Warm the remaining olive oil in a pot over medium heat and sauté onion for 3 minutes. Put in roasted tomatoes, garlic, chicken stock, and red pepper flakes and bring to a boil. Simmer for 15 minutes. Using an immersion blender, purée the soup and stir in Pecorino cheese. Serve right away topped with basil.

Pork Meatball Soup

Total Time: 35 minutes | Serves: 4

Nutrition Info: Per Serving: Calories 380, Fat 18g, Carbs 29g, Protein 18g

INGREDIENTS

2 tbsp olive oil ½ cup white rice ½ lb ground pork Salt and black pepper to taste 2 garlic cloves, minced 1 onion, chopped ½ tsp dried thyme 4 cups beef stock ½ tsp saffron powder 14 oz canned tomatoes, crushed 1 tbsp parsley, chopped

DIRECTIONS

1. In a bowl, mix ground pork, rice, salt, and pepper with your hands. Shape the mixture into ½-inch balls; set aside. Warm the olive oil in a pot over medium heat and cook the onion and garlic for 5 minutes. Pour in beef stock, thyme, saffron powder, and tomatoes and bring to a boil. Add in the pork balls and cook for 20 minutes. Adjust the seasoning with salt and pepper. Serve sprinkled with parsley.

Turkey & Cabbage Soup

Soup Total Time: 40 minutes | Serves: 4

Nutrition Info: Per Serving: Calories 320, Fat 16g, Carbs 25g, Protein 19g

INGREDIENTS

2 tbsp olive oil ½ lb turkey breast, cubed 2 leeks, sliced 4 spring onions, chopped 1 green cabbage head, shredded 4 celery sticks, chopped 4 cups vegetable stock ½ tsp sweet paprika ½ tsp ground nutmeg Salt and black pepper to taste

DIRECTIONS

1. Warm the olive oil in a pot over medium heat and brown turkey for 4 minutes, stirring occasionally. Add in leeks, spring onions, and celery and cook for another minute. Stir in cabbage, vegetable stock, sweet paprika, nutmeg, salt, and pepper and bring to a boil. Cook for 30 minutes. Serve immediately.

Green Lentil & Ham Easy Soup

Soup Total Time: 30 minutes | Serves: 6

Nutrition Info: Per Serving: Calories 270, Fat 12g, Carbs 25g, Protein 15g

INGREDIENTS

½ lb ham, cubed 1 onion, chopped 2 tbsp olive oil 2 tsp parsley, dried 1 potato, chopped 3 garlic cloves, chopped Salt and black pepper to taste 1 carrot, chopped ½ tsp paprika ½ cup green lentils, rinsed 4 cups vegetable stock 3 tbsp tomato paste 2 tomatoes, chopped

DIRECTIONS

1. Warm the olive oil in a pot over medium heat and cook ham, onion, carrot, and garlic for 4 minutes. Stir in tomato paste, paprika, and tomatoes for 2-3 minutes. Pour in lentils, vegetable stock, ham, and potato and bring to a boil. Cook for 18-20 minutes. Adjust the seasoning with salt and pepper and sprinkle with parsley. Serve warm.

Soup With Lamb & Spinach

Soup Total Time: 50 minutes | Serves: 4

Nutrition Info: Per Serving: Calories 290, Fat 29g, Carbs 3g, Protein 6g

INGREDIENTS

2 tbsp olive oil ½ lb lamb meat, cubed 3 eggs, whisked 4 cups beef broth 5 spring onions, chopped 2 tbsp mint, chopped 2 lemons, juiced Salt and black pepper to taste 1 cup baby spinach

DIRECTIONS

1. Warm the olive oil in a pot over medium heat and cook lamb for 10 minutes, stirring occasionally. Add in spring onions and cook for another 3 minutes. Pour in beef broth, salt, and pepper and simmer for 30 minutes. Whisk eggs with lemon juice and some soup and pour into the pot along with the spinach and cook for an additional 5 minutes. Sprinkle with mint and serve immediately.

Lemon Chicken Soup

Soup Total Time: 40 minutes | Serves: 4

Nutrition Info: Per Serving: Calories 240, Fat 12g, Carbs 15g, Protein 13g

INGREDIENTS

2 tbsp olive oil 1 onion, chopped 2 garlic cloves, minced 1 celery stalk, chopped 1 carrot, chopped 4 cups chicken stock Salt and black pepper to taste ¼ cup lemon juice 1 chicken breast, cubed ½ cup stelline pasta 6 mint leaves, chopped

DIRECTIONS

1. Warm the olive oil in a pot over medium heat and sauté onion, garlic, celery, and carrot for 5 minutes until tender. Add in the chicken and cook for another 4-5 minutes, stirring occasionally. Pour in chicken stock and bring to a boil; cook for 10 minutes. Add in the stelline past and let simmer for 10 minutes. Stir in lemon juice and adjust the seasoning with salt and pepper. Sprinkle with mint and ladle the soup into bowls. Serve immediately.

Spanish Chorizo & Bean Special Soup

Soup Total Time: 45 minutes | Serves: 4

Nutrition Info: Per Serving: Calories 580, Fat 27g, Carbs 38g, Protein 27g

INGREDIENTS

DIRECTIONS

2 tbsp olive oil 1 lb Spanish chorizo, sliced 1 carrot, chopped 1 yellow onion, chopped 1 celery stalk, chopped 2 garlic cloves, minced ½ lb kale, chopped 4 cups chicken stock 1 cup canned Borlotti beans, drained 1 tsp rosemary, dried Salt and black pepper to taste ½ cup Manchego cheese, grated

1. Warm the olive oil in a large pot over medium heat and cook sausage for 5 minutes or until the fat is rendered and the chorizo is browned. Add in onion and continue to cook for another 3 minutes until soft and translucent. Stir in garlic and let it cook for 30-40 seconds until fragrant. Lastly, add the carrots and celery and cook for 4-5 minutes or so until tender. Now, pour in the chicken stock, drained and washed beans, rosemary, salt, and pepper and bring to a boil. Reduce the heat to low, cover the pot and simmer for 30 minutes. Stir periodically, checking to make sure there is enough liquid. Five minutes before the end, add the kale. Adjust the seasoning. Ladle your soup into bowls and serve topped with Manchego cheese.

Turkish Chicken Soup with Buckwheat

Total Time: 40 minutes | Serves: 6

Nutrition Info: Per Serving: Calories 320, Fat 9g, Carbs 18g, Protein 24g

INGREDIENTS

DIRECTIONS

1 tbsp olive oil 1 lb chicken breasts, cubed Salt and black pepper to taste 2 celery stalks, chopped 1 carrot, chopped 1 red onion, chopped 6 cups chicken stock ½ cup parsley, chopped ½ cup buckwheat 1 tsp lime juice 1 lime, sliced

1. Warm the olive oil in a pot over medium heat. Season chicken breasts with salt and pepper and cook for 8 minutes. Stir in onion, carrot, and celery and sauté for another 3 minutes or until soft and aromatic. Put in chicken stock and buckwheat and bring to a boil. Reduce the heat to low. Let it simmer for about 20 minutes and add in lime juice. Sprinkle with parsley. Ladle your soup into individual bowls and serve warm with gremolata toast and the lime slices. Yummy!

COOK BOOK

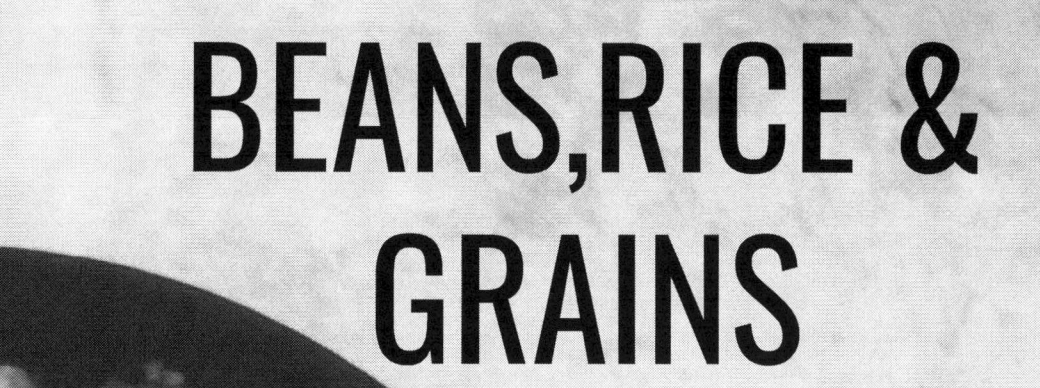

BEANS, RICE & GRAINS

Flavors Taco Rice Bowl

Preparation Time: 10 minutes | Cooking Time: 14 minutes | Servings: 8

Nutrition Info: Calories 464 Fat 15.3 g Carbohydrates 48.9 g Sugar 2.8 g Protein 32.2 g Cholesterol 83 m g

INGREDIENTS

1 lb ground beef 8 oz cheddar cheese, shredded 14 oz can red beans 2 oz taco seasoning 16 oz salsa 2 cups of water 2 cups brown rice Pepper Salt

DIRECTIONS

1. Set instant pot on sauté mode. Add meat to the pot and sauté until brown. Add water, beans, rice, taco seasoning, pepper, and salt and stir well. Top with salsa. Seal pot with lid and cook on high for 14 minutes. Once done, release pressure using quick release. Remove lid. Add cheddar cheese and stir until cheese is melted. Serve and enjoy.

Cucumber Olive Rice

Preparation time: 1 hours 30 minutes | Servings: 6

Nutrition Info: Calories 229 Fat 5.1 g Carbohydrates 40.2 g Sugar 1.6 g Protein 4.9 g Cholesterol 0 mg

INGREDIENTS

2 cups rice, rinsed 1/2 cup olives, pitted 1 cup cucumber, chopped 1 tbsp red wine vinegar 1 tsp lemon zest, grated 1 tbsp fresh lemon juice 2 tbsp olive oil 2 cups vegetable broth 1/2 tsp dried oregano 1 red bell pepper, chopped 1/2 cup onion, chopped 1 tbsp olive oil Pepper Salt

DIRECTIONS

1. Add oil into the inner pot of instant pot and set the pot on sauté mode. Add onion and sauté for 3 minutes. Add bell pepper and oregano and sauté for 1 minute. Add rice and broth and stir well. Seal pot with lid and cook on high for 6 minutes. Once done, allow to release pressure naturally for 10 minutes then release remaining using quick release. Remove lid. Add remaining ingredients and stir everything well to mix. Serve immediately and enjoy it.

Cheese Basil Tomato Rice

Preparation Time: 10 minutes | Cooking Time: 26 minutes | Servings: 8

Nutrition Info: Calories 208 Fat 5.6 g Carbohydrates 32.1 g Sugar 2.8 g Protein 8.3 g Cholesterol 8 mg

INGREDIENTS

1 1/2 cups brown rice 1 cup parmesan cheese, grated 1/4 cup fresh basil, chopped 2 cups grape tomatoes, halved 8 oz can tomato sauce 1 3/4 cup vegetable broth 1 tbsp garlic, minced 1/2 cup onion, diced 1 tbsp olive oil Pepper Salt

DIRECTIONS

1. Add oil into the inner pot of instant pot and set the pot on sauté mode. Add garlic and onion and sauté for 4 minutes. Add rice, tomato sauce, broth, pepper, and salt and stir well. Seal pot with lid and cook on high for 22 minutes. Once done, allow to release pressure naturally for 10 minutes then release remaining using quick release. Remove lid. Add remaining ingredients and stir well. Serve and enjoy.

Fiber Packed Chicken Rice

Preparation Time: 10 minutes | Cooking Time: 16 minutes | Servings: 6

Nutrition Info: Calories 399 Fat 6.4 g Carbohydrates 53.4 g Sugar 3 g Protein 31.6 g Cholesterol 50 mg

INGREDIENTS

1 lb chicken breast, skinless, boneless, and cut into chunks 14.5 oz can cannellini beans 4 cups chicken broth 2 cups wild rice 1 tbsp Italian seasoning 1 small onion, chopped 1 tbsp garlic, chopped 1 tbsp olive oil Pepper Salt

DIRECTIONS

1. Add oil into the inner pot of instant pot and set the pot on sauté mode. Add garlic and onion and sauté for 2 minutes. Add chicken and cook for 2 minutes. Add remaining ingredients and stir well. Seal pot with lid and cook on high for 12 minutes. Once done, release pressure using quick release. Remove lid. Stir well and serve.

Bulgur Salad

Preparation Time: 10 minutes | Cooking Time: 1 minute | Servings: 2

Nutrition Info: Calories 430 Fat 32.2 g Carbohydrates 31.5 g Sugar 3 g Protein 8.9 g Cholesterol 22 mg

INGREDIENTS

1/2 cup bulgur wheat 1/4 cup fresh parsley, chopped 1 tbsp fresh mint, chopped 1/3 cup feta cheese, crumbled 2 tbsp fresh lemon juice 2 tbsp olives, chopped 1/4 cup olive oil 1/2 cup tomatoes, chopped 1/3 cup cucumber, chopped 1/2 cup water Salt

DIRECTIONS

1. Add the bulgur wheat, water, and salt into the instant pot. Seal pot with lid and cook on high for 1 minute. Once done, release pressure using quick release. Remove lid. Transfer bulgur wheat to the mixing bowl. Add remaining ingredients to the bowl and mix well. Serve and enjoy.

Herb Polenta

Preparation Time: 10 minutes | Cooking Time: 12 minutes | Servings: 6

Nutrition Info: Calories 196 Fat 7.8 g Carbohydrates 23.5 g Sugar 1.7 g Protein 8.2 g Cholesterol 6 mg

INGREDIENTS

1 cup polenta 1/4 tsp nutmeg 3 tbsp fresh parsley, chopped 1/4 cup milk 1/2 cup parmesan cheese, grated 4 cups vegetable broth 2 tsp thyme, chopped 2 tsp rosemary, chopped 2 tsp sage, chopped 1 small onion, chopped 2 tbsp olive oil Salt

DIRECTIONS

1. Add oil into the inner pot of instant pot and set the pot on sauté mode. Add onion and herbs and sauté for 4 minutes. Add polenta, broth, and salt and stir well. Seal pot with lid and cook on high for 8 minutes. Once done, allow to release pressure naturally. Remove lid. Stir in remaining ingredients and serve.

Quinoa & Black Bean Stuffed Sweet Potatoes

Cooking Time: 60 minutes | Servings: 8

Nutrition Info: Calories: 243; Carbs: 37.6g; Protein: 8.5g; Fat: 7.3 g

INGREDIENTS

4 sweet potatoes ½ onion, diced 1 garlic glove, crushed and diced ½ large bell pepper diced (about 2/3 cups) Handful of diced cilantro ½ cup cooked quinoa ½ cup black beans 1 tbsp olive oil 1 tbsp chili powder ½ tbsp cumin ½ tbsp paprika ½ tbsp oregano 2 tbsp lime juice 2 tbsp honey Sprinkle salt 1 cup shredded cheddar cheese Chopped spring onions, for garnish (optional)

DIRECTIONS

1. Preheat oven to 400oF. Wash and scrub outside of potatoes. Poke with fork a few times and then place on parchment paper on cookie sheet. Bake for 40-45 minutes or until it is cooked. While potatoes are baking, sauté onions, garlic, olive oil and spices in a pan on the stove until onions are translucent and soft. In the last 10 minutes while the potatoes are cooking, in a large bowl combine the onion mixture with the beans, quinoa, honey, lime juice, cilantro and ½ cup cheese. Mix well. When potatoes are cooked, remove from oven and let cool slightly. When cool to touch, cut in half (hot dog style) and scoop out most of the insides. Leave a thin ring of potato so that it will hold its shape. You can save the sweet potato guts for another recipe, such as my veggie burgers (recipe posted below). Fill with bean and quinoa mixture. Top with remaining cheddar cheese. (If making this a freezer meal, stop here. Individually wrap potato skins in plastic wrap and place on flat surface to freeze. Once frozen, place all potatoes in large zip lock container or Tupperware.) Return to oven for an additional 10 minutes or until cheese is melted.

Quinoa Buffalo Bites

Cooking Time: 15 minutes | Servings: 4

Nutrition Info: Calories: 212; Carbs: 30.6g; Protein: 15.9g; Fat: 3.0g

INGREDIENTS

2 cups cooked quinoa 1 cup shredded mozzarella 1/2 cup buffalo sauce 1/4 cup +1 Tbsp flour 1 egg 1/4 cup chopped cilantro 1 small onion, diced

DIRECTIONS

1. Preheat oven to 350oF. Mix all ingredients in large bowl. Press mixture into greased mini muffin tins. Bake for approximately 15 minutes or until bites are golden. Enjoy on its own or with blue cheese or ranch dip.

Raw Tomato Sauce & Brie on Linguine

Cooking Time: 12 minutes | Servings: 4

Nutrition Info: Calories: 274.7; Carbs: 30.9g; Protein: 14.6g; Fat: 10.3g

INGREDIENTS

¼ cup grated low-fat Parmesan cheese ½ cup loosely packed fresh basil leaves, torn 12 oz whole wheat linguine 2 cups loosely packed baby arugula 2 green onions, green parts only, sliced thinly 2 tbsp balsamic vinegar 2 tbsp extra virgin olive oil 3 large vine-ripened tomatoes 3 oz low-fat Brie cheese, cubed, rind removed and discarded 3 tbsp toasted pine nuts Pepper and salt to taste

DIRECTIONS

1. Toss together pepper, salt, vinegar, oil, onions, Parmesan, basil, arugula, Brie and tomatoes in a large bowl and set aside. Cook linguine following package instructions. Reserve 1 cup of pasta cooking water after linguine is cooked. Drain and discard the rest of the pasta. Do not run under cold water, instead immediately add into bowl of salad. Let it stand for a minute without mixing. Add ¼ cup of reserved pasta water into bowl to make a creamy sauce. Add more pasta water if desired. Toss to mix well. Serve and enjoy.

Red Wine Risotto

Cooking Time: 25 minutes | Servings: 8

Nutrition Info: Calories: 231; Carbs: 33.9g; Protein: 7.9g; Fat: 5.7g

INGREDIENTS

Pepper to taste

1 cup finely shredded Parmigian-Reggiano cheese, divided 2 tsp tomato paste 1 ¾ cups dry red wine ¼ tsp salt 1 ½ cups Italian 'risotto' rice 2 cloves garlic, minced 1 medium onion, freshly chopped 2 tbsp extra-virgin olive oil 4 ½ cups reduced sodium beef broth

DIRECTIONS

1. On medium high fire, bring to a simmer broth in a medium fry pan. Lower fire so broth is steaming but not simmering. On medium low heat, place a Dutch oven and heat oil. Sauté onions for 5 minutes. Add garlic and cook for 2 minutes. Add rice, mix well, and season with salt. Into rice, add a generous splash of wine and ½ cup of broth. Lower fire to a gentle simmer, cook until liquid is fully absorbed while stirring rice every once in a while. Add another splash of wine and ½ cup of broth. Stirring once in a while. Add tomato paste and stir to mix well. Continue cooking and adding wine and broth until broth is used up. Once done cooking, turn off fire and stir in pepper and ¾ cup cheese. To serve, sprinkle with remaining cheese and enjoy.

Seafood Paella with Couscous

Cooking Time: 15 minutes | Servings: 4

Nutrition Info: Calories: 117; Carbs: 11.7g; Protein: 11.5g; Fat: 3.1g

INGREDIENTS

½ cup whole wheat couscous 4 oz small shrimp, peeled and deveined 4 oz bay scallops, tough muscle removed ¼ cup vegetable broth 1 cup freshly diced tomatoes and juice Pinch of crumbled saffron threads ¼ tsp freshly ground pepper ¼ tsp salt ½ tsp fennel seed ½ tsp dried thyme 1 clove garlic, minced 1 medium onion, chopped 2 tsp extra virgin olive oil

DIRECTIONS

1. Put on medium fire a large saucepan and add oil. Stir in the onion and sauté for three minutes before adding: saffron, pepper, salt, fennel seed, thyme, and garlic. Continue to sauté for another minute. Then add the broth and tomatoes and let boil. Once boiling, reduce the fire, cover and continue to cook for another 2 minutes. Add the scallops and increase fire to medium and stir occasionally and cook for two minutes. Add the shrimp and wait for two minutes more before adding the couscous. Then remove from fire, cover and set aside for five minutes before carefully mixing.

Spanish Rice Casserole with Cheesy Beef

Cooking Time: 32 minutes | Servings: 2

Nutrition Info: Calories: 460; Carbohydrates: 35.8g; Protein: 37.8g; Fat: 17.9 g

INGREDIENTS

2 tablespoons chopped green bell pepper 1/4 teaspoon Worcestershire sauce 1/4 teaspoon ground cumin 1/4 cup shredded Cheddar cheese 1/4 cup finely chopped onion 1/4 cup chile sauce 1/3 cup uncooked long grain rice 1/2-pound lean ground beef 1/2 teaspoon salt 1/2 teaspoon brown sugar 1/2 pinch ground black pepper 1/2 cup water 1/2 (14.5 ounce) can canned tomatoes 1 tablespoon chopped fresh cilantro

DIRECTIONS

1. Place a nonstick saucepan on medium fire and brown beef for 10 minutes while crumbling beef. Discard fat. Stir in pepper, Worcestershire sauce, cumin, brown sugar, salt, chile sauce, rice, water, tomatoes, green bell pepper, and onion. Mix well and cook for 10 minutes until blended and a bit tender. Transfer to an ovenproof casserole and press down firmly. Sprinkle cheese on top and cook for 7 minutes at 400oF preheated oven. Broil for 3 minutes until top is lightly browned. Serve and enjoy with chopped cilantro.

Stuffed Tomatoes with Green Chili

Cooking Time: 55 minutes | Servings: 6

Nutrition Info: Calories: 276; Carbs: 46.3g; Protein: 13.4g; Fat: 4.1g

INGREDIENTS

4 oz Colby-Jack shredded cheese ¼ cup water 1 cup uncooked quinoa 6 large ripe tomatoes ¼ tsp freshly ground black pepper ¾ tsp ground cumin 1 tsp salt, divided 1 tbsp fresh lime juice 1 tbsp olive oil 1 tbsp chopped fresh oregano 1 cup chopped onion 2 cups fresh corn kernels 2 poblano chilie s

DIRECTIONS

1. Preheat broiler to high. Slice lengthwise the chilies and press on a baking sheet lined with foil. Broil for 8 minutes. Remove from oven and let cool for 10 minutes. Peel the chilies and chop coarsely and place in medium sized bowl. Place onion and corn in baking sheet and broil for ten minutes. Stir two times while broiling. Remove from oven and mix in with chopped chilies. Add black pepper, cumin, ¼ tsp salt, lime juice, oil and oregano. Mix well. Cut off the tops of tomatoes and set aside. Leave the tomato shell intact as you scoop out the tomato pulp. Drain tomato pulp as you press down with a spoon. Reserve 1 ¼ cups of tomato pulp liquid and discard the rest. Invert the tomato shells on a wire rack for 30 mins and then wipe the insides dry with a paper towel. Season with ½ tsp salt the tomato pulp. On a sieve over a bowl, place quinoa. Add water until it covers quinoa. Rub quinoa grains for 30 seconds together with hands; rinse and drain. Repeat this procedure two times and drain well at the end. In medium saucepan bring to a boil remaining salt, ¼ cup water, quinoa and tomato liquid. Once boiling, reduce heat and simmer for 15 minutes or until liquid is fully absorbed. Remove from heat and fluff quinoa with fork. Transfer and mix well the quinoa with the corn mixture. Spoon ¾ cup of the quinoa-corn mixture into the tomato shells, top with cheese and cover with the tomato top. Bake in a preheated 350oF oven for 15 minutes and then broil high for another 1.5 minutes.

"Mari & Monti" Fried Rice

Cooking Time: 20 minutes | Servings: 4

Nutrition Info: Calories: 556; Carbs: 60.2g; Protein: 20.2g; Fat: 25.2g

INGREDIENTS

4 cups cold cooked rice 1/2 cup peas 1 medium yellow onion, diced 5 tbsp olive oil 4 oz frozen medium shrimp, thawed, shelled, deveined and chopped finely 6 oz roast pork 3 large eggs Salt and freshly ground black pepper 1/2 tsp cornstarch

DIRECTIONS

1. Combine the salt and ground black pepper and 1/2 tsp cornstarch, coat the shrimp with it. Chop the roasted pork. Beat the eggs and set aside. Stir-fry the shrimp in a wok on high fire with 1 tbsp heated oil until pink, around 3 minutes. Set the shrimp aside and stir fry the roasted pork briefly. Remove both from the pan. In the same pan, stir-fry the onion until soft, Stir the peas and cook until bright green. Remove both from pan. Add 2 tbsp oil in the same pan, add the cooked rice. Stir and separate the individual grains. Add the beaten eggs, toss the rice. Add the roasted pork, shrimp, vegetables and onion. Toss everything together. Season with salt and pepper to taste.

Turkey and Quinoa Stuffed Peppers

Cooking Time: 55 minutes | Servings: 6

Nutrition Info: Calories: 255.6; Carbs: 21.6g; Protein: 14.4g; Fat: 12.4g

INGREDIENTS

3 large red bell peppers 2 tsp chopped fresh rosemary 2 tbsp chopped fresh parsley 3 tbsp chopped pecans, toasted ¼ cup extra virgin olive oil ½ cup chicken stock ½ lb. fully cooked smoked turkey sausage, diced ½ tsp salt 2 cups water 1 cup uncooked quinoa

DIRECTIONS

1. On high fire, place a large saucepan and add salt, water and quinoa. Bring to a boil. Once boiling, reduce fire to a simmer, cover and cook until all water is absorbed around 15 minutes. Uncover quinoa, turn off fire and let it stand for another 5 minutes. Add rosemary, parsley, pecans, olive oil, chicken stock and turkey sausage into pan of quinoa. Mix well. Slice peppers lengthwise in half and discard membranes and seeds. In another boiling pot of water, add peppers, boil for 5 minutes, drain and discard water. Grease a 13 x 9 baking dish and preheat oven to 350oF. Place boiled bell pepper onto prepared baking dish, evenly fill with the quinoa mixture and pop into oven. Bake for 15 minutes.

Veggies and Sun-Dried Tomato Alfredo

Cooking Time: 30 minutes | Servings: 4

Nutrition Info: : 439; Carbs: 52.0g; Protein: 16.3g; Fat: 19.5g

INGREDIENTS

2 tsp finely shredded lemon peel ½ cup finely shredded Parmesan cheese 1 ¼ cups milk 2 tbsp all-purpose flour 8 fresh mushrooms, sliced 1 ½ cups fresh broccoli florets 4 oz fresh trimmed and quartered Brussels sprouts 4 oz trimmed fresh asparagus spears 1 tbsp olive oil 4 tbsp butter ½ cup chopped dried tomatoes 8 oz dried fettuccine

DIRECTIONS

1. In a boiling pot of water, add fettuccine and cook following manufacturer's instructions. Two minutes before the pasta is cooked, add the dried tomatoes. Drain pasta and tomatoes and return to pot to keep warm. Set aside. On medium high fire, in a big fry pan with 1 tbsp butter, fry mushrooms, broccoli, Brussels sprouts and asparagus. Cook for eight minutes while covered, transfer to a plate and put aside. Using same fry pan, add remaining butter and flour. Stirring vigorously, cook for a minute or until thickened. Add Parmesan cheese, milk and mix until cheese is melted around five minutes. Toss in the pasta and mix. Transfer to serving dish. Garnish with Parmesan cheese and lemon peel before serving.

Sausage & Bean Casserole

Total Time: 45 minutes | Serves: 4

Nutrition Info: : Calories 862, Fat 43.6g, Carbs 76.2g, Protein 43.4g

INGREDIENTS

1 lb Italian sausages 1 (15.5-oz) can cannellini beans, drained 1 carrot, chopped 2 tbsp olive oil 1 onion, chopped 2 garlic cloves, minced 1 tsp paprika 1 (14-oz) can tomatoes in juice, chopped ¼ cup chopped fresh parsley 1 celery stalk, chopped Salt and black pepper to taste

DIRECTIONS

1. Preheat oven to 350 F. Warm olive oil in a pot over medium heat and sauté onion, garlic, celery, and carrot for 3-4 minutes, stirring often until softened. Add in sausages and cook for another 3 minutes, turning occasionally. Stir in paprika for 30 seconds. Turn the heat off and mix in tomatoes, beans, salt, and pepper. Pour into a baking dish and bake for 30 minutes. Serve topped with parsley.

Moroccan Spiced Couscous

Total Time: 25 minutes | Serves: 4

Nutrition Info: Calories 246, Fat 7.4g, Carbs 41.8g, Protein 5.2g

INGREDIENTS

1 cup instant couscous 2 tbsp dried apricots, chopped 2 tbsp dried sultanas 2 tbsp olive oil ½ onion, minced 1 orange, juiced and zested ¼ tsp paprika ¼ tsp turmeric ½ tsp garlic powder ½ tsp ground cumin ¼ tsp ground cinnamon Salt and black pepper to taste

DIRECTIONS

1. Warm olive oil in a pot over medium heat and sauté onion for 3 minutes. Add in orange juice, orange zest, garlic powder, cumin, salt, paprika, turmeric, cinnamon, black pepper, and 2 cups of water and bring to a boil. Stir in apricots, couscous, and sultanas. Remove from the heat and let sit covered for 5 minutes. Fluff the couscous using a fork. Serve.

Parmesan & Collard Green Oats

Total Time: 15 minutes | Serves: 4

Nutrition Info: Calories 192, Fat 11.2g, Carbs 19.8g, Protein 5.3g

INGREDIENTS

2 cups collard greens, torn into pieces ½ cup black olives, pitted and sliced 1 cup rolled oats 2 tomatoes, diced 2 spring onions, chopped 1 tsp garlic powder ½ tsp hot paprika A pinch of salt 2 tbsp fresh parsley, chopped 1 tbsp lemon juice 2 tbsp olive oil ½ cup Parmesan cheese, grated

DIRECTIONS

1. Put 2 cups of water in a pot over medium heat. Bring to a boil, then lower the heat, and add the rolled oats. Cook for 4-5 minutes. Mix in tomatoes, spring onions, hot paprika, garlic powder, salt, collard greens, black olives, parsley, lemon juice, and olive oil. Cook for another 5 minutes. Ladle into bowls and top with Parmesan cheese. Serve warm.

Vegetable Rice Bowl

Total Time: 25 minutes | Serves: 4

Nutrition Info: : Calories 391, Fat 9.4g, Carbs 67.6g, Protein 9.8g

INGREDIENTS

12 oz broccoli cuts 3 cups fresh baby spinach 1 red chili, seeded and chopped 1 ½ cups cooked brown rice 2 tbsp olive oil 1 onion, chopped 1 garlic clove, minced 1 orange, juiced and zested 1 cup vegetable broth Salt and black pepper to taste

DIRECTIONS

1. Warm olive oil in a pan over medium heat and sauté onion for 5 minutes, then add in broccoli cuts and cook for 4-5 minutes until tender. Stir-fry garlic and chili for 30 seconds. Pour in orange zest, orange juice, broth, salt, and pepper and bring to a boil. Stir in the rice and spinach and cook for 4 minutes until the liquid is reduced. Serve.

Italian Cannellini Beans with Egg Noddles

Total Time: 20 minutes | Serves: 4

Nutrition Info: Calories 641, Fat 19.6g, Carbs 92.1g, Protein 28.7g

INGREDIENTS

12 oz egg noodles 1 (14.5-oz) can diced tomatoes 1 (13-oz) can Cannellini beans, drained ½ cup heavy cream 1 cup vegetable stock 2 garlic cloves, minced 1 onion, chopped 3 tbsp olive oil 1 cup spinach, chopped 1 tsp dill 1 tsp thyme ½ tsp red pepper, crushed 1 lemon, juiced and zested 1 tbsp fresh basil leaves, chopped

DIRECTIONS

1. Boil the egg noodles in plenty of salted water for 6 minutes or until al dente. Drain and set aside. Warm the olive oil in a pot over medium heat. Add in onion and garlic and cook for 3 minutes. Stir in dill, thyme, and red pepper for 1 minute. Add in spinach, vermicelli, vegetable stock, and tomatoes. Bring to a boil, cover, and lower the heat. Cook for 5-7 minutes. Put in beans and cook until heated through. Combine the heavy cream, lemon juice, lemon zest, and basil. Serve the dish garnished with parsley and the creamy lemon sauce on the side.

Awesome Chickpea & Spinach Bowl

Total Time: 20 minutes | Serves: 4

Nutrition Info: Calories 512, Fat 1.8g, Carbs 76.6g, Protein 24.8g

INGREDIENTS

1 lb canned chickpeas, drained 10 oz spinach 1 tsp coriander seeds 1 red onion, finely chopped 2 tomatoes, pureed 1 garlic clove, minced 2 tbsp olive oil ½ tbsp rosemary ½ tsp smoked paprika 1 bay leaf Salt and white pepper to taste

DIRECTIONS

1. Heat the olive oil in a pot over medium heat. Add in the onion, garlic, coriander seeds, salt, and pepper and cook for 3 minutes until translucent. Stir in tomatoes, rosemary, paprika, salt, black pepper, and bay leaf. Bring to a boil, then lower the heat, and simmer for 10 minutes. Add in chickpeas and spinach and cook covered until the spinach wilts. Serve immediately.

Cavolo Nero & Pea Farro Pilaf

Total Time: 50 minutes | Serves: 4

Nutrition Info: Calories 362, Fat 10.7g, Carbs 57.6g, Protein 10.3g

INGREDIENTS

1 cup green peas 4 cups cavolo nero, torn into pieces ½ cup hummus ½ cup scallions, sliced 1 garlic clove, minced 1 cup farro 2 cups water 1 cup chopped tomatoes 1 tbsp tomato paste 1 tsp cumin ½ tsp oregano 2 tbsp fresh cilantro, chopped 2 tbsp olive oil Salt and black pepper to taste

DIRECTIONS

1. Heat the olive oil in a skillet over medium heat. Add in scallions, sauté until tender. Add in garlic, cumin, and oregano and cook for another 30 seconds. Stir in farro, water, chopped tomatoes, and tomato paste. Bring to a boil, then lower the heat, and simmer for 30-40 minutes. Stir in peas, cavolo nero, salt, and black pepper. Let sit covered for 8 minutes. Serve topped with hummus and cilantro.

Lentil & Potato Stew with Goat Cheese

Total Time: 35 minutes | Serves: 4

Nutrition Info: Calories 330, Fat 18g, Carbs 27g, Protein 17g

INGREDIENTS

1 tbsp olive oil 1 carrot, sliced 1 onion, chopped 1 celery stalk, chopped 2 garlic cloves, minced 1 lb potatoes, cubed 1 cup lentils ½ tsp paprika Salt and black pepper to taste 14 oz canned tomatoes, chopped 2 tbsp cilantro, chopped 4 oz goat cheese, sliced

DIRECTIONS

1. S Warm the olive oil in a pot over medium heat and sauté onion, garlic, celery, and carrot for 5 minutes. Stir in potatoes, lentils, paprika, salt, pepper, and tomatoes. Pour in 2 cups of water and bring to a boil. Simmer for 20 minutes. Sprinkle with cilantro and top with goat cheese slices to serve.

Spanish Rice with Chicken

Total Time: 50 minutes | Serves: 4

Nutrition Info: Calories 502, Fat 16.6g, Carbs 43.8g, Protein 39.8g

INGREDIENTS

1 lb chicken thighs, skinless 1 cup arroz bomba (Spanish rice), rinsed 2 cups chicken broth ½ cup spring onions, chopped ½ red bell pepper, thinly chopped ¼ cup tomato paste 2 garlic cloves, minced ¼ cup white wine ½ tsp sweet paprika ¼ tsp turmeric ½ tsp dried basil ½ tsp dried tarragon 2 tbsp olive oil Aioli, for garnish Salt and black pepper to taste

DIRECTIONS

1. Warm the olive oil in a saucepan over medium heat and stir-fry the chicken for 8-10 minutes. Remove to a plate to cool. Add spring onions, bell pepper, and garlic to the saucepan and cook for 3 minutes. Pour in white wine to scrape off any bits from the bottom. Discard the bones from the chicken and shred it with a fork. Return to the saucepan and sprinkle with salt, black pepper, paprika, turmeric, tarragon, and basil. Stir in the rice, tomato paste, and chicken broth. Cook covered for about 20 minutes. Serve garnished with aioli

Chicken & Olive Rice

Total Time: 45 minutes | Serves: 4

Nutrition Info: Calories 450, Fat 19g, Carbs 28g, Protein 26g

INGREDIENTS

4 chicken thighs, bone-in and skin-on 1 cup arborio rice 2 lemons, juiced 1 tsp oregano, dried 1 red onion, chopped Salt and black pepper to taste 2 garlic cloves, minced 2 tbsp olive oil 2 ½ cups chicken stock 1 cup green olives, pitted and sliced 2 tbsp parsley, chopped ½ cup Parmesan cheese, crumbled

DIRECTIONS

1. Warm the olive oil in a skillet over medium heat and brown chicken thighs skin-side down for 3-4 minutes, turn, and cook for 3 minutes. Remove to a plate. Place garlic and onion in the same skillet and sauté for 3 minutes. Stir in rice, salt, pepper, oregano, and lemon juice. Add 1 cup of chicken stock, reduce the heat and simmer the rice while stirring until it is absorbed. Add another cup of chicken broth and continue simmering until the stock is absorbed. Pour in the remaining chicken stock and return the chicken; cook until the rice is tender. Turn the heat off. Stir in Parmesan cheese and top with olives and parsley. Serve into plates. Enjoy!

Lima Bean Stew

Total Time: 70 minutes | Serves: 4

Nutrition Info: Calories 310, Fat 16g, Carbs 30g, Protein 16g

INGREDIENTS

2 tbsp olive oil 3 tomatoes, cubed 1 yellow onion, chopped 1 celery stalk, chopped 2 tbsp parsley, chopped 2 garlic cloves, minced 1 cup lima beans, soaked 1 tsp paprika 1 tsp dried oregano ½ tsp dried thyme Salt and black pepper to taste

DIRECTIONS

1. S Cover the lima beans with water in a pot and place over medium heat. Bring to a boil and cook for 30 minutes. Drain and set aside. Warm olive oil in the pot over medium heat and cook onion and garlic for 3 minutes. Stir in tomatoes, celery, oregano, thyme, and paprika and cook for 5 minutes. Pour in 3 cups water and return the lima beans; season with salt and pepper. Simmer for 30 minutes. Sprinkle with parsley and serve.

Garbanzo Bean & Pork Stew

Total Time: 50 minutes | Serves: 4

Nutrition Info: Calories 430, Fat 16g, Carbs 28g, Protein 44g

INGREDIENTS

2 tbsp olive oil 2 lb pork stew meat, cubed 1 leek, chopped 1 red bell pepper, chopped 3 garlic cloves, minced 2 tsp sage 4 oz canned garbanzo beans, drained 1 cup chicken stock 2 zucchinis, chopped 2 tbsp tomato paste 2 tbsp parsley, chopped

DIRECTIONS

1. S Warm the olive oil in a pot over medium heat and sear pork meat for 10 minutes, stirring occasionally. Add in leek, bell pepper, garlic, and zucchini and sauté for 5 minutes. Stir in tomato paste and sage for 1 minute and pour in garbanzo beans and chicken stock. Cover and bring to a boil, then reduce the heat and simmer for 30 minutes. Adjust the seasoning and serve garnished with parsley.

Caper & Brown Rice Pilaf

Total Time: 30 minutes | Serves: 4

Nutrition Info: Calories 230, Fat 9g, Carbs 16g, Protein 7g

INGREDIENTS

1 cup brown rice 2 tbsp olive oil 1 onion, chopped 1 celery stalk, chopped 2 garlic cloves, minced ½ cup capers, rinsed Salt and black pepper to taste 2 tbsp parsley, chopped

DIRECTIONS

1. Warm the olive oil in a skillet over medium heat and sauté celery, garlic, and onion for 10 minutes. Stir in rice, capers, 2 cups of water, salt, and pepper and cook for 25 minutes. Serve topped with parsley

Valencian Mussel & Rice Stew

Total Time: 40 minutes | Serves: 4

Nutrition Info: Calories 310, Fat 15g, Carbs 17g, Protein 12g

INGREDIENTS

2 tbsp olive oil 2 garlic cloves, minced 1 yellow onion, chopped 2 tomatoes, chopped 2 cups fish stock 1 lb mussels, cleaned and debearded 1 cup white rice 1 bunch parsley, chopped Salt and white pepper to the taste

DIRECTIONS

1. Warm the olive oil in a pot over medium heat and cook onion and garlic for 5 minutes. Stir in rice for 1 minute. Pour in tomatoes and fish stock and bring to a boil. Add in the mussels and simmer for 20 minutes. Discard any unopened mussels. Serve topped with parsley.

Chili Zucchini Millet

Total Time: 30 minutes | Serves: 4

Nutrition Info: : Calories 230, Fat 11g, Carbs 15g, Protein 3g

INGREDIENTS

2 tomatoes, chopped 2 zucchinis, chopped 3 tbsp olive oil 1 cup millet 2 spring onions, chopped ½ cup cilantro, chopped 1 tsp chili paste ½ cup lemo n juice Salt and black pepper to taste

DIRECTIONS

1. Warm the olive oil in a skillet over medium heat and sauté millet for 1-2 minutes. Pour in 2 cups of water, salt, and pepper and bring to a simmer. Cook for 15 minutes. Mix in spring onions, tomatoes, zucchini, chili paste, and lemon juice. Serve topped with cilantro.

Couscous with Apricots & Chickpeas

Total Time: 30 minutes | Serves: 4

Nutrition Info: Calories 270, Fat 12g, Carbs 23g, Protein 8g

INGREDIENTS

2 tbsp olive oil 1 red onion, chopped 2 garlic cloves, minced 14 oz canned chickpeas, drained 2 cups veggie stock 2 cups couscous, cooked 2 tbsp cilantro, chopped ½ cup dried apricots, chopped Salt and black pepper to taste

DIRECTIONS

1. Warm the olive oil in a skillet over medium heat and cook onion and garlic for 5 minutes. Put in chickpeas, stock, cilantro, apricots, salt, and pepper and cook for 15 minutes. Ladle couscous into bowls. Top with chickpea mixture to serve.

Basil and Pecorino Risotto

Total Time: 35 minutes | Serves: 4

Nutrition Info: Calories 430, Fat 9g, Carbs 57g, Protein 8g

INGREDIENTS

2 tbsp olive oil 2 cups chicken stock 1 onion, chopped 10 oz sundried tomatoes in olive oil, drained and chopped 1 cup Arborio rice Salt and black pepper to taste 1 cup Pecorino cheese, grated ¼ cup basil leaves, chopped

DIRECTIONS

1. Warm the olive oil in a skillet over medium heat and cook onion and sundried tomatoes for 5 minutes. Stir in rice, chicken stock, salt, pepper, and basil and bring to a boil. Cook for 20 minutes. Mix in Pecorino cheese and serve.

Risotto Milanese

Total Time: 10 minutes | Serves: 4

Nutrition Info:: Calories 250, Fat 10g, Carbs 18g, Protein 5g

INGREDIENTS

1 cup Arborio rice, cooked 2 tbsp olive oil ½ cup white wine 2 tbsp butter, softened 1 onion, chopped Salt and black pepper to taste 2 cups hot chicken stock 1 pinch of saffron, soaked ½ cup Parmesan cheese, grated

DIRECTIONS

1. Warm the olive oil in a skillet over medium heat and sauté onion for 3 minutes. Stir in rice, salt, and pepper for 1 minute. Pour in white wine and saffron and stir to deglaze the bottom of the skillet. Gradually add in the chicken stock while stirring; cook for 15-18 minutes. Turn off the heat and mix in butter and Parmesan cheese. Serve immediately.

Thyme Pork with Rice

Total Time: 8 hours and 10 minutes |

Nutrition Info: Calories 280, Fat 15g, Carbs 17g, Protein 15g

INGREDIENTS

3 tbsp olive oil 2 lb pork loin, sliced 1 cup chicken stock ½ tbsp chili powder 2 tsp thyme, dried ½ tbsp garlic powder Salt and black pepper to taste 2 cups rice, cooked

DIRECTIONS

1. Place pork, chicken stock, oil, chili powder, garlic powder, salt, and pepper in your slow cooker. Cover with the lid and cook for 8 hours on Low. Share pork into plates with a side of rice and garnish with sage to serve.

Asparagus Brown Rice

Total Time: 20 minutes | Serves: 4

Nutrition Info: Calories 330, Fat 12g, Carbs 17g, Protein 11g

INGREDIENTS

1 tbsp olive oil 1 lb asparagus, steamed and chopped 3 tbsp balsamic vinegar 1 cup brown rice 2 tsp mustard Salt and black pepper to taste 5 oz baby spinach ½ cup parsley, chopped 1 tbsp tarragon, chopped

DIRECTIONS

1. Bring to a boil a pot of salted water over medium heat. Add in brown rice and cook for 7-9 minutes until al dente. Drain and place in a bowl. Add the asparagus to the same pot and blanch them for 4-5 minutes. Remove them to the rice bowl. Mix in spinach, olive oil, balsamic vinegar, mustard, salt, pepper, parsley, and tarragon. Serve.

Feta Couscous with Kale & Cucumber

Total Time: 20 minutes | Serves: 4

Nutrition Info: Calories 210, Fat 7g, Carbs 16g, Protein 5g

INGREDIENTS

2 tbsp olive oil 1 cup couscous 1 cup kale, chopped 1 tbsp parsley, chopped 3 spring onions, chopped 1 cucumber, chopped 1 tsp allspice ½ lemon, juiced and zested 4 oz feta cheese, crumbled

DIRECTIONS

1. In a bowl, place couscous and cover with hot water. Let sit for 10 minutes and fluff. Warm the olive oil in a skillet over medium heat and sauté onions and allspice for 3 minutes. Stir in the remaining ingredients and cook for 5-6 minutes more.

Mediterranean-Style Quinoa

Total Time: 35 minutes | Serves: 4

Nutrition Info: : Calories 200, Fat 8g, Carbs 6g, Protein 2g

INGREDIENTS

2 tbsp olive oil 2 cups chicken stock 2 tbsp olive oil 1 cup quinoa, rinsed 1 red onion, chopped 1 tbsp garlic, minced 1 tsp lemon zest, grated 2 tbsp lemon juice Salt and black pepper to taste 2 tbsp rosemary, chopped 1 cup arugula

DIRECTIONS

1. Warm the olive oil in a skillet over medium heat and cook onion and garlic for 5 minutes. Stir in quinoa, chicken stock, lemon zest, lemon juice, salt, pepper, and rosemary and cook for another 15 minutes, stirring often. Transfer to a serving platter and top with arugula to serve.

Hot Vegetarian Two-Bean Cassoulet

Total Time: 40 minutes | Serves: 4

Nutrition Info: Calories 361, Fat 8.4g, Carbs 55.7g, Protein 17.1g

INGREDIENTS

1 cup canned pinto beans, drained 1 cup canned can kidney beans, drained 2 red bell peppers, seeded and chopped 1 onion, chopped 1 celery stalk, chopped 2 garlic cloves, minced 1 (14-oz) can crushed tomatoes 2 tbsp olive oil 1 tbsp red pepper flakes 1 tsp ground cumin Salt and black pepper to taste ¼ tsp ground coriander

DIRECTIONS

1. Warm olive oil in a pot over medium heat and sauté bell peppers, celery, garlic, and onion for 5 minute s until tender. Stir in ground cumin, ground coriander, salt, and pepper for 1 minute. Pour in beans, tomatoes, and red pepper flakes. Bring to a boil, then decrease the heat and simmer for another 20 minutes. Serve immediately.

Bulgur Tabbouleh

Total Time: 30 minutes | Serves: 4

Nutrition Info: Per Serving: Calories 290, Fat 29g, Carbs 3g, Protein 6g

INGREDIENTS

8 cherry tomatoes, quartered 1 cucumber, peeled and chopped 1 cup bulgur, rinsed 4 scallions, chopped ½ cup fresh parsley, chopped 1 lemon, juiced ¼ cup extra-virgin olive oil Salt and black pepper to taste

DIRECTIONS

1. Place the bulgur in a large pot with plenty of salted water, cover, and boil for 13-15 minutes. Drain and let it cool completely. Add scallions, tomatoes, cucumber, and parsley to the cooled bulgur and mix to combine. In another bowl, whisk the lemon juice, olive oil, salt, and pepper. Pour the dressing over the bulgur mixture and toss to combine. Serve chilled.

Italian Barley with Artichoke Hearts

Total Time: 50 minutes | Serves: 4

Nutrition Info: Per Serving: Calories 240, Fat 12g, Carbs 15g, Protein 13g

INGREDIENTS

1 cup pearl barley ½ cup artichoke hearts, chopped 2 tbsp grated Parmesan cheese 1 bay leaf 1 fresh cilantro sprig 1 fresh thyme sprig 2 tbsp olive oil 1 onion, chopped 1 tbsp Italian seasoning 3 garlic cloves, minced 1 cup chicken broth 1 lemon, zested Salt and black pepper to taste

DIRECTIONS

1. Place barley, cilantro, bay leaf, and thyme in a pot over medium heat and cover with water. Bring to a boil, then lower the heat and simmer for 25 minutes. Drain, discard the bay leaf, rosemary, and thyme and reserve. Warm olive oil in a pan over medium heat. Sauté onion, artichoke, and Italian seasoning for 5 minutes. Add garlic and stir-fry for 40 seconds. Pour in some broth and cook until the liquid absorbs, then add more, and keep stirring until absorbed. Mix in lemon zest, salt, pepper, and cheese and stir for 2 minutes until the cheese has melted. Pour over the barley and serve.

Cherry Tomato Rice Pilaf with Pistachios

Total Time: 30 minutes | Serves: 4

Nutrition Info: Calories 305, Fat 11.4g, Carbs 43.8g, Protein 8g

INGREDIENTS

1 cup basmati rice 1 carrot, shredded ½ cup scallions, chopped 1 cup cherry tomatoes, halved 1 oz pistachios, crushed 2 cups vegetable broth 1 garlic clove, minced 2 tbsp olive oil 1 tsp ground coriander 2 tbsp fresh parsley, chopped

DIRECTIONS

1. Heat olive oil in a saucepan over medium heat. Add in the carrot, garlic, and scallions and cook for 3-4 minutes, stirring often. Stir in the rice for 1-2 minutes. Pour in 2 vegetable broth. Bring to a quick boil and sprinkle with ground coriander. Lower the heat and simmer covered for 10-12 minutes until the liquid has absorbed. Fluff the rice with a fork and transfer to a serving plate. Top with cherry tomatoes and pistachios and sprinkle with parsley. Serve warm.

Spicy Garbanzo Bowl with Feta Cheese

Total Time: 10 minutes | Serves: 4

Nutrition Info: Calories 330, Fat 11.6g, Carbs 42.7g, Protein 16.8g

INGREDIENTS

2 cups canned garbanzo beans, drained 2 tomatoes, diced 1 cucumber, thinly sliced 1 tsp garlic, minced 1 red onion, chopped 2 green hot peppers, chopped 1 red bell pepper, thinly sliced 2 tbsp fresh parsley, chopped 1 fresh lemon, juiced 1 cup feta cheese, crumbled 1 tsp harissa ¼ tsp chili flakes Salt and black pepper to taste Fresh mint leaves, chopped

DIRECTIONS

1. In a bowl, combine the garbanzo beans with cucumber, garlic, onion, hot peppers, tomatoes, bell pepper, parsley, lemon juice, chili flakes, harissa, salt, and black pepper. Adjust the seasonings. Serve topped with crumbled feta cheese and freshly chopped mint leaves.

Lemony Shrimp & Quinoa Bowl

Total Time: 20 minutes | Serves: 4

Nutrition Info: Calories 662, Fat 20.9g, Carbs 37.8g, Protein 78.8g

INGREDIENTS

1 cup quinoa 1 lemon, cut in wedges, to garnish 12 tiger shrimp, peeled and cooked ¼ cup olive oil 2 tomatoes, sliced 2 bell peppers, thinly sliced ½ cup black olives, pitted and halved 1 red onion, chopped 1 tsp dried dill 1 tbsp fresh parsley, chopped Salt and black pepper to taste

DIRECTIONS

1. Place the quinoa in a pot and cover with 2 cups of water over medium heat. Bring to a boil, reduce the heat, and simmer for 12-15 minutes or until tender. Remove from heat and fluff it with a fork. Mix in the quinoa with olive oil, dill, parsley, salt, and black pepper. Stir in tomatoes, bell peppers, olives, and onion. Serve decorated with shrimp and lemon wedges.

Harissa Farro & Chickpea Stew

Total Time: 35 minutes | Serves: 4

Nutrition Info: : Calories 680, Fat 16g, Carbs 88g, Protein 28g

INGREDIENTS

3 tbsp olive oil 1 cup faro Salt and black pepper to taste 1 eggplant, cubed 1 yellow onion, chopped 14 oz canned tomatoes, chopped 14 oz canned chickpeas, drained 3 garlic cloves, minced 2 tbsp harissa paste 2 tbsp cilantro, chopped

DIRECTIONS

1. Warm the olive oil in a skillet over medium heat and sauté eggplant, salt, and pepper for 10 minutes; reserve. In the same skillet, add and sauté onion for 3-4 minutes. Stir in garlic, salt, pepper, harissa paste, chickpeas, tomatoes, and faro, and 2 cups of water. Cook for 15-20 minutes. Stir in eggplant for another 5 minutes. Garnish with cilantro and serve.

Greek Lentils with Chicken

Total Time: 1 hour 20 minutes | Serves: 4

Nutrition Info: Calories 320, Fat 14g, Carbs 18g, Protein 14g

INGREDIENTS

1 lb chicken thighs, skinless, boneless, and cubed 1 tbsp coriander seeds 1 bay leaf 1 tbsp tomato paste 2 tbsp olive oil 2 carrots, chopped 1 onion, chopped 2 garlic cloves, chopped ½ tsp red chili flakes 4 cups chicken stock 1 cup brown lentils Salt and black pepper to taste

DIRECTIONS

1. Warm the olive oil in a pot over medium heat and cook chicken, onion, and garlic for 6-8 minutes. Stir in carrots, tomato paste, coriander seeds, Turkish bay leaf, red chili pepper, and paprika for 3 minutes. Pour in the chicken stock and bring to a boil. Simmer for 25 minutes. Add in lentils, season with salt and pepper and cook for another 15 minutes. Discard bay leaf and serve right away.

Caper & Tuna Pearl Barley

Total Time: 50 minutes | Serves: 4

Nutrition Info: Calories 260, Fat 12g, Carbs 17g, Protein 24sg

INGREDIENTS

3 cups chicken stock 10 oz canned tuna, flaked 1 cup barley Salt and black pepper to taste 1 cup cherry tomatoes, halved ½ cup pepperoncini, sliced 2 tbsp olive oil ¼ cup capers, drained ½ lemon, juiced

DIRECTIONS

1. Boil chicken stock in a saucepan over medium heat and add in barley. Cook covered for 40 minutes. Fluff the barley and remove to a bowl. Stir in tuna, salt, pepper, tomatoes, pepperoncini, olive oil, capers, and lemon juice. Serve.

Slow-Cooked Bean & Pork Cassoulet

Total Time: 8 hours 10 minutes | Serves: 4

Nutrition Info: Calories 290, Fat 13g, Carbs 30g, Protein 26g

INGREDIENTS

2 lb pork stew meat, cubed ½ cup vegetable stock 1 tbsp ginger, grated 1 tsp coriander, ground 2 tsp cumin, ground Salt and black pepper to taste 14 oz canned tomatoes, chopped 1 red onion, chopped 2 garlic cloves, minced ½ cup apricots, cut into quarters 15 oz canned cannellini beans, drained 1 tbsp cilantro, chopped

DIRECTIONS

1. Place pork, beef stock, ginger, coriander, cumin, salt, pepper, tomatoes, onion, garlic, and apricots in your slow cooker. Put the lid and cook for 6 hours on Low. Open the lid and add in beans and cook for another 2 hours on Low. Adjust the seasoning, top with cilantro, and serve.

Pressure Cooker Pork with Rice

Total Time: 35 minutes | Serves: 4

Nutrition Info: Calories 310, Fat 16g, Carbs 18g, Protein 23g

INGREDIENTS

3 tbsp olive oil 1 lb pork stew meat, cubed Salt and black pepper to taste 2 chicken broth 1 leek, sliced 2 bay leaves 1 carrot, sliced 1 cup brown rice 2 garlic cloves, minced 2 tbsp cilantro, chopped

DIRECTIONS

1. Set your IP to Sauté and heat the olive oil. Place in pork and cook for 4-5 minutes, stirring often. Add in onion, leek, garlic, and carrot and sauté for 3 more minutes. Stir in brown rice for 1 minute and pour in chicken broth; return the pork. Lock the lid in place, select Manual, and cook for 20 minutes on High. When done, do a quick pressure release. Adjust the seasoning and serve topped with cilantro.

Veggie Brown Rice Bowl

Total Time: 25 minutes | Serves: 4

Nutrition Info: Calories 320, Fat 5g, Carbs 23g, Protein 5g

INGREDIENTS

2 tbsp olive oil 1 onion, sliced 1 red bell pepper, cut into strips ½ lb broccoli rabe, halved lengthways ½ cup green peas 1 carrot, chopped 1 celery stalk, chopped 1 garlic clove, minced ½ cup brown rice 2 cups vegetable broth Salt and black pepper to taste ½ tsp dried thyme ¾ tsp paprika 2 green onions, chopped

DIRECTIONS

1. Warm the olive oil in a skillet over medium heat and sauté onion, garlic, carrot, celery, and bell pepper for 10 minutes. Stir in rice, vegetable broth, salt, pepper, thyme. paprika, and green onions and bring to a simmer. Cook for 15 minutes. Add in broccoli rabe and green peas and cook for 5 minutes. Serve.

Feta & Chard Couscous

Total Time: 20 minutes | Serves: 4

Nutrition Info: Calories 310, Fat 8g, Carbs 18g, Protein 7g

INGREDIENTS

2 tbsp olive oil 10 oz couscous 2 garlic cloves, minced 1 cup raisins ½ cup feta cheese, crumbled 1 bunch of Swiss chard, chopped

DIRECTIONS

1. In a bowl, place couscous and coevr with hot water. Let sit covered for 10 minutes. Using a fork fluff it. Warm the olive oil in a skillet over medium heat and sauté garlic for a minute. Stir in couscous, raisins, and chard. Serve topped with feta cheese.

Parmesan & Sage Faro

Total Time: 50 minutes | Serves: 4

Nutrition Info: Calories 220, Fat 7g, Carbs 9g, Protein 4

INGREDIENTS

2 tbsp olive oil 1 cup faro 1 red onion, chopped 5 sage leaves 1 garlic clove, minced ½ tbsp Parmesan cheese, grated 6 cups veggie stock Salt and black pepper to taste

DIRECTIONS

1. Warm the olive oil in a skillet over medium heat and cook onion and garlic for 5 minutes. Stir in sage leaves, faro, veggie stock, salt, and pepper and bring to a simmer. Cook for 40 minutes. Mix in Parmesan cheese and serve.

Lemon Chickpeas with Carrots & Capers

Total Time: 35 minutes | Serves: 4

Nutrition Info: Calories 210, Fat 5g, Carbs 7g, Protein 4g

INGREDIENTS

3 tbsp olive oil 3 tbsp capers, drained 1 lemon, juiced and zested 1 red onion, chopped 14 oz canned chickpeas, drained 4 carrots, peeled and cubed 1 tbsp parsley, chopped Salt and black pepper to taste

DIRECTIONS

1. Warm the olive oil in a skillet over medium heat and cook onion, lemon zest, lemon juice, and capers for 5 minutes. Stir in chickpeas, carrots, parsley, salt, and pepper and cook for another 20 minutes. Serve.

Cannellini Beans with Cherry Tomatoes

Total Time: 10 minutes | Serves: 4

Nutrition Info: : Calories 300, Fat 8g, Carbs 26g, Protein 13g

INGREDIENTS

2 tbsp olive oil 15 oz canned cannellini beans, drained 1 cup cherry tomatoes, halved 2 spring onions, chopped 1 tsp paprika Salt and black pepper to taste ½ tsp ground cumin 1 tbsp lime juice

DIRECTIONS

1. Place beans, cherry tomatoes, spring onions, olive oil, paprika, salt, pepper, cumin, and lime juice in a bowl and toss to combine. Transfer to the fridge for 10 minutes and serve.

Lamb with Mint

Soup Total Time: 50 minutes | Serves: 4

Nutrition Info: Per Serving: Calories 290, Fat 29g, Carbs 3g, Protein 6g

INGREDIENTS

2 tbsp olive oil ½ lb lamb meat, cubed 3 eggs, whisked 4 cups beef broth 5 spring onions, chopped 2 tbsp mint, chopped 2 lemons, juiced Salt and black pepper to taste 1 cup baby spinach

DIRECTIONS

1. Warm the olive oil in a pot over medium heat and cook lamb for 10 minutes, stirring occasionally. Add in spring onions and cook for another 3 minutes. Pour in beef broth, salt, and pepper and simmer for 30 minutes. Whisk eggs with lemon juice and some soup and pour into the pot along with the spinach and cook for an additional 5 minutes. Sprinkle with mint and serve immediately.

Cheesy Mushroom Wild Rice

Total Time: 30 minutes | Serves: 4

Nutrition Info: Calories 230, Fat 6g, Carbs 13g, Protein 6g

INGREDIENTS

2 cups chicken stock 1 cup wild rice 1 onion, chopped ½ lb white mushrooms, sliced 2 garlic cloves, minced 1 lemon, juiced and zested 1 tbsp chives, chopped ½ cup mozzarella cheese, grated Salt and black pepper to taste

DIRECTIONS

1. Warm chicken stock in a pot over medium heat and add in wild rice, onion, mushrooms, garlic, lemon juice, lemon zest, salt, and pepper. Bring to a simmer and cook for 20 minutes. Transfer to a baking tray and top with mozzarella cheese. Place the tray under the broiler for 4 minutes until the cheese is melted. Sprinkle with chives and serve.

Ricotta & Rice Stuffed Peppers

Total Time: 35 minutes | Serves: 4

Nutrition Info: Calories 285, Fat 6.7g, Carbs 48.3g, Protein 8.4g

INGREDIENTS

2 lb mixed bell peppers, halved 1 cup white rice, rinsed ½ cup ricotta cheese, crumbled 2 tomatoes, pureed 1 onion, chopped 1 tsp ground cumin 1 tsp ground fennel seeds 1 tbsp olive oil Salt and black pepper to taste

DIRECTIONS

1. Blanch the peppers in a pot with salted water over medium heat for 1-2 minutes, drain and set aside. Add the rice to the pot, bring to a boil and simmer for 15 minutes. Drain and remove to a bowl. Add in olive oil, cumin, ground fennel seeds, onion, tomatoes, salt, and pepper and stir to combine. Divide the mixture between the pepper halves and top with ricotta cheese. Bake for 8-10 minutes. Serve right away.

Lamb & Mint Risotto

Total Time: 1 hour 30 minutes | Serves: 4

Nutrition Info: Calories 310, Fat 14g, Carbs 17g, Protein 15g

INGREDIENTS

2 garlic cloves, minced 1 onion, chopped 1 lb lamb, cubed 2 tbsp olive oil Salt and black pepper to taste 2 cups vegetable stock 1 cup arborio rice 2 tbsp mint, chopped 1 cup Parmesan cheese, grated

DIRECTIONS

1. Warm the olive oil in a pot over medium heat. Season chicken breasts with salt and pepper and cook for 8 minutes. Stir in onion, carrot, and celery and sauté for another 3 minutes or until soft and aromatic. Put in chicken stock and buckwheat and bring to a boil. Reduce the heat to low. Let it simmer for about 20 minutes and add in lime juice. Sprinkle with parsley. Ladle your soup into individual bowls and serve warm with gremolata toast and the lime slices. Yummy!a Warm the olive oil in a skillet over medium heat and cook the onion for 5 minutes. Put in lamb and cook for another 5 minutes. Stir in garlic, salt, pepper, and stock and bring to a simmer; cook for 1 hour. Stir in rice and cook for 18-20 minutes. Mix in mint and serve.

Hot Vegetable Stew with Green Beans & Rice

Total Time: 45 minutes | Serves: 4

Nutrition Info: Calories 153, Fat 7.9g, Carbs 19g, Protein 5.7g

INGREDIENTS

1 cup rice 1 lb green beans, trimmed and chopped 2 zucchinis, sliced 1 bell pepper, deveined and sliced 1 jalapeño pepper, chopped 1 carrot, trimmed and chopped 2 spring onions, chopped 2 cloves garlic, minced 2 tomatoes, pureed 1 cup vegetable broth 2 tbsp olive oil 1 cup water ½ tsp dried sage 1 tsp paprika Salt and black pepper to taste

DIRECTIONS

1. Cook the rice in a pot with 2 cups of water for about 20 minutes. Using a fork, fluff the rice and set aside. Heat the olive oil in a pot over medium heat. Add in the zucchinis, bell pepper, jalapeño pepper, carrot, spring onions, tomatoes, and garlic and stir-fry for 10 minutes or until the veggies are softened. Pour in vegetable broth, sage, paprika, salt, and black pepper. Cook covered for 7 minutes. Distribute the rice across bowls and top with the veggie mixture. Serve hot.

Parmesan Mushroom Pilaf

Total Time: 30 minutes | Serves: 4

Nutrition Info: Calories 250, Fat 10g, Carbs 28g, Protein 13g

INGREDIENTS

2 tbsp olive oil 1 cup rice, rinsed 2 greens onions, chopped 2 cups chicken stock 1 cup white mushrooms, sliced 1 garlic clove, minced Salt and black pepper to taste ½ cup Parmesan cheese, grated 2 tbsp cilantro, chopped

DIRECTIONS

1. Warm the olive oil in a skillet over medium heat and cook onion, garlic, and mushrooms for 5 minutes until tender. Stir in rice, salt, and pepper for 1 minute. Pour in chicken stock and cook for 15-18 minutes. Transfer to a platter, scatter Parmesan cheese all over, and sprinkle with cilantro to serve.

Tasty Greek Rice

Preparation Time: 10 minutes | Cooking Time: 10 minutes | Servings: 6

Nutrition Info: Calories 285 Fat 9.1 g Carbohydrates 45.7 g Sugar 1.2 g Protein 6 g Cholesterol 0 mg

INGREDIENTS

1 3/4 cup brown rice, rinsed and drained 3/4 cup roasted red peppers, chopped 1 cup olives, chopped 1 tsp dried oregano 1 tsp Greek seasoning 1 3/4 cup vegetable broth 2 tbsp olive oil Salt

DIRECTIONS

1. Add oil into the inner pot of instant pot and set the pot on sauté mode. Add rice and cook for 5 minutes. Add remaining ingredients except for red peppers and olives and stir well. Seal pot with lid and cook on high for 5 minutes. Once done, allow to release pressure naturally for 10 minutes then release remaining using quick release. Remove lid. Add red peppers and olives and stir well. Serve and enjoy.

Perfect Herb Rice

Preparation Time: 10 minutes | Cooking Time: 4 minutes | Servings: 4

Nutrition Info: Calories 264 Fat 9.9 g Carbohydrates 36.7 g Sugar 0.4 g Protein 7.3 g Cholesterol 0 mg

INGREDIENTS

1 cup brown rice, rinsed 1 tbsp olive oil 1 1/2 cups water 1/2 cup fresh mix herbs, chopped 1 tsp salt

DIRECTIONS

1. Add all ingredients into the inner pot of instant pot and stir well. Seal pot with lid and cook on high for 4 minutes. Once done, allow to release pressure naturally for 10 minutes then release remaining using quick release. Remove lid. Stir well and serve.

Quinoa and Three Beans Recipe

Cooking Time: 35 minutes | Servings: 8

Nutrition Info: Calories: 249; Carbs: 31.0g; Protein: 8.0g; Fat: 10.0g

INGREDIENTS

1 cup grape tomatoes, sliced in half 1 cup quinoa 1 cup seedless cucumber, chopped 1 red bell pepper, seeds removed and chopped 1 tablespoon balsamic vinegar 1 yellow bell pepper, seeds removed and chopped 1/2-pound green beans, trimmed and snapped into 2-inch pieces 1/3 cup pitted kalamata olives, cut in half 1/4 cup chopped fresh basil 1/4 cup diced red onion 1/4 cup feta cheese crumbles 1/4 cup olive oil 1/4 teaspoon dried basil 1/4 teaspoon dried oregano 15 ounces garbanzo beans, drained and rinsed 15 ounces white beans, drained and rinsed 2 cups water 2 garlic cloves, smashed kosher salt and freshly ground black pepper to taste

DIRECTIONS

1. Bring water and quinoa to a boil in a medium saucepan. Cover, reduce heat to low, and cook until quinoa is tender, around 15 minutes. Remove from heat and let stand for 5 minutes, covered. Remove lid and fluff with a fork. Transfer to a large salad bowl. Meanwhile. Bring a large pot of salted water to a boil and blanch the green beans for two minutes. Drain and place in a bowl of ice water. Drain well. Add the fresh basil, olives, feta cheese, red onion, tomatoes, cucumbers, peppers, white beans, garbanzo beans, and green beans in bowl of quinoa. In a small bowl, whisk together the pepper, salt, oregano, dried basil, balsamic, and olive oil. Pour dressing over the salad and gently toss salad until coated with dressing. Season with additional salt and pepper if needed. Serve and enjoy.

Raisins, Nuts and Beef on Hashweh Rice

Cooking Time: 50 minutes | Servings: 8

Nutrition Info: Calories: 357; Carbs: 39.0g; Protein: 16.7g; Fat: 15.9g

INGREDIENTS

½ cup dark raisins, soaked in 2 cups water for an hour 1/3 cup slivered almonds, toasted and soaked in 2 cups water overnight 1/3 cup pine nuts, toasted and soaked in 2 cups water overnight ½ cup fresh parsley leaves, roughly chopped Pepper and salt to taste ¾ tsp ground cinnamon, divided ¾ tsp cloves, divided 1 tsp garlic powder 1 ¾ tsp allspice, divided 1 lb. lean ground beef or lean ground lamb 1 small red onion, finely chopped Olive oil 1 ½ cups medium grain rice

DIRECTIONS

1. For 15 to 20 minutes, soak rice in cold water. You will know that soaking is enough when you can snap a grain of rice easily between your thumb and index finger. Once soaking is done, drain rice well. Meanwhile, drain pine nuts, almonds and raisins for at least a minute and transfer to one bowl. Set aside. On a heavy cooking pot on medium high fire, heat 1 tbsp olive oil. Once oil is hot, add red onions. Sauté for a minute before adding ground meat and sauté for another minute. Season ground meat with pepper, salt, ½ tsp ground cinnamon, ½ tsp ground cloves, 1 tsp garlic powder, and 1 ¼ tsp allspice. Sauté ground meat for 10 minutes or until browned and cooked fully. Drain fat. In same pot with cooked ground meat, add rice on top of meat. Season with a bit of pepper and salt. Add remaining cinnamon, ground cloves, and allspice. Do not mix. Add 1 tbsp olive oil and 2 ½ cups of water. Bring to a boil and once boiling, lower fire to a simmer. Cook while covered until liquid is fully absorbed, around 20 to 25 minutes. Turn of fire. To serve, place a large serving platter that fully covers the mouth of the pot. Place platter upside down on mouth of pot, and invert pot. The inside of the pot should now rest on the platter with the rice on bottom of plate and ground meat on top of it. Garnish the top of the meat with raisins, almonds, pine nuts, and parsley. Serve and enjoy.

Red Quinoa Peach Porridge

Cooking Time: 30 minutes | Servings: 1,

Nutrition Info: Calories: 456.6; Carbs: 77.3g; Protein: 16.6g; Fat: 9g

INGREDIENTS

¼ cup old fashioned rolled oats ¼ cup red quinoa ½ cup milk 1 ½ cups water 2 peaches, peeled and sliced

DIRECTIONS

1. On a small saucepan, place the peaches and quinoa. Add water and cook for 30 minutes. Add the oatmeal and milk last and cook until the oats become tender. Stir occasionally to avoid the porridge from sticking on the bottom of the pan.

Rice & Currant Salad Mediterranean Style

Cooking Time: 50 minutes | Servings: 4

Nutrition Info: Calories: 450; Carbs: 50.0g; Protein: 9.0g; Fat: 24.0g

INGREDIENTS

1 cup basmati rice 2 1/2 Tablespoons lemon juice 1 teaspoon grated orange zest 2 Tablespoons fresh orange juice 1/4 cup olive oil 1/2 teaspoon cinnamon Salt and pepper to taste 4 chopped green onions 1/2 cup dried currants 3/4 cup shelled pistachios or almonds 1/4 cup chopped fresh parsley

DIRECTIONS

1. Place a nonstick pot on medium high fire and add rice. Toast rice until opaque and starts to smell, around 10 minutes. Add 4 quarts of boiling water to pot and 2 tsp salt. Boil until tender, around 8 minutes uncovered. Drain the rice and spread out on a lined cookie sheet to cool completely. In a large salad bowl, whisk well the oil, juices and spices. Add salt and pepper to taste. Add half of the green onions, half of parsley, currants, and nuts. Toss with the cooled rice and let stand for at least 20 minutes. If needed adjust seasoning with pepper and salt. Garnish with remaining parsley and green onions.

Shrimp Paella Made with Quinoa

Cooking Time: 40 minutes | Servings: 7

Nutrition Info: Calories: 324.4; Protein: 22g; Carbs: 33g; Fat: 11.6g

INGREDIENTS

1 lb. large shrimp, peeled, deveined and thawed 1 tsp seafood seasoning 1 cup frozen green peas 1 red bell pepper, cored, seeded & membrane removed, sliced into ½" strips ½ cup sliced sun-dried tomatoes, packed in olive oil Salt to taste ½ tsp black pepper ½ tsp Spanish paprika ½ tsp saffron threads (optional turmeric) 1 bay leaf ¼ tsp crushed red pepper flakes 3 cups chicken broth, fat free, low sodium 1 ½ cups dry quinoa, rinse well 1 tbsp olive oil 2 cloves garlic, minced 1 yellow onion, diced

DIRECTIONS

1. 1 lb. large shrimp, peeled, deveined and thawed 1 tsp seafood seasoning 1 cup frozen green peas 1 red bell pepper, cored, seeded & membrane removed, sliced into ½" strips ½ cup sliced sun-dried tomatoes, packed in olive oil Salt to taste ½ tsp black pepper ½ tsp Spanish paprika ½ tsp saffron threads (optional turmeric) 1 bay leaf ¼ tsp crushed red pepper flakes 3 cups chicken broth, fat free, low sodium 1 ½ cups dry quinoa, rinse well 1 tbsp olive oil 2 cloves garlic, minced 1 yellow onion, diced

Squash and Eggplant Casserole

Cooking Time: 45 minutes | Servings: 2

Nutrition Info: Calories: 579.3; Carbs: 79.2g; Protein: 22.2g; Fat: 19.3g

INGREDIENTS

½ cup dry white wine 1 eggplant, halved and cut to 1-inch slices 1 large onion, cut into wedges 1 red bell pepper, seeded and cut to julienned strips 1 small butternut squash, cut into 1-inch slices 1 tbsp olive oil 12 baby corn 2 cups low sodium vegetable broth Salt and pepper to taste Polenta Ingredients ¼ cup parmesan cheese, grated 1 cup instant polenta 2 tbsp fresh oregano, chopped Topping Ingredients 1 garlic clove, chopped 2 tbsp slivered almonds 5 tbsp parsley, chopped Grated zest of 1 lemon

DIRECTIONS

1. Preheat the oven to 350 degrees Fahrenheit. In a casserole, heat the oil and add the onion wedges and baby corn. Sauté over medium high heat for five minutes. Stir occasionally to prevent the onions and baby corn from sticking at the bottom of the pan. Add the butternut squash to the casserole and toss the vegetables. Add the eggplants and the red pepper. Cover the vegetables and cook over low to medium heat. Cook for about ten minutes before adding the wine. Let the wine sizzle before stirring in the broth. Bring to a boil and cook in the oven for 30 minutes. While the casserole is cooking inside the oven, make the topping by spreading the slivered almonds on a baking tray and toasting under the grill until they are lightly browned. Place the toasted almonds in a small bowl and mix the remaining ingredients for the toppings. Prepare the polenta. In a large saucepan, bring 3 cups of water to boil over high heat. Add the polenta and continue whisking until it absorbs all the water. Reduce the heat to medium until the polenta is thick. Add the parmesan cheese and oregano. Serve the polenta on plates and add the casserole on top. Sprinkle the toppings on top.

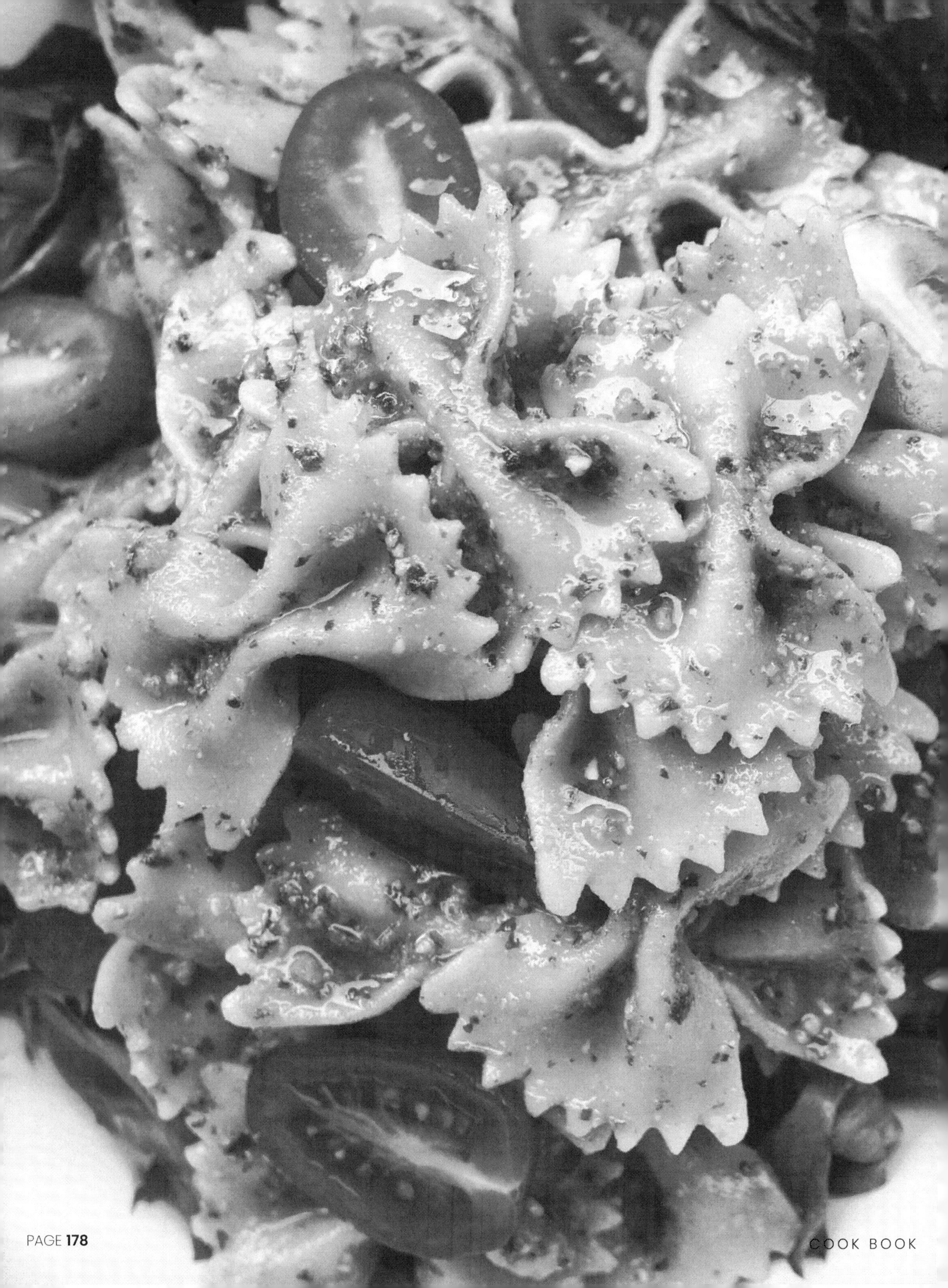

PIZZA & PASTA

Asiago & Artichoke Pizza

Total Time : 1 hour 20 minutes | Serves : 4

Nutrition Info: Calories 254, Fat 9.5g, Carbs 34.3g, Protein 8g

INGREDIENTS

1 cup canned passata
2 cups flour
1 cup lukewarm water
1 pinch of sugar
1 tsp active dry yeast
¾ tsp salt
2 tbsp olive oil
1 ½ cups frozen artichoke hearts
¼ cup grated Asiago cheese
½ onion, minced
3 garlic cloves, minced
1 tbsp dried oregano
1 cup sun-dried tomatoes, chopped
½ tsp red pepper flakes
5-6 basil leaves, torn

DIRECTIONS

1. Sift the flour and salt in a bowl and stir in yeast. Mix lukewarm water, olive oil, and sugar in another bowl. Add the wet mixture to the dry mixture and whisk until you obtain a soft dough. Place the dough on a lightly floured work surface and knead it thoroughly for 4-5 minutes until elastic. Transfer the dough to a greased bowl. Cover with cling film and leave to rise for 50-60 minutes in a warm place until doubled in size. Roll out the dough to a thickness of around 12 inches.

2. Preheat oven to 400 F. Warm oil in a saucepan over medium heat and sauté onion and garlic for 3-4 minutes. Mix in tomatoes and oregano and bring to a boil. Decrease the heat and simmer for another 5 minutes. Transfer the pizza crust to a baking sheet. Spread the sauce all over and top with artichoke hearts and sun-dried tomatoes. Scatter the cheese and bake for 15 minutes until golden. Top with red pepper flakes and basil leaves and serve sliced.

Balsamic-Glazed Pizza with Arugula & Olives

Total Time : 1 hour 30 minutes | Serves : 4

Nutrition Info: Per Serving : Calories 350, Fat 15.4g, Carbs 47.1g, Protein 6.4g

INGREDIENTS

2 cups flour
1 cup lukewarm water
1 pinch of sugar
1 tsp active dry yeast
2 tbsp olive oil
2 tbsp honey
½ cup balsamic vinegar
4 cups arugula
Salt and black pepper to taste
1 cup mozzarella cheese, grated
¾ tsp dried oregano
6 black olives, drained

DIRECTIONS

1. Sift the flour and ¾ tsp salt in a bowl and stir in yeast. Mix lukewarm water, olive oil, and sugar in another bowl. Add the wet mixture to the dry mixture and whisk until you obtain a soft dough. Place the dough on a lightly floured work surface and knead it thoroughly for 4-5 minutes until elastic. Transfer the dough to a greased bowl. Cover with cling film and leave to rise for 50-60 minutes in a warm place until doubled in size. Roll out the dough to a thickness of around 12 inches.

2. Place the balsamic vinegar and honey in a saucepan over medium heat and simmer for 5 minutes until syrupy. Preheat oven to 390 F. Transfer the pizza crust to a baking sheet and sprinkle with oregano and mozzarella cheese; bake for 10-15 minutes. Remove the pizza from the oven and top with arugula. Sprinkle with balsamic glaze and black olives and serve.

Pepperoni Fat Head Pizza

Total Time : 35 minutes | Serves : 4

Nutrition Info: Per Serving : Calories 229; Fats 7.1g; Carbs 0.4g; Protein 36.4g

INGREDIENTS

2 cups flour

1 cup lukewarm water

1 pinch of sugar

1 tsp active dry yeast

¾ tsp salt

2 tbsp olive oil

1 tsp dried oregano

2 cups mozzarella cheese

1 cup sliced pepperoni

DIRECTIONS

1. Sift the flour and salt in a bowl and stir in yeast. Mix lukewarm water, olive oil, and sugar in another bowl. Add the wet mixture to the dry mixture and whisk until you obtain a soft dough. Place the dough on a lightly floured work surface and knead it thoroughly for 4-5 minutes until elastic. Transfer the dough to a greased bowl. Cover with cling film and leave to rise for 50-60 minutes in a warm place until doubled in size. Roll out the dough to a thickness of around 12 inches.

2. Preheat oven to 400 F. Line a round pizza pan with parchment paper. Spread the dough on the pizza pan and top with the mozzarella cheese, oregano, and pepperoni slices. Bake in the oven for 15 minutes or until the cheese melts. Remove the pizza, slice and serve.

Extra Cheesy Pizza

Total Time : 35 minutes | Serves : 4

Nutrition Info: Per Serving : Calories 193; Fats 10.2g; Carbs 3.2g; Protein 19.5g

INGREDIENTS

½ cup almond flour
¼ tsp salt
2 tbsp ground psyllium husk
1 tbsp olive oil
1 cup lukewarm water
For the topping
½ cup sugar-free pizza sauce
1 cup sliced mozzarella cheese
1 cup grated mozzarella cheese
3 tbsp grated Parmesan cheese
2 tsp Italian seasoning

DIRECTIONS

1. Preheat the oven to 400 F. Line a baking sheet with parchment paper. In a medium bowl, mix the almond flour, salt, psyllium powder, olive oil, and lukewarm water until dough forms. Spread the mixture on the pizza pan and bake in the oven until crusty, 10 minutes. When ready, remove the crust and spread the pizza sauce on top. Add the sliced mozzarella, grated mozzarella, Parmesan cheese, and Italian seasoning. Bake in the oven for 18 minutes or until the cheeses melt. Serve warm.

Spanish-Style Pizza de Jamon

Total Time : 45 minutes | Serves : 4

Nutrition Info: Per Serving : Calories 160; Fats 6.2g; Carbs 0.5g; Protein 21.9g

INGREDIENTS

2 cups flour
1 cup lukewarm water
1 pinch of sugar
1 tsp active dry yeast
¾ tsp salt
2 tbsp olive oil
For the topping
½ cup tomato sauce
½ cup sliced mozzarella cheese
4 oz jamon serrano, sliced
7 fresh basil leaves

DIRECTIONS

1. Sift the flour and salt in a bowl and stir in yeast. Mix lukewarm water, olive oil, and sugar in another bowl. Add the wet mixture to the dry mixture and whisk until you obtain a soft dough. Place the dough on a lightly floured work surface and knead it thoroughly for 4-5 minutes until elastic. Transfer the dough to a greased bowl. Cover with cling film and leave to rise for 50-60 minutes in a warm place until doubled in size. Roll out the dough to a thickness of around 12 inches.

2. Preheat the oven to 400 F. Line a pizza pan with parchment paper. Spread the tomato sauce on the crust. Arrange the mozzarella slices on the sauce and then the jamon serrano. Bake for 15 minutes or until the cheese melts. Remove from the oven and top with the basil. Slice and serve warm.

Spicy & Smoky Pizza

Total Time : 45 minutes | Serves : 4

Nutrition Info: Per Serving : Calories 302; Fats 17g; Carbs 1.4g; Protein 31.6g

INGREDIENTS

2 cups flour
1 cup lukewarm water
1 pinch of sugar
1 tsp active dry yeast
¾ tsp salt
2 tbsp olive oil
For the topping
1 tbsp olive oil
1 cups sliced chorizo
¼ cup sugar-free marinara sauce
1 cup sliced smoked mozzarella cheese
1 jalapeño pepper, deseeded and sliced
¼ red onion, thinly sliced

DIRECTIONS

1. Sift the flour and salt in a bowl and stir in yeast. Mix lukewarm water, olive oil, and sugar in another bowl. Add the wet mixture to the dry mixture and whisk until you obtain a soft dough. Place the dough on a lightly floured work surface and knead it thoroughly for 4-5 minutes until elastic. Transfer the dough to a greased bowl. Cover with cling film and leave to rise for 50-60 minutes in a warm place until doubled in size. Roll out the dough to a thickness of around 12 inches.
2. Preheat the oven to 400 F. Line a pizza pan with parchment paper. Heat the olive oil and cook the chorizo until brown, 5 minutes. Spread the marinara sauce on the crust, top with the mozzarella cheese, chorizo, jalapeño pepper, and onion. Bake in the oven until the cheese melts, 15 minutes. Remove from the oven, slice, and serve warm.

Turkey Pizza with Pesto Topping

Total Time : 35 minutes | Serves : 4

Nutrition Info: Per Serving : Calories 684, Fat 54g; Carbs 22g; Protein 31.5g

INGREDIENTS

Pizza Crust
3 cups flour
3 tbsp olive oil
½ tsp salt
3 large eggs
Pesto Chicken Topping
½ lb turkey ham, chopped
2 tbsp cashew nuts
Salt and black pepper to taste
1 ½ tbsp olive oil
1 green bell pepper, seeded and sliced
1 ½ cups basil pesto
1 cup mozzarella cheese, grated
1 ½ tbsp Parmesan cheese, grated
1½ tbsp fresh basil leaves
A pinch of red pepper flakes

DIRECTIONS

1. In a bowl, mix flour, 3 tbsp of olive oil, salt, and eggs until a dough forms. Mold the dough into a ball and place it in between two full parchment papers on a flat surface. Roll it out into a circle of a ¼ -inch thickness. After, slide the pizza dough into the pizza pan and remove the parchment paper. Place the pizza pan in the oven and bake the dough for 20 minutes at 350°F.
2. Once the pizza bread is ready, remove it from the oven, fold and seal the extra inch of dough at its edges to make a crust around it. Apply 2/3 of the pesto on it and sprinkle half of the mozzarella cheese too.
3. Toss the chopped turkey ham in the remaining pesto and spread it on top of the pizza. Sprinkle with the remaining mozzarella, bell peppers, and cashew nuts and put the pizza back in the oven to bake for 9 minutes. When it is ready, remove from the oven to cool slightly, garnish with the basil leaves and sprinkle with parmesan cheese and red pepper flakes. Slice and serve.

Baby Spinach Pizza with Sweet Onion

Total Time : 1 hour 30 minutes | Serves : 4

Nutrition Info: Per Serving : Calories 399, Fat 22.7g, Carbs 42.9g, Protein 8.1g

INGREDIENTS

For the crust
2 cups flour
1 cup lukewarm water
1 pinch of sugar
1 tsp active dry yeast
¾ tsp salt
2 tbsp olive oil
For the caramelized onion
1 onion, sliced
1 tsp sugar
2 tbsp olive oil
½ tsp salt
For the pizza
¼ cup shaved Pecorino Romano cheese
2 tbsp olive oil
½ cup grated mozzarella cheese
1 cup baby spinach
¼ cup chopped fresh basil leaves
½ red bell pepper, sliced

DIRECTIONS

1. Sift the flour and salt in a bowl and stir in yeast. Mix lukewarm water, olive oil, and sugar in another bowl. Add the wet mixture to the dry mixture and whisk until you obtain a soft dough. Place the dough on a lightly floured work surface and knead it thoroughly for 4-5 minutes until elastic. Transfer the dough to a greased bowl. Cover with cling film and leave to rise for 50-60 minutes in a warm place until doubled in size. Roll out the dough to a thickness of around 12 inches.
2. Warm olive oil in a skillet over medium heat and sauté onion with salt and sugar for 3 minutes. Lower the heat and brown for 20-35 minutes until caramelized. Preheat oven to 390 F. Transfer the pizza crust to a baking sheet. Drizzle the crust with olive oil and top with onion. Cover with bell pepper and mozzarella. Bake for 10-15 minutes. Serve topped with baby spinach, basil, and Pecorino cheese.

Italian Mushroom Pizza

Total Time : 45 minutes | Serves : 4

Nutrition Info: Per Serving : Calories 203; Fats 8.6g; Carbs 2.6g; Protein 24.3g

INGREDIENTS

For the crust
2 cups flour
1 cup lukewarm water
1 pinch of sugar
1 tsp active dry yeast
¾ tsp salt
2 tbsp olive oi l
For the topping
1 tsp olive oil
2 medium cremini mushrooms, sliced
1 garlic clove, minced
½ cup sugar-free tomato sauce
1 tsp sugar
1 bay leaf
1 tsp dried oregano
1tsp dried basil
Salt and black pepper to taste
½ cup grated mozzarella cheese
½ cup grated Parmesan cheese
6 black olives, pitted and sliced

DIRECTIONS

1. Sift the flour and salt in a bowl and stir in yeast. Mix lukewarm water, olive oil, and sugar in another bowl. Add the wet mixture to the dry mixture and whisk until you obtain a soft dough. Place the dough on a lightly floured work surface and knead it thoroughly for 4-5 minutes until elastic. Transfer the dough to a greased bowl. Cover with cling film and leave to rise for 50-60 minutes in a warm place until doubled in size. Roll out the dough to a thickness of around 12 inches.
2. Preheat the oven to 400 F. Line a pizza pan with parchment paper. Heat the olive oil in a medium skillet and sauté the mushrooms until softened, 5 minutes. Stir in the garlic and cook until fragrant, 30 seconds.
3. Mix in the tomato sauce, sugar, bay leaf, oregano, basil, salt, and black pepper. Cook for 2 minutes and turn the heat off. Spread the sauce on the crust, top with the mozzarella and Parmesan cheeses, and then, the olives. Bake in the oven until the cheeses melts, 15 minutes. Remove the pizza, slice, and serve warm.

Broccoli-Pepper Pizza

Total Time : 25 minutes | Serves : 4

Nutrition Info: Per Serving : Calories 180; Fats 9g; Carbs 3.6g; Protein 17g

INGREDIENTS

For the crust
½ cup almond flour
¼ tsp salt
2 tbsp ground psyllium husk
1 tbsp olive oil
1 cup lukewarm water
For the topping
1 tbsp olive oil
1 cup sliced fresh mushrooms
1 white onion, thinly sliced
3 cups broccoli florets
4 garlic cloves, minced
½ cup pizza sauce
4 tomatoes, sliced
1 ½ cup grated mozzarella cheese
½ cup grated Parmesan cheese

DIRECTIONS

1. Preheat the oven to 400 F. Line a baking sheet with parchment paper. In a bowl, mix the almond flour, salt, psyllium powder, olive oil, and lukewarm water until dough forms. Spread the mixture on the pizza pan and bake in the oven until crusty, 10 minutes. When ready, remove the crust and allow cooling.
2. Heat olive oil in a skillet and sauté the mushrooms, onion, garlic, and broccoli until softened, 5 minutes. Spread the pizza sauce on the crust and top with the broccoli mixture, tomato, mozzarella and Parmesan cheeses. Bake for 5 minutes.

Caramelized Onion and Goat Cheese Pizza

Total Time : 35 minutes | Serves : 4

Nutrition Info: Per Serving : Calories 317; Fats 20g; Carbs 1g; Protein 28g

INGREDIENTS

For the crust
2 cups flour
1 cup lukewarm water
1 pinch of sugar
1 tsp active dry yeast
¾ tsp salt
2 tbsp olive oil
For the topping:
2 tbsp butter
2 red onions, thinly sliced
Salt and black pepper to taste
1 cup crumbled goat cheese
1 tbs almond milk
1 cup fresh curly endive, chopped

DIRECTIONS

1. Sift the flour and salt in a bowl and stir in yeast. Mix lukewarm water, olive oil, and sugar in another bowl. Add the wet mixture to the dry mixture and whisk until you obtain a soft dough. Place the dough on a lightly floured work surface and knead it thoroughly for 4-5 minutes until elastic. Transfer the dough to a greased bowl. Cover with cling film and leave to rise for 50-60 minutes in a warm place until doubled in size. Roll out the dough to a thickness of around 12 inches.
2. Preheat the oven to 400 F. Line a pizza pan with parchment paper. Melt the butter in a large skillet and stir in the onions. Reduce the heat to low, season the onions with salt, black pepper, and cook with frequent stirring until caramelized, 15 to 20 minutes. Turn the heat. In a medium bowl, mix the goat cheese with the almond milk and spread on the crust. Top with the caramelized onions. Bake in the oven for 10 minutes and take out after. Top with the curly endive, slice, and serve warm.

Vegetarian Spinach-Olive Pizza

Total Time : 40 minutes | Serves : 4

Nutrition Info: Per Serving : Calories 95; Fats 4.3g; Carbs 1.8g; Protein 9.7g

INGREDIENTS

For the crust
½ cup almond flour
¼ tsp salt
2 tbsp ground psyllium husk
1 tbsp olive oil
1 cup lukewarm water
For the topping
½ cup tomato sauce
½ cup baby spinach
1 cup grated mozzarella cheese
1 tsp dried oregano
3 tbsp sliced black olives

DIRECTIONS

1. Preheat the oven to 400 F. Line a baking sheet with parchment paper. In a medium bowl, mix the almond flour, salt, psyllium powder, olive oil, and water until dough forms. Spread the mixture on the pizza pan and bake in the oven until crusty, 10 minutes. When ready, remove the crust and spread the tomato sauce on top. Add the spinach, mozzarella cheese, oregano, and olives. Bake until the cheese melts, 15 minutes. Take out of the oven, slice and serve warm.

Chicken Bacon Ranch Pizza

Total Time : 45 minutes | Serves : 4

Nutrition Info: Per Serving : Calories 528; Fats 27.8g; Carbs 4.9g; Protein 61.2g

INGREDIENTS

For the crust
2 cups flour
1 cup lukewarm water
1 pinch of sugar
1 tsp active dry yeast
¾ tsp salt
2 tbsp olive oil
For the ranch sauce
1 tbsp butter
2 garlic cloves, minced
1 tbsp cream cheese
¼ cup half and half
1 tbsp dry Ranch seasoning mix
For the topping
3 bacon slices, chopped
2 chicken breasts
Salt and black pepper to taste
1 cup grated mozzarella cheese
6 fresh basil leaves

DIRECTIONS

1. Sift the flour and salt in a bowl and stir in yeast. Mix lukewarm water, olive oil, and sugar in another bowl. Add the wet mixture to the dry mixture and whisk until you obtain a soft dough. Place the dough on a lightly floured work surface and knead it thoroughly for 4-5 minutes until elastic. Transfer the dough to a greased bowl. Cover with cling film and leave to rise for 50-60 minutes in a warm place until doubled in size. Roll out the dough to a thickness of around 12 inches.
2. Preheat the oven to 400 F. Line a pizza pan with parchment paper. In a bowl, mix the sauce's ingredients butter, garlic, cream cheese, half and half, and ranch mix. Set aside. Heat a grill pan over medium heat and cook the bacon until crispy and brown, 5 minutes. Transfer to a plate and set aside.
3. Season the chicken with salt, pepper and grill in the pan on both sides until golden brown, 10 minutes. Remove to a plate, allow cooling and cut into thin slices. Spread the ranch sauce on the pizza crust, followed by the chicken and bacon, and then, mozzarella cheese and basil. Bake for 5 minutes or until the cheese melts. Slice and serve warm.

Tagliatelle with Sardines & Capers

Total Time : 20 minutes | Serves : 4

Nutrition Info: Per Serving : Calories 412, Fat 13g, Carbs 47g, Protein 23g

INGREDIENTS

- 8 oz tagliatelle
- 1 tbsp olive oil
- ¼ cup chopped onion
- 2 garlic cloves, minced
- 1 tsp tomato paste
- 16 canned sardines in olive oil
- 1 tbsp capers
- ½ cup grated Parmesan cheese
- Salt and black pepper to taste
- 1 tbsp chopped parsley
- 1 tsp chopped oregano

DIRECTIONS

1. Boil water in a pot over medium heat and place in the pasta. Cook for 8-10 minutes for al dente. Drain and set aside; reserve ½ cup of the cooking liquid. Warm the olive oil in a pan over medium heat. Place in onion, garlic, and oregano and cook for 5 minutes until soft. Stir in salt, tomato paste, pepper, and ½ cup of reserved liquid for 1 minute. Mix in cooked pasta, capers, and sardines and toss to coat. Serve topped with Parmesan cheese and parsley.

Fall Baked Vegetable with Rigatoni

Total Time : 45 minutes | Serves : 6

Nutrition Info: Per Serving : Calories 186, Fat 11g, Carbs 15g, Protein 10g

INGREDIENTS

- 1 lb pumpkin, chopped
- 1 zucchini, chopped
- 2 tbsp grated Pecorino-Romano cheese
- 1 onion, chopped
- 1 lb rigatoni
- 2 tbsp olive oil
- Salt and black pepper to taste
- ½ tsp garlic powder
- ½ cup dry white wine

DIRECTIONS

1. Preheat oven to 420 F. Combine zucchini, pumpkin, onion, and olive oil in a bowl. Arrange on a lined aluminum foil sheet and season with salt, pepper, and garlic powder. Bake for 30 minutes until tender. In a pot of boiling water, cook rigatoni for 8-10 minutes until al dente. Drain and set aside.
2. In a food processor, place ½ cup of the roasted veggies and wine and pulse until smooth. Transfer to a skillet over medium heat. Stir in rigatoni and cook until heated through. Top with the remaining roasted vegetables and Pecorino cheese to serve.
3. 248.Broccoli Pesto Fusill i

Broccoli Pesto Fusilli

Total Time : 23 minutes | Serves : 4

Nutrition Info: Per Serving : Calories 385, Fat 22g, Carbs 38g, Protein 12g

INGREDIENTS

4 Roma tomatoes, diced
1 cup broccoli florets
1 lb fusilli
2 tsp tomato paste
2 garlic cloves, minced
1 tbsp chopped fresh oregano
½ tsp salt
1 cup vegetable broth
1 packed cup fresh basil leaves
¼ cup grated Parmesan cheese
¼ cup olive oil
¼ cup pine nuts

DIRECTIONS

1. Place the pasta in a pot with salted boiling water and cook for 8-10 minutes until al dente. Drain and set aside. In a pan over medium heat, sauté tomato paste, tomatoes, broth, oregano, garlic, and salt for 10 minutes.
2. In a food processor, place basil, broccoli, Parmesan, olive oil, and pine nuts; pulse until smooth. Pour into the tomato mixture. Stir in pasta, cook until heated through and the pasta is well coated. Serve.

Pasta Salad

Total Time : 25 minutes | Serves : 4

Nutrition Info: Per Serving : Calories 377, Fat 16.6g, Carbs 44.3g, Protein 11.5g

INGREDIENTS

½ cup crumbled ricotta cheese
2 tbsp black olives, halved
4 cups fresh baby spinach, chopped
2 tbsp scallions, chopped
16 oz farfalle pasta
¼ cup red wine vinegar
¼ cup extra-virgin olive oil
1½ tsp freshly squeezed lemon juice
Salt and black pepper to taste

DIRECTIONS

1. Cook the farfalle pasta to pack instructions, drain and let it to cool. Mix the scallions, spinach, and cooled pasta in a bowl. Top with ricotta and olives. Combine the vinegar, olive oil, lemon juice, salt, and pepper in another bowl. Pour over the pasta mixture and toss to combine. Serve chilled.

Fettuccine a la Puttanesca

Total Time : 20 minutes | Serves : 4

Nutrition Info: Per Serving : Calories 443, Fat 13.7g, Carbs 65g, Protein 18.1g

INGREDIENTS

20 Kalamata olives, pitted and chopped
¼ cup fresh basil, chopped
4 garlic cloves, minced
2 anchovy fillets, chopped
¼ tsp red pepper flakes
3 tbsp capers
2 (14-oz) cans crushed tomatoes
1 (14-oz) can chopped tomatoes, drained
8 oz fettuccine pasta
2 tbsp extra-virgin olive oil
2 tbsp Parmesan cheese, grated
Salt and black pepper to taste

DIRECTIONS

1. Preheat the pan with the olive oil and the garlic. When hot, add fresh basil, anchovys, olives, tomatoes and the other sauce ingredients.
2. Cook the pasta in salted boiling water and pour into the sauce. Serve.

Walnut Pesto Pasta

Total Time : 10 minutes | Serves : 4

Nutrition Info: Per Serving : Calories 559, Fat 17.4g, Carbs 91.2g, Protein 20.5g

INGREDIENTS

8 oz whole-wheat pasta
¼ cup walnuts, chopped
3 garlic cloves, finely minced
½ cup fresh dill, chopped
¼ cup grated Parmesan cheese
3 tbsp extra-virgin olive oil

DIRECTIONS

1. Cook the whole-wheat pasta to pack instructions, drain and let it cool. Place the olive oil, dill, garlic, Parmesan cheese, and walnuts in a food processor and blend for 15 seconds or until paste forms. Pour over the cooled pasta and toss to combine. Serve immediately.

Broccoli Pasta with Basil Pesto

Total Time : 40 minutes | Serves : 4

Nutrition Info: Per Serving : Calories 190, Fat 4g, Carbs 9g, Protein 8g

INGREDIENTS

1 lb broccoli florets
16 oz penne pasta
1 cup vegetable stock
Salt and black pepper
2 tbsp basil pesto
2 cups mozzarella cheese, shredded
1/3 cup Parmesan cheese, grated
2 green onions, chopped

DIRECTIONS

1. Bring to a bowl salted water over medium heat and add in the pasta. Cook for 7-9 minutes until al dente. Drain and set aside. Preheat the oven to 380 F. Place pasta, vegetable stock, salt, pepper, basil pesto, broccoli, and green onions in a greased baking pan and combine. Scatter with mozzarella and parmesan cheeses and bake for 30 minutes. Serve.

Garlic Shrimp with Tie Pasta

Total Time : 25 minutes | Serves : 4

Nutrition Info:Per Serving : Calories 493; Fats 31.8g; Carbs 16.1g; Protein 33.7g

INGREDIENTS

1 tbsp olive oil
1 lb shrimp, peeled and deveined
Salt and black pepper to taste
2 tbsp unsalted butter
6 garlic cloves, minced
½ cup dry white wine
1 ½ cups heavy cream
½ cup grated Asiago cheese
2 tbsp chopped fresh parsley
16 oz bow tie pasta
Salt to season

DIRECTIONS

1. In a pot of boiling water, cook the tie pasta for 8-10 minutes until al dente. Drain and set aside.
2. Heat the olive oil in a large skillet, season the shrimp with salt and black pepper, and cook in the oil on both sides until pink and opaque, 2 minutes. Set aside. Melt the butter in the skillet and sauté the garlic until fragrant. Stir in the white wine and cook until reduced by half, scraping the bottom of the pan to deglaze. Reduce the heat to low and stir in the heavy cream. Allow simmering for 1 minute and stir in the Asiago cheese to melt. Return the shrimp to the sauce and sprinkle the parsley on top. Adjust the taste with salt and black pepper, if needed. Top the pasta with the sauce and serve.

Creamy Salmon Fettucine

Total Time : 35 minutes | Serves : 4

Nutrition Info: Per Serving : Calories 795; Fats 45.8g; Carbs 20.1g; Protein 72.2g

INGREDIENTS

16 oz fettuccine
5 tbsp butter
4 salmon fillets, cut into 2-inch cubes
Salt and black pepper to taste
3 garlic cloves, minced
1 ¼ cups heavy cream
½ cup dry white wine
1 tsp grated lemon zest
1 cup baby spinach
Lemon wedges for garnishing

DIRECTIONS

1. In a pot of boiling water, cook the fettuccine pasta for 8-10 minutes until al dente. Drain and set aside.
2. Melt half of the butter in a large skillet; season the salmon with salt, black pepper, and cook in the butter until golden brown on all sides and flaky within, 8 minutes. Transfer to a plate and set aside. Add the remaining butter to the skillet to melt and stir in the garlic. Cook until fragrant, 1 minute. Mix in heavy cream, white wine, lemon zest, salt, and pepper.
3. Allow boiling over low heat for 5 minutes. Stir in spinach, allow wilting for 2 minutes and stir in fettuccine and salmon until well-coated in the sauce. Garnish with the lemon wedges.

Beef Carbonara

Total Time : 30 minutes | Serves : 4

Nutrition Info: Per Serving : Calories 470; Fats 35.5g; Carbs 8.9g; Protein 25.4 g

INGREDIENTS

DIRECTIONS

Ingredients
16 oz linguine
4 bacon slices, chopped
1 ¼ cups heavy whipping cream
¼ cup mayonnaise
Salt and black pepper to taste
4 egg yolks
1 cup grated Parmesan cheese

1. In a pot of boiling water, cook the linguine pasta for 8-10 minutes until al dente. Drain and set aside.
2. Add the bacon to a skillet and cook over medium heat until crispy, 5 minutes. Set aside. Pour heavy cream into a pot and allow simmering for 5 minutes. Whisk in mayonnaise and season with salt and pepper. Cook for 1 minute and spoon 2 tablespoons of the mixture into a medium bowl. Allow cooling and mix in the egg yolks. Pour the mixture into the pot and mix quickly. Stir in Parmesan and fold in the pasta. Garnish with more Parmesan. Cook for 1 minute to warm the pasta.

Pork Loin with Green Beans & Fettuccine

Total Time : 40 minutes | Serves : 4

Nutrition Info: Per Serving : Calories 586; Fats 32.3g; Carbs 9g; Protein 59g

INGREDIENTS

DIRECTIONS

16 oz fettuccine
1 tbsp olive oil
4 pork loin medallions, cut into strips
Salt and black pepper to taste
½ cup green beans, chopped
1 lemon, zested and juiced
¼ cup chicken broth
1 cup crème fraiche
6 basil leaves, chopped
1 cup shaved Parmesan cheese

1. In a pot of boiling water, cook the fettuccine pasta for 8-10 minutes until al dente. Drain and set aside.
2. Heat olive oil in a skillet, season the pork with salt, pepper, and cook for 10 minutes. Mix in green beans and cook for 5 minutes. Stir in lemon zest, lemon juice, and chicken broth. Cook for 5 more minutes or until the liquid reduces by a quarter. Add crème fraiche and mix well. Pour in pasta and basil and cook for 1 minute. Top with Parmesan cheese.

Garlic-Butter Steak Bites with Fusilli

Total Time : 30 minutes | Serves : 4

Nutrition Info: Per Serving : Calories 422; Fats 22.4g; Carbs 17.3g; Protein 36.5g

INGREDIENTS

1 lb thick-cut New York strip steaks, cut into 1-inch cubes
16 oz fusilli pasta
4 tbsp butter
Salt and black pepper to taste
4 garlic cloves, minced
2 tbsp chopped fresh parsley
1 cup grated Pecorino Romano cheese

DIRECTIONS

1. In a pot of boiling water, cook the fusilli pasta for 8-10 minutes until al dente. Drain and set aside.
2. Melt the butter in a large skillet, season the steaks with salt, black pepper and cook in the butter until brown, and cooked through, 10 minutes. Stir in the garlic and cook until fragrant, 1 minute. Mix in the parsley and fusilli pasta; toss well and season with salt and black pepper. Dish the food, top with the Pecorino Romano cheese and serve immediately.

Beef Ragu with Veggies

Total Time : 20 minutes | Serves : 4

Nutrition Info: Per Serving : Calories 451; Fats 25.7g; Carbs 6.6g; Protein 39.8g

INGREDIENTS

16 oz tagliatelle pasta
2 tbsp butter
1 lb ground beef
Salt and black pepper to taste
¼ cup tomato sauce
1 green bell pepper, chopped
1 red bell pepper, chopped
1 small red onion, chopped
1 cup grated Parmesan cheese

DIRECTIONS

1. In a pot of boiling water, cook the tagliatelle pasta for 8-10 minutes until al dente. Drain and set aside.
2. Heat half of the butter in a medium skillet and cook the beef until brown, 5 minutes. Season with salt and black pepper. Stir in the tomato sauce and cook for 10 minutes or until the sauce reduces by a quarter. Stir in the bell peppers and onion; cook for 1 minute and turn the heat off. Adjust the taste with salt and black pepper and mix in the tagliatelle. Dish the food onto serving plates. Garnish with the Parmesan cheese and serve warm.

Tuscan Chicken Linguine

Total Time : 35 minutes | Serves : 4

Nutrition Info: Per Serving : Calories 941; Fats 60.7g; Carbs 10.7g; Protein 79.3 g

INGREDIENTS

16 oz linguine
2 tbsp olive oil
4 chicken breasts
1 medium white onion, chopped
1 cup sundried tomatoes in oil, chopped
1 red bell pepper, deseeded and chopped
5 garlic cloves, minced
¾ cup chicken broth
1 ½ cups heavy cream
¾ cup grated Pecorino Romano cheese
1 cup baby kale, chopped
Salt and black pepper to taste

DIRECTIONS

1. In a pot of boiling water, cook the linguine pasta for 8-10 minutes until al dente. Drain and set aside.
2. Heat the olive oil in a large skillet, season the chicken with salt, black pepper, and cook in the oil until golden brown on the outside and cooked within, 7 to 8 minutes. Transfer the chicken to a plate and cut into 4 slices each. Set aside.
3. Add the onion, sundried tomatoes, bell pepper to the skillet and sauté until softened, 5 minutes. Mix in the garlic and cook until fragrant, 1 minute. Deglaze the skillet with the chicken broth and mix in the heavy cream. Simmer for 2 minutes and stir in the Pecorino Romano cheese until melted, 2 minutes. Once the cheese melts, stir in the kale to wilt and adjust the taste with salt and black pepper. Mix in the linguine and chicken until well coated in the sauce. Dish the food and serve warm.

Beef-Asparagus Rotini Pasta

Total Time : 40 minutes | Serves : 4

Nutrition Info: Per Serving : Calories 513; Fats 24.7g; Carbs 21.4g; Protein 43.8g

INGREDIENTS

16 oz rotini pasta
1 lb ground beef
3 tbsp olive oil
1 lb asparagus, cut into 1-inch pieces
2 large shallots, finely chopped
3 garlic cloves, minced
Salt and black pepper to taste
1 cup finely grated Parmesan cheese for topping

DIRECTIONS

1. In a pot of boiling water, cook the rotini pasta for 8-10 minutes until al dente. Drain and set aside.
2. Heat a large non-stick skillet over medium heat and add the beef. Cook while breaking the lumps that form until brown, 10 minutes. Use a slotted spoon to transfer the beef to a plate and discard the drippings. Heat olive oil in a skillet and sauté asparagus until tender, 7 minutes. Stir in shallots and garlic and cook for 2 minutes. Season with salt and pepper.
3. Stir in the beef and rotini pasta and toss until well combined. Adjust the taste with salt and black pepper as desired. Dish the food between serving plates and garnish generously with the Parmesan cheese.

Classic Beef Lasagna

Total Time : 70 minutes | Serves : 4

Nutrition Info: Per Serving : Calories 557; Fats 29.6g; Carbs 4.6g; Protein 60.2g

INGREDIENTS

1 lb lasagne sheets
2 tbsp olive oil
1 lb ground beef
1 medium white onion, chopped
1 tsp Italian seasoning
Salt and black pepper to taste
1 cup marinara sauce
½ cup grated Parmesan cheese

DIRECTIONS

1. Preheat oven to 350 F. Warm olive oil in a skillet and add the beef and onion. Cook until the beef is brown, 7-8 minutes. Season with Italian seasoning, salt, and pepper. Cook for 1 minute and mix in the marinara sauce. Simmer for 3 minutes.
2. Spread a layer of the beef mixture in a lightly greased baking sheet and make a first single layer on the beef mixture. Top with a single layer of lasagna sheets. Repeat the layering two more times using the remaining ingredients in the same quantities. Sprinkle with the Parmesan cheese. Bake in the oven until the cheese melts and is bubbly with the sauce, 20 minutes. Remove the lasagna, allow cooling for 2 minutes and dish onto serving plates. Serve warm.

Cauliflower Casserole with Macaroni

Total Time : 45 minutes | Serves : 4

Nutrition Info: Per Serving : Calories 301; Fats 20.8g; Carbs 13.4g; Protein 11.6g

INGREDIENTS

16 oz elbow pasta
1 head cauliflower, cut into florets
1 cup heavy cream
1 cup grated mozzarella cheese
1 tsp dried thyme
1 tsp smoked paprika
Salt to taste
½ tsp red chili flakes

DIRECTIONS

1. In a pot of boiling water, cook the macaroni for 8-10 minutes until al dente. Drain and set aside.
2. Preheat the oven to 350 F and grease a baking dish with cooking spray. Set aside. Bring 4 cups of water to a boil in a large pot and blanch the cauliflower for 4 minutes. Drain through a colander. In a large bowl, mix the cauliflower, macaroni, heavy cream, half of the mozzarella cheese, thyme, paprika, salt, and red chili flakes until well-combined. Transfer the mixture to the baking dish and top with the remaining cheese. Bake for 30 minutes. Allow cooling for 2 minutes and serve afterwards.

Mussels with Spaghetti

Total Time : 25 minutes | Serves : 4

Nutrition Info: Per Serving : Calories 471; Fats 33.8g; Carbs 18.9g; Protein 18.8g

INGREDIENTS

16 oz spaghetti, broken in half
1 lb mussels, debearded and rinsed
1 cup white wine
4 tbsp olive oil
3 shallots, finely chopped
6 garlic cloves, minced
2 tsp red chili flakes
½ cup fish stock
1 ½ cups heavy cream
2 tbsp chopped fresh parsley
Salt and black pepper to taste

DIRECTIONS

1. Boil water in a pot over medium heat and place in the pasta. Cook for 8-10 minutes for al dente. Drain and set aside.
2. Pour mussels and white wine into a pot, cover, and cook for 4 minutes. Occasionally stir until the mussels have opened. Strain the mussels and reserve the cooking liquid. Allow cooling, discard any mussels with closed shells, and remove the meat out of ¾ of the mussel shells. Set aside with the remaining mussels in the shells.
3. Heat olive oil in a skillet and sauté shallots, garlic, and chili flakes for 3 minutes. Mix in reduced wine and fish stock. Allow boiling and whisk in the remaining butter and then the heavy cream. Taste the sauce and adjust the taste with salt, pepper, and mix in parsley. Pour in the pasta, mussels and toss well in the sauce. Serve afterwards.

One-Pot Spicy Pasta

Total Time : 35 minutes | Serves : 4

Nutrition Info: Per Serving : Calories 763; Fats 34g; Carbs 17.9g; Protein 82.7g

INGREDIENTS

16 oz whole-wheat pasta
4 chicken breasts
1 medium yellow onion, minced
3 garlic cloves, minced
1 tsp Italian seasoning
½ tsp garlic powder
¼ tsp red chili flakes
¼ tsp cayenne pepper
1 cup marinara sauce
1 cup grated mozzarella cheese
½ cup grated cheddar cheese
Salt and black pepper to taste

DIRECTIONS

1. In a pot of boiling water, cook the whole-wheat pasta according to the package directions. Drain and set aside.
2. Heat the olive oil in a large pot, season the chicken with salt, black pepper, and cook in the oil until golden brown on both sides and cooked within, 10 minutes. Transfer to a plate, cut into cubes and set aside. Add the onion and garlic to the pan and cook until softened and fragrant, 3 minutes. Season with Italian seasoning, garlic powder, chili flakes, and cayenne pepper.
3. Cook for 1 minute. Stir in marinara sauce and simmer for 5 minutes. Adjust the taste with salt and black pepper. Reduce heat to low and return the chicken to the sauce and pasta, mozzarella and cheddar cheeses. Stir until the cheese melts. Serve.

Spicy Veggie Pasta Bake

Total Time : 45 minutes | Serves : 4

Nutrition Info: Per Serving : Calories 248; Fats 11.5g; Carbs 4.9g; Protein 26.8g

INGREDIENTS

- 16 oz penne
- 1 tbsp olive oil
- 1 cup mixed chopped bell peppers
- 1 yellow squash, chopped
- 1 red onion, halved and sliced
- 1 cup sliced white button mushrooms
- Salt and black pepper to taste
- ¼ tsp red chili flakes
- 1 cup marinara sauce
- 1 cup grated mozzarella cheese
- 1 cup grated Parmesan cheese
- ¼ cup chopped fresh basil

DIRECTIONS

1. In a pot of boiling water, cook the penne pasta for 8-10 minutes until al dente. Drain and set aside.
2. Heat the olive oil in a cast iron and sauté the bell peppers, squash, onion, and mushrooms. Cook until softened, 5 minutes. Stir in garlic and cook until fragrant, 30 seconds. Season with salt, pepper, and red chili flakes. Mix in marinara sauce and cook for 5 minutes. Stir in the penne and spread the mozzarella and Parmesan cheeses on top. Bake in the oven until the cheeses melt and golden brown on top, 15 minutes. Allow cooling for 2 minutes and dish onto serving plates. Serve warm.

Tomato Kale Chicken with Pappardelle

Total Time : 30 minutes + chilling time | Serves : 4

Nutrition Info: Per Serving : Calories 740; Fats 52.9g; Carbs 15.1g; Carbs 6.1g; Protein 50.2g

INGREDIENTS

- 16 oz pappardelle pasta
- 3 tbsp olive oil
- 4 chicken thighs, cut into 1-inch pieces
- Salt and black pepper to taste
- 1 yellow onion, chopped
- 4 garlic cloves, minced
- 1 cup cherry tomatoes, halved
- ½ cup chicken broth
- 2 cups baby kale, chopped
- 1 cup grated Parmigiano-Reggiano cheese
- 2 tbsp pine nuts for topping

DIRECTIONS

1. In a pot of boiling water, cook the pappardelle pasta for 8-10 minutes until al dente. Drain and set aside.
2. Heat the olive oil in a medium pot, season the chicken with salt, black pepper, and sear in the oil until golden brown on the outside. Transfer to a plate and set aside. Add the onion and garlic to the oil and cook until softened and fragrant, 3 minutes. Mix in tomatoes and chicken broth and cook over low heat until the tomatoes soften and the liquid reduces by half. Season with salt and pepper. Return the chicken to the pot and stir in the kale. Allow wilting for 2 minutes. Spoon the pappardelle onto serving plates, top with kale sauce and then the Parmigianino-Reggiano cheese. Garnish with pine nuts and serve.

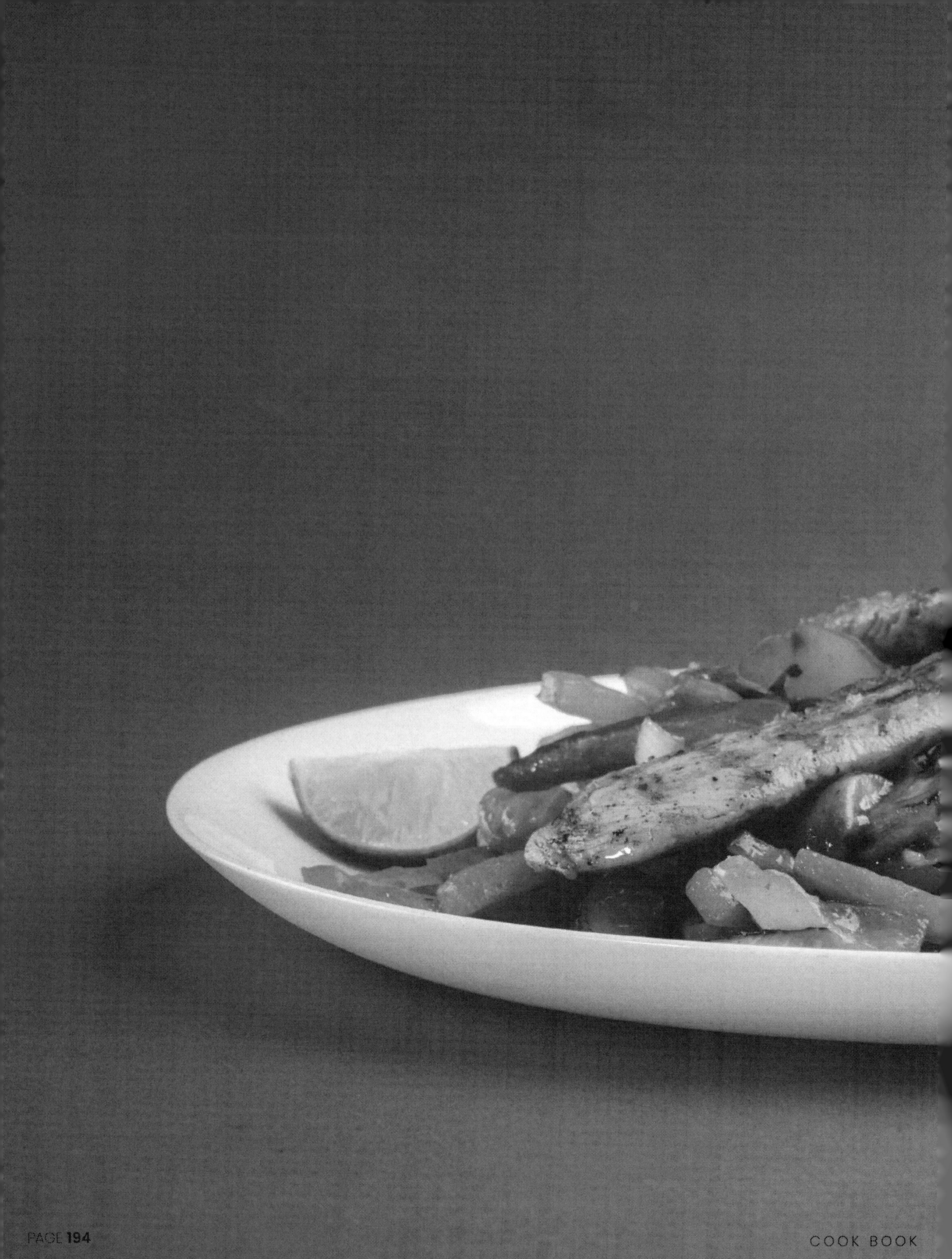

MAIN COURSES

Peppered Pork & Parsnip Bake

Total Time : 1 hour 30 minutes | Serves : 4

Nutrition Info: Per Serving : Calories 230, Fat 8g, Carbs 22g, Protein 16g

INGREDIENTS

2 lb pork loin, sliced
2 parsnips, chopped
2 tbsp olive oil
1 tsp black peppercorns, crushed
2 red onions, chopped
2 cups Greek yogurt
1 tsp mustard
Salt and black pepper to taste

DIRECTIONS

1. Preheat the oven to 360 F.
2. Warm the olive oil in a skillet over medium heat and sear pork for 8 minutes on all sides. Remove to a bowl. In the same skillet, cook onions, parsnips, and peppercorns and cook for 5 minutes. Put the pork back along with the yogurt, mustard, salt, and pepper and stir and bake for 1 hour. Serve warm.

One-Pan Lamb with Cherry Tomatoes

Total Time : 30 minutes | Serves : 4

Nutrition Info: Per Serving : Calories 324, Fat 10g, Carbs 22g, Protein 16g

INGREDIENTS

2 garlic cloves, minced
1 lemon, juiced and zested
1 ½ lb ground lamb
3 tbsp olive oil
Salt and black pepper to taste
1 lb cherry tomatoes, halved
1 red onion, chopped
2 tbsp tomato paste
1 tbsp mint leaves, chopped

DIRECTIONS

1. Warm the olive oil in a skillet over medium heat and cook lamb and garlic for 5 minutes. Stir in lemon zest, lemon juice, salt, pepper, cherry tomatoes, onion, tomato paste, and mint and cook for 15 minutes. Serve right away.

Tomato & Dill Lamb

Total Time : 40 minutes | Serves : 4

Nutrition Info: Per Serving : Calories 300, Fat 14g, Carbs 16g, Protein 19 g

INGREDIENTS

16 oz whole-wheat pasta
4 chicken breasts
1 medium yellow onion, minced
3 garlic cloves, minced
1 tsp Italian seasoning
½ tsp garlic powder
¼ tsp red chili flakes
¼ tsp cayenne pepper
1 cup marinara sauce
1 cup grated mozzarella cheese
½ cup grated cheddar cheese
Salt and black pepper to taste

DIRECTIONS

1. Warm the olive oil in a skillet over medium heat and cook onion and garlic for 5 minutes. Put in lamb and cook for another 5 minutes. Stir in celery, salt, pepper, tomatoes, stock, nutmeg, and dill and bring to a boil. Cook for 20 minutes. Serve.

Easy Lamb Stew

Total Time : 35 minutes | Serves : 4

Nutrition Info: Per Serving : Calories 300, Fat 22g, Carbs 26g, Protein 20g

INGREDIENTS

1 carrot, chopped
4 potatoes, diced
1 tsp ground nutmeg
½ tsp cinnamon
2 tbsp olive oil
1 lb lamb stew meat, cubed
½ cup sweet chili sauce
½ cup vegetable stock
1 tbsp cilantro, chopped
Salt and black pepper to taste

DIRECTIONS

1. Warm the olive oil in a skillet over medium heat and sear lamb for 5 minutes. Stir in chili sauce, carrot, potatoes, stock, nutmeg, cinnamon, cilantro, salt, and pepper and bring to a boil. Cook for another 20 minutes. Serve immediately

Creamy Lamb with Pears

Total Time : 35 minutes | Serves : 4

Nutrition Info: Per Serving : Calories 340, Fat 18g, Carbs 23g, Protein 16g

INGREDIENTS

2 pears, cored, peeled, and cubed
2 tbsp olive oil
1 lemon, juiced
1 lb lamb stew meat, cubed
2 tbsp dill, chopped
2 oz heavy cream
Salt and black pepper to taste

DIRECTIONS

1. Warm the olive oil in a skillet over medium heat and sear lamb for 5 minutes. Stir in pears, lemon juice, dill, heavy cream, salt, and pepper and bring to a boil. Simmer for 20 minutes. Serve right away.

Juicy Pork Chops

Total Time : 40 minutes | Serves : 4

Nutrition Info: Per Serving : Calories 230, Fat 19g, Carbs 12g, Protein 13g

INGREDIENTS

DIRECTIONS

4 pork chops
½ cup tomato puree
Salt and black pepper to taste
2 tbsp olive oil
1 tbsp Italian seasoning
1 tbsp rosemary, chopped

1. Preheat the oven to 380 F. Warm olive oil in a skillet over medium heat. Sear pork. Stir in salt, pepper, tomato purée, Italian seasoning, and rosemary and bake for 20 minutes. Serve warm.

Balsamic Lamb with Walnuts

Total Time : 30 minutes | Serves : 4

Nutrition Info: Per Serving : Calories 310, Fat 15g, Carbs 17g, Protein 19g

INGREDIENTS

DIRECTIONS

1 ½ lb lamb meat, cubed
2 tbsp lime juice
1 tbsp balsamic vinegar
5 garlic cloves, minced
3 tbsp olive oil
Salt and black pepper to taste
2 tbsp walnuts, toasted and chopped
2 scallions, chopped

1. Warm the olive oil in a skillet over medium heat and sear lamb for 8 minutes on both sides. Put in scallions and garlic and cook for another 2 minutes. Stir in lime juice, vinegar, salt, pepper, and walnuts and cook for an additional 10 minutes.

Hot Pork Meatballs

Total Time : 30 minutes | Serves : 4

Nutrition Info: Per Serving : Calories 240, Fat 19g, Carbs 12g, Protein 15 g

INGREDIENTS

DIRECTIONS

1 lb ground pork
3 tbsp olive oil
2 tbsp parsley, chopped
2 green onions, chopped
4 garlic cloves, minced
1 red chili, chopped
1 cup veggie stock
2 tbsp hot paprika

1. Combine pork, parsley, green onions, garlic, and red chili in a bowl and form medium balls out of the mixture.
2. Warm olive oil in a skillet over medium heat. Sear meatballs for 8 minutes on all sides. Stir in stock and hot paprika and simmer for another 12 minutes. Serve warm.

Peppercorn Pork Chops

Total Time : 30 minutes | Serves : 4

Nutrition Info:Per Serving : Calories 240, Fat 10g, Carbs 14g, Protein 25g

INGREDIENTS

4 pork chops
1 cup red onion, sliced
1 tbsp black peppercorns, crushed
¼ cup vegetable stock
¼ cup dry white wine
2 garlic cloves, minced
Salt and black pepper to taste
2 tbsp olive oil

DIRECTIONS

1. Warm the olive oil in a skillet over medium heat and sear pork chops for 8 minutes on both sides. Put in onion and garlic and cook for another 2 minutes. Mix in stock, white winw, salt, and pepper and cook for 10 minutes, stirring often. Serve.

Orange Lamb with Dates

Total Time : 40 minutes | Serves : 4

Nutrition Info: Per Serving : Calories 298, Fat 14g, Carbs 19g, Protein 17g

INGREDIENTS

2 tbsp olive oil
1 tbsp dates, chopped
1 lb lamb, cubed
1 garlic clove, minced
1 onion, grated
2 tbsp orange juice
Salt and black pepper to taste
1 cup vegetable stock

DIRECTIONS

1. Warm the olive oil in a skillet over medium heat and cook onion and garlic for 5 minutes. Put in lamb and cook for another 5 minutes. Stir in dates, orange juice, salt, pepper, and stock and bring to a boil; cook for 20 minutes. Serve right away.

Rosemary Lamb with Broccoli

Total Time : 1 hour 10 minutes | Serves : 4

Nutrition Info: Per Serving : Calories 350, Fat 16g, Carbs 23g, Protein 24g

INGREDIENTS

- 1 lb lamb meat, roughly cubed
- 2 tbsp olive oil
- 1 garlic clove, minced
- 1 onion, chopped
- 1 tsp rosemary, chopped
- 1 cup vegetable stock
- 2 cups broccoli florets
- 2 tbsp sweet paprika
- Salt and black pepper to taste

DIRECTIONS

1. Warm the olive oil in a skillet over medium heat and cook onion and garlic for 5 minutes. Put in lamb meat and cook for another 5-6 minutes. Stir in rosemary, stock, broccoli, paprika, salt, and pepper and cook for 50 minutes. Serve hot

---

Slow Cooker Pork with Pearl Onions

Total Time : 8 hours 10 minutes | Serves : 4

Nutrition Info: Per Serving : Calories 340, Fat 15g, Carbs 19g, Protein 25g

INGREDIENTS

- 2 lb pork loin, sliced
- 1 lb pearl onions
- 1 tbsp olive oil
- Salt and white pepper to taste
- 1 tsp Italian seasoning
- 1 cup vegetable stock
- 1 tbsp tomato paste
- 2 bay leaves

DIRECTIONS

1. Place pork, olive oil, salt, pepper, pearl onions, Italian seasoning, stock, tomato paste, and bay leaves in your slow cooker. Cover with the lid and cook for 8 hours on Low. Discard the bay leaves and serve.

Slow Cooker Pork & Mushroom Stew

Total Time : 8 hours 10 minutes | Serves : 4

Nutrition Info: Per Serving : Calories 340, Fat 18g, Carbs 13g, Protein 17 g

INGREDIENTS

- 2 lb pork stew meat, cubed
- 1 lb white mushrooms, chopped
- Salt and black pepper to taste
- 2 cups chicken stock
- 2 tbsp olive oil
- 1 carrot, chopped
- 1 yellow onion, chopped
- 2 tbsp thyme, chopped
- 2 garlic cloves, minced
- 2 cups tomatoes, chopped
- ½ cup parsley, chopped

DIRECTIONS

1. Place pork meat, salt, pepper, stock, olive oil, onion, carrot, garlic, mushrooms, and tomatoes in your slow cooker. Cover with the lid and cook for 8 hours on Low. Serve warm topped with parsley.

Saffron Pork with Green Onions

Total Time : 35 minutes | Serves : 4

Nutrition Info: Per Serving : Calories 300, Fat 14g, Carbs 14g, Protein 15g

INGREDIENTS

- 3 tbsp olive oil
- 1 ½ lb pork shoulder, cubed
- 2 garlic cloves, minced
- Salt and black pepper to taste
- ½ cup vegetable stock
- ½ tsp saffron powder
- ¼ tsp cumin, ground
- 4 green onions, sliced

DIRECTIONS

1. Warm the olive oil in a skillet over medium heat and cook garlic, green onions, saffron, and cumin for 5 minutes. Put in pork and cook for another 5 minutes. Stir in salt, pepper, stock, and cumin and bring to a boil. Cook for an additional 15 minutes. Serve immediately.

White Wine Leg of Lamb

Total Time : 2 hours 20 minutes | Serves : 4

Nutrition Info: Per Serving : Calories 320, Fat 13g, Carbs 23g, Protein 15g

INGREDIENTS

- 2 lb leg of lamb, boneless
- 2 tbsp tomato paste
- 2 tbsp yellow mustard
- ½ cup butter
- 2 tbsp basil, chopped
- 2 garlic cloves, minced
- Salt and black pepper to taste
- 1 cup white wine
- ½ cup sour cream

DIRECTIONS

1. Preheat oven to 360 F. Warm butter in a skillet over medium heat. Sear leg of lamb for 10 minutes on all sides. Stir in mustard, basil, tomato paste, garlic, salt, pepper, wine, and sour cream and bake for 2 hours. Serve right away.

Minty Lamb Chops with Bell Peppers

Total Time : 1 hour 40 minutes | Serves : 4

Nutrition Info: Per Serving : Calories 310, Fat 15g, Carbs 17g, Protein 25g

INGREDIENTS

DIRECTIONS

1 lb lamb chops
1 red bell pepper, sliced
1 green bell pepper, sliced
1 yellow bell pepper, sliced
2 tbsp olive oil
2 tbsp fresh oregano, chopped
4 garlic cloves, minced
½ cup chicken stock
Salt and black pepper to taste

1. Preheat oven to 360 F. Warm olive oil in a skillet over medium heat. Sear lamb chops for 8 minutes on both sides. Stir in bell peppers, oregano, garlic, stock, salt, and pepper and bake for 80 minutes. Serve warm.

Baked Lamb Ribs

Total Time : 2 hours 10 minutes | Serves : 4

Nutrition Info: Per Serving : Calories 300, Fat 10g, Carbs 18g, Protein 25g

INGREDIENTS

DIRECTIONS

2 lb lamb ribs
2 garlic cloves, minced
1 onion, chopped
½ cup chicken stock
2 tbsp olive oil
1 tbsp ground fennel seeds

1. Preheat oven to 360 F. Mix garlic, onion, stock, olive oil, lemon juice, fennel seeds, salt, pepper, and lamb ribs in a roasting pan and bake for 2 hours. Serve hot with salad.

Jalapeño Lamb

Total Time : 25 minutes | Serves : 4

Nutrition Info: Per Serving : Calories 320, Fat 13g, Carbs 19g, Protein 18g

INGREDIENTS

DIRECTIONS

1 lb lamb fillets
3 jalapeños, chopped
2 tbsp balsamic vinegar
1 cup mint leaves, chopped
Salt and black pepper to taste
2 tbsp olive oil
1 tbsp sweet paprika

1. Warm half of oil in a skillet over medium heat and sauté jalapeños, balsamic vinegar, mint, salt, pepper, and paprika for 5 minutes. Preheat grill over medium heat. Rub lamb fillets with the remaining oil, salt, and pepper and grill for 6 minutes on both sides. Top with mint vinaigrette and serve.

Cilantro Lamb

Total Time : 8 hours 10 minutes | Serves : 4

Nutrition Info: Per Serving : Calories 360, Fat 16g, Carbs 19g, Protein 16g

INGREDIENTS

- 1 ½ lb lamb shoulder, cubed
- ½ cup chicken stock
- 2 tomatoes, chopped
- 2 garlic cloves, minced
- 1 tbsp cinnamon powder
- Salt and black pepper to taste
- 2 tbsp cilantro, chopped

DIRECTIONS

1. Place lamb, tomatoes, garlic, cinnamon, salt, pepper, chicken stock, and cilantro in your slow cooker. Cover with the lid and cook for 8 hours on Low. Serve immediately.

Spicy Lamb in Peach Sauce

Total Time : 1 hour 10 minutes | Serves : 4

Nutrition Info: Per Serving : Calories 310, Fat 16g, Carbs 17g, Protein 16g

INGREDIENTS

- 1 lb lamb, cubed
- 2 cups Greek yogurt
- 2 peaches, peeled and cubed
- 1 onion, chopped
- 2 tbsp parsley, chopped
- ½ tsp red pepper flakes
- Salt and black pepper to taste
- 2 tbsp olive oil

DIRECTIONS

1. Warm the olive oil in a skillet over medium heat and sear lamb for 5 minutes. Put in onion and cook for another 5 minutes. Stir in yogurt, peaches, parsley, red pepper flakes, salt, pepper, and cinnamon powder and bring to a boil. Cook for 45 minutes. Serve right away.

Bell Pepper Pork Chops

Total Time : 35 minutes | Serves : 4

Nutrition Info: Per Serving : Calories 230, Fat 19g, Carbs 18g, Protein 13g

INGREDIENTS

- 4 pork chops
- 4 bell peppers, chopped
- 1 tsp rosemary, dried
- 2 tsp olive oil
- 2 tbsp wine vinegar
- 2 spring onions, chopped
- ½ green cabbage head, shredded
- Salt and black pepper to taste

DIRECTIONS

1. Warm half of oil in a skillet over medium heat and cook spring onions for 3 minutes. Stir in vinegar, cabbage, sweet peppers, salt, and pepper, and simmer for 10 minutes. Turn the heat off.
2. Preheat the grill over medium heat. Sprinkle pork chops with remaining oil, salt, pepper, and rosemary and grill for 10 minutes on both sides. Share chops into plates with cabbage mixture on the side. Serve immediately.

Lamb with Eggplants

Total Time : 1 hour 10 minutes | Serves : 4

Nutrition Info: Per Serving : Calories 310, Fat 19g, Carbs 23g, Protein 15g

INGREDIENTS

- 1 cup chicken stock
- 1 ½ lb lamb meat, cubed
- 2 eggplants, cubed
- 2 tbsp olive oil
- 2 onions, chopped
- 2 tbsp tomato paste
- 2 tbsp parsley, chopped
- 4 garlic cloves, mince d

DIRECTIONS

1. Warm the olive oil in a skillet over medium heat and cook onions and garlic for 4 minutes. Put in lamb and cook for 6 minutes. Stir in eggplants, bell pepper, and tomato paste for 5 minutes. Pour in stock and bring to a boil. Cook for another 50 minutes, stirring often. Serve garnished with parsley.

Moroccan Lamb Stew

Total Time : 1 hour 20 minutes | Serves : 4

Nutrition Info: Per Serving : Calories 420, Fat 18g, Carbs 26g, Protein 35g

INGREDIENTS

- 3 tbsp olive oil
- 2 lb lamb shoulder, cubed
- Salt and black pepper to taste
- 1 onion, chopped
- 2 garlic cloves, minced
- 3 tomatoes, grated
- 1 tsp red chili flakes
- 2 cups chicken stock
- 1 cup couscous
- ¾ cup green olives, pitted and sliced
- 1 tbsp cilantro, chopped

DIRECTIONS

1. Warm the olive oil in a pot over medium heat and cook lamb for 5 minutes until brown, stirring often. Add in onion and garlic and cook for another 5 minutes. Stir in tomatoes, salt, pepper, chicken stock, olives, and red chili flakes. Bring to a boil and simmer for 1 hour. Cover the couscous with boiling water in a bowl, cover, and let sit for 4-5 minutes until the water has been absorbed. Fluff with a fork and season with salt and pepper. Pour the stew over, scatter with cilantro and serve.

Beef & Mushroom Stew

Total Time : 60 minutes | Serves : 4

Nutrition Info: Per Serving : Calories 230, Fat 9g, Carbs 35g, Protein 9g

INGREDIENTS

2 tbsp olive oil
2 tbsp tomato paste
1 ½ lb beef meat, cubed
1 carrot, chopped
2 garlic cloves, chopped
1 large onion, chopped
2 cups beef stock
1 tsp thyme, chopped
2 bay leaves
1 lb cremini mushrooms, sliced
1 oz dried button mushrooms
Salt and black pepper to taste

DIRECTIONS

1. Soak the button mushrooms in water for 10 minutes. Warm the olive oil in a pot over medium heat. Season the beef with salt and pepper and cook for 5 minutes, stirring often.
2. Add in onion and garlic and cook for another 3 minutes. Stir in carrot, tomato paste, thyme, bay leaves, and mushrooms. for 5 minutes. Pour in the button mushrooms with the water, beef stock, and tomatoes and simmer for 40 minutes. Adjust the seasoning and serve right away.

Grilled Beef Meatballs

Total Time : 25 minutes | Serves : 4

Nutrition Info: Per Serving : Calories 240, Fat 15g, Carbs 17g, Protein 13g

INGREDIENTS

1 lb ground beef meat
1 onion, chopped
3 tbsp cilantro, chopped
1 garlic clove, minced
Salt and black pepper to taste
2 tbsp olive oil

DIRECTIONS

1. Combine beef, onion, cilantro, garlic, salt, and pepper in a bowl and form meatballs out of the mixture. Sprinkle with oil. Preheat the grill over medium heat and grill them for 14 minutes on all sides. Serve with salad.

Pork Stew with Apricots

Total Time : 50 minutes | Serves : 4

Nutrition Info: Per Serving : Calories 320, Fat 17g, Carbs 22g, Protein 35g

INGREDIENTS

- 1 ½ lb pork stew meat, roughly cubed
- 3 tbsp olive oil
- Salt and black pepper to taste
- 1 cup red onions, chopped
- 1 cup apricots, dried and chopped
- 2 garlic cloves, minced
- 1 cup canned tomatoes, crushed
- 2 tbsp parsley, chopped

DIRECTIONS

1. Warm olive oil in a skillet over medium heat. Sear pork meat for 5 minutes. Put in onions and cook for another 5 minutes. Stir in salt, pepper, apricots, garlic, tomatoes, and parsley and bring to a simmer and cook for an additional 30 minutes.

Lamb & Fig Stew

Total Time : 1 hour 55 minutes | Serves : 4

Nutrition Info: Per Serving : Calories 360, Fat 15g, Carbs 23g, Protein 16 g

INGREDIENTS

- 3 tbsp olive oil
- ½ cup mint leaves, chopped
- Salt and black pepper to taste
- 1 ½ lb stewing lamb, cubed
- 1 carrot, chopped
- 1 onion, chopped
- 1 celery rib, chopped
- 14 oz canned tomatoes, crushed
- 1 garlic clove, minced
- 1 cup dried figs, chopped
- 6 tbsp Greek yogurt

DIRECTIONS

1. Warm 2 tbsp of oil in a pot over medium heat and cook lamb for 5 minutes until brownes, stirring occasionally. Stir in carrot, onion, celery, and garlic for another 5 minutes. Pour in tomatoes, figs, and 2 cups of water. Season with salt and pepper and bring to a boil. Reduce the heat and simmer for 90 minutes. Serve topped with yogurt.

Parsley Pork with Olives & Capers

Total Time : 30 minutes | Serves : 4

Nutrition Info: Per Serving : Calories 260, Fat 13g, Carbs 22g, Protein 14g

INGREDIENTS

- 2 lb pork loin, sliced
- 4 garlic cloves, minced
- 1 cup green olives, pitted and halved
- 1 tbsp capers
- 2 tbsp olive oil
- ½ cup tomato puree
- Salt and black pepper to taste
- 2 tbsp parsley, chopped
- Salt and black pepper to taste
- Juice of 1 lime

DIRECTIONS

1. Warm the olive oil in a skillet over medium heat and cook garlic and pork for 5 minutes. Stir in green olives, capers, tomato purée, salt, pepper, cilantro, and lime juice and bring to a simmer. Cook for another 15 minutes. Serve immediately

Creamy Pork with Green Sauce

Total Time : 30 minutes | Serves : 4

Nutrition Info: Per Serving : Calories 280, Fat 12g, Carbs 21g, Protein 19g

INGREDIENTS

1 lb pork stew meat, cubed
½ cup olive oil
1 tbsp walnuts, chopped
2 tbsp cilantro, chopped
2 tbsp basil, chopped
2 garlic cloves, minced
Salt and black pepper to taste
2 cups Greek yogurt

DIRECTIONS

1. In a food processor, blend cilantro, basil, garlic, walnuts, yogurt, salt, pepper, and half of the oil until smooth.
2. Warm the remaining oil in a skillet over medium heat. Brown pork meat for 5 minutes. Pour parsley sauce over meat and bring to a boil. Cook for another 15 minutes. Serve right away.

Saucy Dill Pork

Total Time : 30 minutes | Serves : 4

Nutrition Info: Per Serving : Calories 330, Fat 15g, Carbs 15g, Protein 18g

INGREDIENTS

1 lb pork tenderloin, sliced
2 tbsp olive oil
Salt and black pepper to taste
3 tbsp ground caraway seeds
1/3 cup half-and-half
½ cup dill, chopped

DIRECTIONS

1. Warm the olive oil in a skillet over medium heat and sear pork for 8 minutes on all sides. Stir in salt, pepper, ground caraway seeds, half-and-half, and dill and bring to a boil. Cook for another 12 minutes. Serve warm.

Simple Pork Stew

Total Time : 50 minutes | Serves : 4

Nutrition Info: Per Serving : Calories 360, Fat 24g, Carbs 18g, Protein 25g

INGREDIENTS

2 tbsp olive oil
1 red onion, chopped
2 garlic cloves, minced
2 lb ground pork
2 tbsp milk
¼ cup Colby cheese, grated
1 egg, whisked
1/3 cup black olives, pitted and chopped
2 tbsp oregano, chopped
Salt and black pepper to taste

DIRECTIONS

1. Warm the olive oil in a pot over medium heat and cook pork meat for 5 minutes until brown, stirring occasionally. Add in shallots and garlic and cook for an additional 3 minutes. Stir in beef stock, paprika, thyme, coriander seeds, salt, and pepper and bring to a boil; cook for 30 minutes. Serve warm.

Cheesy Pork Meatloaf

Total Time : 1 hour 30 minutes | Serves : 6

Nutrition Info: Per Serving : Calories 471; Fats 33.8g; Carbs 18.9g; Protein 18.8g

INGREDIENTS

1 ½ lb pork loin
1/2 tbsp oregano, chopped
1 garlic clove, minced
1 tbsp onion, minced
2 tbsp milk
1 cup Corby cheese
1 Egg
Salt and black pepper to taste
½ cup Olives, chopped

DIRECTIONS

1. Preheat oven to 360 F. Combine, onion, garlic, pork, milk, Colby cheese, egg, olives, oregano, salt, and pepper in a bowl and form a meatloaf. Transfer to the pan and bake for 80 minutes. Serve sliced.

Pork with Capers & Ricotta

Total Time : 1 hour 10 minutes | Serves : 4

Nutrition Info: Per Serving : Calories 310, Fat 15g, Carbs 17g, Protein 34g

INGREDIENTS

1 ½ lb pork loin, cubed
2 tbsp marjoram, chopped
1 garlic clove, minced
1 tbsp capers, drained
2 tbsp olive oil
1 cup chicken stock
Salt and black pepper to taste
½ cup ricotta cheese, crumbled

DIRECTIONS

1. Warm the olive oil in a skillet over medium heat and sear pork for 5 minutes. Stir in marjoram, garlic, capers, stock, salt, and pepper and bring to a boil. Cook for 30 minutes. Mix in cheese and serve.

Braised Beef & Vegetable Stew

Total Time : 8 hours 10 minutes | Serves : 4

Nutrition Info: Per Serving : Calories 370, Fat 17g, Carbs 28g, Protein 35g

INGREDIENTS

2 tbsp canola oil
2 lb beef stew meat, cubed
Salt and black pepper to taste
2 cups beef stock
2 shallots, chopped
2 tbsp thyme, chopped
2 garlic cloves, minced
1 carrot, chopped
3 celery stalks, chopped
28 oz canned tomatoes, crushed
2 tbsp parsley, chopped

DIRECTIONS

1. Place the beef meat, salt, pepper, beef stock, olive oil, shallots, thyme, garlic, carrot, celery, and tomatoes in your slow cooker. Put the lid and cook for 8 hours on Low. Sprinkle with parsley and serve warm.

Chili Beef with Zucchini

Total Time : 20 minutes | Serves : 4

Nutrition Info: Per Serving : Calories 360, Fat 12g, Carbs 26g, Protein 37g

INGREDIENTS

2 tbsp olive oil
1 lb beef steaks, sliced
2 zucchinis, spiralized
½ cup sweet chili sauce
1 cup carrot, grated
3 tbsp water
1 tbsp chives, chopped
Salt and black pepper to taste

DIRECTIONS

1. Warm the olive oil in a skillet over medium heat and brown beef steaks for 8 minutes on both side; set aside and cover with foil to keep warm. Stir zucchini noodles, chili sauce, carrot, water, salt, and pepper and cook for an additional 3-4 minutes. Remove the foil form the steaks and pour the zucchini mix over to serve.

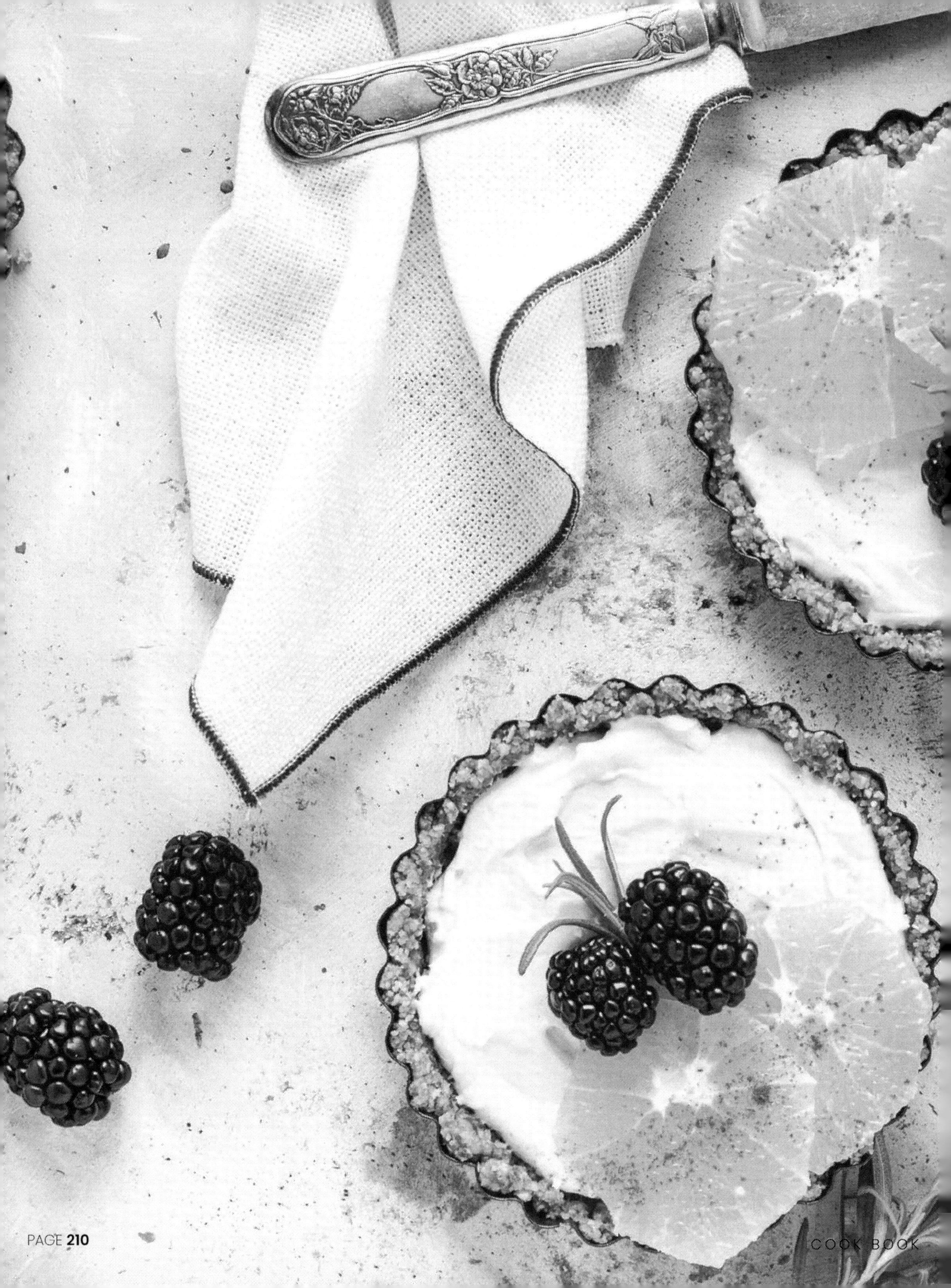

DESSERTS & SNACKS

COOK BOOK

PAGE **211**

Apple Tart

Ready in 25 minutes |Servings 8 |Difficulty: Hard

Nutrition Info:Calories 182, fat 5mg, fiber 4mg, carb 15mg, protein 5mg

INGREDIENTS

Four apples, cored, diced, and trimmed
1/4 cup of natural juice for apples
Cranberries for 1/2 cup, dried
Two spoonfuls of cornstarch
Two teaspoons of sugar coconut
Extract 1 teaspoon of vanilla
1/4 teaspoon of dried cinnamon
Concerning the crust:
One and a quarter cup of whole wheat flour
Two teaspoons sugar
Coconut oil for Three teaspoons, melted
1/4 cup of ice water

DIRECTIONS

1. Integrate the cranberries with the apple juice in a cup.
2. Integrate the apples with the cornstarch in another pan, swirl, and apply the cranberry mixture.
3. Mix it all up, add vanilla and cinnamon, then mix it all up again.
4. Sift the flour with the sugar, oil, and chilled water in a different bowl and stir until the dough is finished.
5. Move the dough, flatten well, roll into a circle and move to a pastry pan to a surface of the workpiece.
6. Push the crust well into the pan, pour the mixture of apples over the crust, place it in the oven, cook for 25 minutes at 375 ° lower the temperature, slice, and serve.

Fresh Parfait

Ready in 10 minutes |Servings 6 |Difficulty: Easy

Nutrition Info: Calories 200, fat 3g, fiber 4mg, carbs 15mg, protein 10mg

INGREDIENTS

Four cups of yogurt that is non-fat
Stevia, Three tbsp
Two tablespoons of juice with lime
Two lime zest teaspoons, grind
Four grapefruits, chopped and peeled
Cut 1 tablespoon of spice

DIRECTIONS

1. 1. Mix the yogurtwith the stevia, lime juice, lime zest, and mint in a bowl and blend.
2. 2. Split the grapefruits into small cups, add each one to the yogurtmix and serve.

Delicious Peach Pie

Ready in 10 minutes |Servings 4|Difficulty: Normal

Nutrition Info: Calories 199, fat 4mg, fiber 3g, carbs 12mg, protein 9mg

INGREDIENTS

Two peaches, peeled and sliced
½ cup raspberries
½ teaspoon coconut sugar
Three eggs, whisked
Avocado Oil, 1 tablespoon
½ cup almond milk
½ cup whole flour
¼ Cup non-fat yogurt

DIRECTIONS

1. 1. In a container, comb the peaches with sugar and raspberries.
2. 2. In another container, mix the eggs with milk and flour and whisk.
3. 3. Grease a pie pan with the oil, insert eggs paste, then peaches mix, scatter, bake in the oven at 400 degrees F for twenty minutes, slice and serve.

Simple Brownies

Ready in 30 minutes| Servings 8|Difficulty: Normal

Nutrition Info: Calories 144, fat 4mg, fiber 4mg, carbs 9mg, protein 8mg

INGREDIENTS

Dark chocolate Six ounces, diced
Four Egg Whites
1/2 Cup of Hot Water
Extract 1 tsp of vanilla
2/3 cup sugar for coconut
One and 1/2 entire cups of flour
1/2 cup of sliced walnuts
Cooking spray
1 tsp powder for baking

DIRECTIONS

Directions:

1. Integrate the chocolate and the hot water in a cup and shake together very well.

2. Apply the vanilla extract and the whites of the egg and stir again good.

3. Integrate the sugar with the flour, baking powder, and walnuts in another pan. Mix.

4. Combine two blends, mix properly, place into a cooking spray-greased cake tin, spread well, bake for 30 minutes in the oven, cool it down, cut, and serve.

Easy Chocolate Cake

Total Time : 25 minutes | Serves : 4

Nutrition Info: Calories 200, fat 4g, fiber 2mg, carbs 12mg, protein 6mg

INGREDIENTS

Three cups of a grain of whole wheat
One Cup of sugar from coconut
Extract 1 tablespoon of vanilla
Three tbsp of powdered cocoa
Vinegar for 2 tbsp
Two and 1/2 teaspoons of soda for baking
Hot water two cups
1/2 cup of molten coconut oil

DIRECTIONS

1. Mix the flour with the baking soda, sugar, flour, and cocoa powder in a pan. Mix.
2. Place this in a frying pan, add the vanilla extract in one, the oil in the other, and the vinegar in the last one, leaving three holes in this mixture.
3. Add water from the bowl over the mixture, swirl it all for two minutes, put it in the oven at 350 ° F, bake for 25 minutes, chill the cake, slice and serve.

Apple Pancakes

Ready in 10 minutes |Servings 4 |Difficulty: Normal

Nutrition Info: Calories 232, fat 4g, fiber 6mg, carbs 12mg, protein 4mg

INGREDIENTS

1/2 cup of flour for brown rice
1/2 cup of flour for sweet rice
1/4 cup of flour for almonds
1 tsp of soda for baking
1 tsp powder for baking
Flaxseeds with two teaspoons
1/2 cinnamon teaspoon powder
Two teaspoons of sugar of maple
1/2 cup of apple sauce in raw form
1/4 Cup of Water
Cooking Spray
Two apples, cored, sliced, and trimmed

DIRECTIONS

1. Integrate almond flour, sweet rice flour, baking soda, baking powder, flaxseeds, sugar, maple syrup, apple sauce, water, and apples in a cup, and stir thoroughly.
2. Warm a pan over medium-high heat, cooking spray grease, drop some of the batter, spread, bake the pancake on all sides until crispy, and move to a tray.
3. Repeat with the remainder of the batter and deliver the warm pancakes

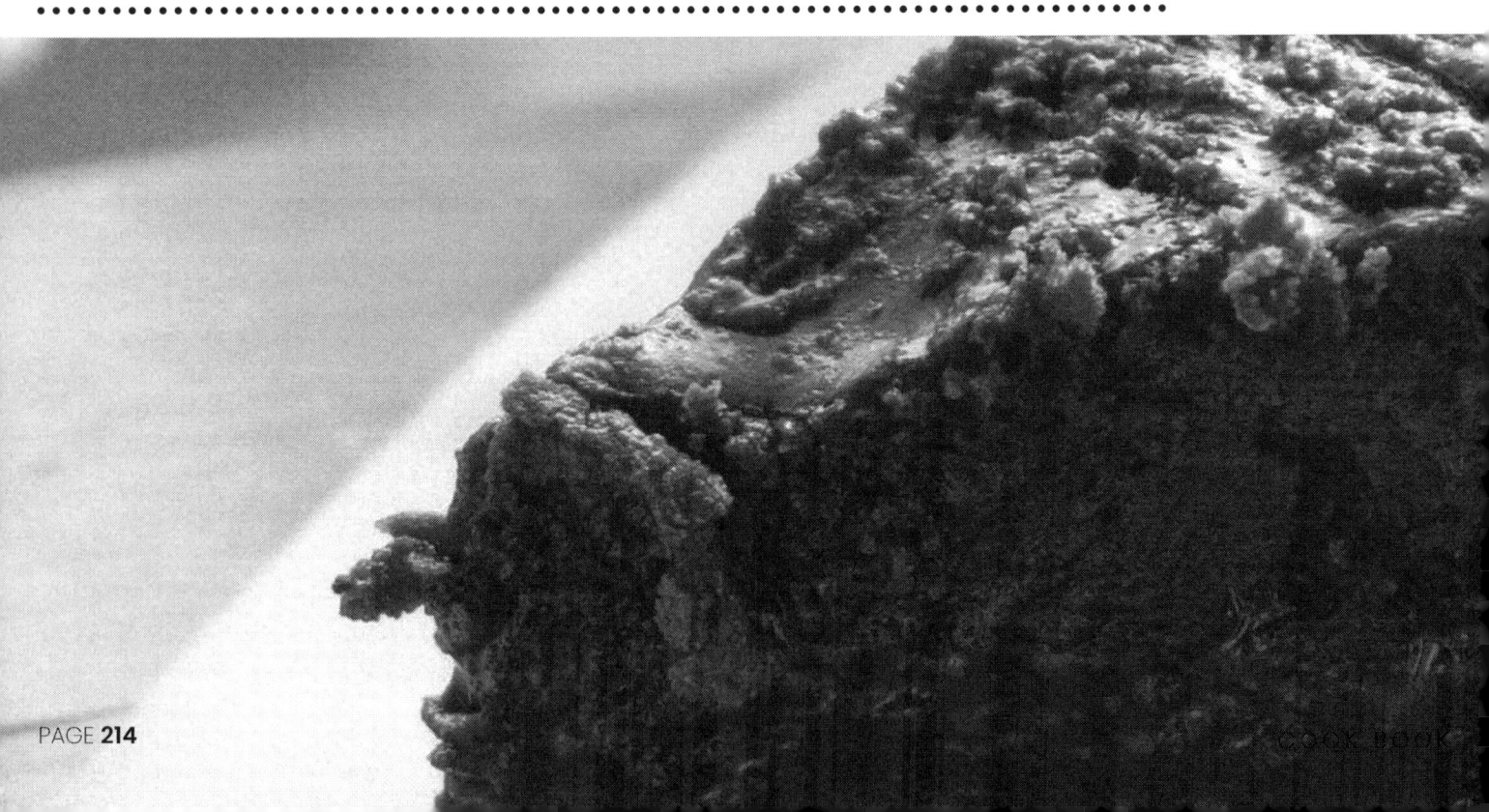

Easy Fudge

Ready in 2 hours |Servings 12 |Difficulty: Normal

Nutrition Info: Calories 154, fat 5g, fiber 5, carbs 16mg, protein 3mg

INGREDIENTS

One cup milk that is non-fat
1/2 cup butter with low-fat content
Two cups of sugar coconut
Dark chocolate 12 ounces, sliced
Extract one teaspoon of vanilla

DIRECTIONS

1. 1. Heat the milk in a pan over medium heat, add the sugar and butter, stir and simmer for seven minutes.
2. 2. Take the heat off, insert the chocolate, and swirl it all together.
3. 3. Layer properly, hold in the fridge for 2 hours, slice into little squares, and serve. Pour this into a lined square pan.

Black Bean Brownies

Ready in 20 minutes |Servings 12 |Difficulty: Easy

Nutrition Info: Calories 200, fat 3g, fiber 3g, carbs 14mg, protein 4mg

INGREDIENTS

One and 1/2 cups of dried, no-salt-added, washed and soaked black beans
Rinsed, rinsed
Two teaspoons of sugar from coconut
1/2 Cup Quick Oats
Two spoonfuls of cocoa powder
1/3 cup of sugar of maple
1/4 cup of molten coconut oil
1/2 teaspoon powder for baking
2 tsp extract of vanilla
Cooking Spray

DIRECTIONS

1. Integrate the black beans with the coconut sugar, oats, oil, baking powder, cocoa powder, maple syrup, and vanilla extract in your mixing bowl and process properly.

2. Grease a square pan with a cooking spray, apply the mix of black beans, scatter, put in the oven, bake for twenty minutes at 350 º F, leave to cool, cut, and serve.

Banana Cake

Ready in 25 minutes| Servings 8 |Difficulty: Easy

Nutrition Info: Calories 197, fat 5g, fiber 6g, carbs 13mg, protein 2mg

INGREDIENTS

Two cups of the grain of whole wheat
1/4 cup powdered cocoa
One banana, smashed and trimmed
1/2 teaspoon of soda for baking
1/2 cup sugar for coconut
3/4 cup of milk with almonds
1/4 cup of molten coconut oil
One single egg
One white egg
Extract 1 teaspoon of vanilla
One tablespoon of juice from a lemon
Cooking Spray

DIRECTIONS

1. Mix the flour with the cocoa powder, baking soda, and sugar in a pan. Mix.
2. Apply the banana, milk, oil, egg, white egg, vanilla, and lemon juice and blend well.
3. Grease the baking spray on a cake pan, put in the cake mix, scatter, bake for 25 minutes in the oven at 350 º F, cool it down, cut, and serve.

Chocolate Pudding

Ready in 10 minutes |Servings 4 |Difficulty: Easy

Nutrition Info: Calories 182, fat 5g, fiber 3g, carbs 16mg, protein 6mg

INGREDIENTS

Two tablespoons of sugar from coconut
Three spoonfuls of cornstarch
Two spoonfuls of cocoa powder
Two cups of milk with almonds
Chocolate chips in 1/3 cup, unsweetened
1/2 teaspoon extract of vanilla

DIRECTIONS

1. Place the cornstarch in a frying pan, stir in the chocolate, sugar, and milk, stir well, and flame for five minutes over moderate flame.
2. Take it off the oven, apply chips of vanilla and chocolate, swirl well, spill into small cups, and serve cold.

Coconut Mousse

Ready in 10 minutes | Servings 12 |Difficulty: Easy

Nutrition Info: Calories 152, fat 5g, fiber 1mg, carbs 11mg, protein 3mg

INGREDIENTS

Two and 3/4 of a cup of coconut milk
1 tsp extract of coconut
Retrieve 1 teaspoon of vanilla
Four teaspoons of sugar from coconut
Toasted 1 cup of coconut,

DIRECTIONS

1. Integrate the coconut milk with the juice of coconut, vanilla extract, coconut, and sugar in a bowl, stir well, split into small cups and serve cold.

Mango Pudding

Ready in 50 minutes| Servings 4 |Difficulty: Normal

Nutrition Info: Calories 251, fat 3g, fiber 4mg, carbs 16mg, protein 7mg

INGREDIENTS

- One Cup of rice brown
- Water, 2 cups
- One mango, diced and peeled
- One Cup of milk with coconut
- Two spoonfuls of sugar from coconut
- Extract 1 teaspoon of vanilla
- 1/2 tsp cinnamon powder

DIRECTIONS

1. Place the water in a pot and put it over a moderate flame to a boil.
2. Include the rice, mix and cover the pan, then simmer for 40 minutes.
3. Add the milk, sugar, cocoa, cinnamon, and mango, mix, cap again, simmer for an additional ten minutes, split into bowls and serve.

Rhubarb Pie

Ready in 10 minutes |Servings 12 |Difficulty: Easy

Nutrition Info: Calories 162, fat 5g, fiber 5mg, carbs 15mg, protein 6g

INGREDIENTS

- Two cups of the grain of whole wheat
- One Cup of butter low in fat, melted
- One Cup of sliced pecans
- One and a fifth of a cup of coconut sugar
- Rhubarb Four cups, diced
- One Cup of sliced strawberries
- Low-fat Eight ounces of cream cheese

DIRECTIONS

1. Combine the flour with the butter, pecans, and 1/4 cup of sugar in a bowl and mix well.
2. Move this to a pie plate, press tightly into the plate, put it in the oven, and bake for 20 minutes at 350-degree Fahrenheit
3. Integrate the strawberries with the rhubarb, cream cheese, and One Cup of sugar in a saucepan, mix well and simmer for four minutes over moderate flame.
4. Put this over the crust of the pie and hold it for a few hours in the fridge before slicing and serve.

Fruit Skewers

Ready in 10 minutes|Servings: 10|Difficulty: Normal

Nutrition Info: Calories 76, fat 1g, fiber 1mg, carbs 10mg, protein 2mg

INGREDIENTS

DIRECTIONS

Five strawberries, sliced in half
1/4 melon, cubed,
Two bananas, chopped into bits
1 apple, cored and chopped into bits

1. Thread cherry, cantaloupe, bananas & apple onto skewers alternately and serve cold.

Berries Mix

Ready in 10 minutes |Servings: 6|Difficulty: Easy

Nutrition Info: Calories 120g, fat 2mg, fiber 3mg, carbs 4mg, protein 4g

INGREDIENTS

DIRECTIONS

Two Lemon Juice Teaspoons
1 lb. of blackberries
Strawberries for 1 pound
Four teaspoons of sugar from coconut

1. Mix the strawberries with the blackberries and sugar in a saucepan, mix, bring to the boil over moderate flame and simmer for ten minutes.
2. Split it into cups and serve it cold.

Blueberry Compote

Ready in 10 minutes |Servings: 6|Difficulty: Easy

Nutrition Info: Calories 120, fat 2g, fiber 3mg, carbs 6mg, protein 9mg

INGREDIENTS

DIRECTIONS

Coconut sugar, Five tbsp
1-ounce of orange juice
Blueberries for 1 pound

1. Integrate the orange juice and blueberry sugar in a bowl, swirl, bring to the boil over a moderate flame, simmer for fifteen minutes, split into bowls and serve cold.

Summer Strawberry Stew

Ready in 10 minutes |Servings: 6 | Difficulty: Easy

Nutrition Info: Calories 160, fat 2mg, fiber 2mg, carbs 6mg, Protein 6g

INGREDIENTS

DIRECTIONS

Sixteen ounces of strawberries, sliced in half
Two spoonfuls of water
Two tablespoons of sugar from coconut
Lemon juice 2 tbsp
Two spoonfuls of cornstarch
1/4 teaspoon extract of almonds

1. 1. Integrate the strawberries with the lemon juice, water, sugar, cornstarch, and almond concentrate in a saucepan, swirl properly, simmer for ten minutes over a moderate flame, split into bowls and serve.

Lemon Apple Mix

Ready in 10 minutes |Servings: 6 | Difficulty:

Nutrition Info: Calories 210, fat 4mg, fiber 3mg, carbs 8mg, Protein 5g

INGREDIENTS

DIRECTIONS

Six apples, cored and diced roughly
Four teaspoons of sugar from coconut
Two teaspoons extract of vanilla
Two Lemon Juice Teaspoons
Two tsp cinnamon powder

1. 1. Integrate the apples with the sugar, vanilla, lemon juice, and cinnamon in a tiny skillet, swirl, fire over a moderate flame, simmer for around 10-15 minutes, split into small plates of dessert and serve.

Minty Rhubarb Drink

Ready in 10 minutes |Servings: 4| Difficulty: Easy

Nutrition Info: Calories 160, fat 2g, fiber 4mg, carbs 8mg, protein 5mg

INGREDIENTS

1/3 of a cup of water
Rhubarb, two pounds, finely chopped
Three teaspoons of sugar from coconut
Sliced one tablespoon of mint

DIRECTIONS

1. 1. In a shallow dish, place the water, heat it over a moderate flame, add the sugar, and whisk well.
2. 2. Add the rhubarb and combine, mix, fry, split into bowls and serve for ten minutes.

Nigella Mango Sweet Mix

Ready in 10 minutes |Servings: 8|Difficulty: Normal

Nutrition Info: Calories 160, fat 3g, fiber 4g, carbs 8g, Protein 3g

INGREDIENTS

One and 1/2 pounds of peeled and cubed mango
One teaspoon seeds of nigella
Three tablespoons of sugar from coconut
1/2 cup of cider vinegar for apples
1tsp cinnamon powder

DIRECTIONS

1. Incorporate the mango, sugar, vinegar, and cinnamon in a small pot with the nigella seeds, swirl, bring to a boil over a moderate flame, cook for 10 minutes, split into bowls and serve.

Blueberry Curd

Ready in 10 minutes | Servings: 4|Difficulty: Normal

Nutrition Info: Calories 201, fat 3g, fiber 2g, carbs 6mg, protein 3mg

INGREDIENTS

Lemon juice 2 tbsp
2 tablespoons of molten coconut oil
3 teaspoons of sugar from coconut
Blueberries, 12 ounces
Two eggs

DIRECTIONS

1. Put the oil in a saucepan, heat over medium heat, add the coconut sugar and lemon juice and whisk well.
2. Attach the eggs and the blueberries, whisk well, simmer for 10 minutes, break into small cups, then eat cold.

Lemon & Coconut Cream

Ready in 10 minutes | Servings: 4|Difficulty: Normal

Nutrition Info: Calories 161, fat 3mg, fiber 5mg, carbs 6mg, protein 4g

INGREDIENTS

- Three cups of coconut milk
- Juice containing 2 lemons
- Two lemons with lemon zest, grated
- 1/2 cup of sugar of maple
- Coconut oil for 3 teaspoons
- 1 single egg
- 2 teaspoons of gelatin
- 1 cup of water

DIRECTIONS

1. Comb coconut milk with lemon juice, maple syrup, lemon zest, coconut oil, egg, and gelatin in your blender, and spin very well.
2. Split and seal them into tiny holes.
3. Place the jars in a tub, add water, place them in the pan and cook for fifteen minutes at 380 degrees F.
4. Serve cold with the sauce.

Almond Peach Mix

Ready in 10 minutes |Servings: 4|Difficulty: Easy

Nutrition Info: Calories 161, fat 3g, fiber 3g, carbs 7g, protein 5g

INGREDIENTS

- Four Cups of Water
- 1 chopped peach
- 2 cups of oats rolled
- Extract 1 teaspoon of vanilla
- Two teaspoons of flaxseed meal
- 1/2 cup chopped almonds

DIRECTIONS

1. Incorporate the oats, almonds vanilla extract, flaxseed meal, and peach with the water in a saucepan, mix, bring to a boil over a moderate flame, cook for ten minutes, split into bowls and serve.

Fruits Stew

Ready in 10 minutes | Servings: 4|Difficulty:Normal

Nutrition Info: Calories 142, fat 4g, fiber 4g, carbs 14mg, protein 7mg

INGREDIENTS

DIRECTIONS

One strawberry, diced and pitted
1 pear, diced and cored
One apple, cored and sliced
Two tbsp of sugar coconut
1/4 of a cup of coconut, shredded
1/2 cinnamon teaspoon powder
Coconut oil for 3 teaspoons, melted
1/4 cup of minced pecans

1. Mix the oil with the coconut, cinnamon, and sugar in a saucepan, whisk and cook over medium heat.
2. Whisk in the plum, pear, apple, and pecans, whisk, simmer for 8 minutes, split into bowls and serve cold.

Easy Pomegranate Mix

Ready in 10 minutes | Servings: 2|Difficulty: Easy

Nutrition Info: Calories 172, fat 4g, fiber 5mg, carbs 10mg, protein 5mg

INGREDIENTS

DIRECTIONS

1 cup of oats cut from steel
Two cups of pomegranate juice
Pomegranate Seeds of 1

1. Integrate the pomegranate juice with the pomegranate seeds and the oats in a shallow dish, flip, cook for 5 minutes over a moderate flame, split into bowls, and serve cold.

Black Rice Pudding

Ready in 10 minutes | Servings: 4|Difficulty: Easy

Nutrition Info: Calories 220, fat 4g, fiber 4mg, carbs 10mg, protein 6mg

INGREDIENTS

DIRECTIONS

The 6 and 1/2 cups of water
1 cup of sugar from coconut
2 cups of washed and rinsed black rice
2 cinnamon powder teaspoons
1/2 cup of shredded coconut

1. Place the water in a saucepan. Warm over medium-high heat, add sugar, rice & coconut, whisk, bring to a boil, lower the heat to mild and cook for 20 minutes. Sprinkle with cinnamon, turn, separate into bowls and serve cold.

Peach Stew

Ready in 10 minutes | Servings: 6|Difficulty: Easy

Nutrition Info: Calories 142, fat 1mg, fiber 2mg, carbs 7mg, protein 2mg

INGREDIENTS	DIRECTIONS

Peaches with five cups, sliced and cut into cubes
Three tbsp of sugar from coconut
1 ginger teaspoon, grated
Water for 2 cups

1. Integrate the peaches with the sugar, ginger, and water in a bowl, toss, bring to a boil over a moderate flame, simmer for ten minutes, split into bowls, and chill.

Coconut Cream

Ready in 1-hour |Servings: 4|Difficulty:

Nutrition Info: Calories 130, fat 5mg, fiber 2mg, carbs 8mg, protein 6mg

INGREDIENTS	DIRECTIONS

Two cups of milk of coconut
One cinnamon powder teaspoon
Three eggs, whisked
Coconut sugar for Five teaspoons
1 lemon zest, grind

1. Incorporate the milk with cinnamon, eggs, sugar, and lemon zest in a shallow saucepan, stir well, boil for ten minutes over a moderate flame, split into ramekins and hold in the refrigerator for 1 hour before eating.

Strawberries and Avocado Salad

Ready in 5 minutes |Servings: 2|Difficulty: Easy

Nutrition Info: Calories 150, fat 4g, fiber 4mg carbs 8mg, protein 6mg

INGREDIENTS

DIRECTIONS

1 banana, sliced and peeled
2 cups of strawberries, sliced in half
Mint 3 tablespoons, chopped
Pitted and peeled 2 avocados

1. Mix the banana and the strawberries, mint, and avocados in a mug, mix, and eat cold.

Blueberry Cream

Ready in 5 minutes | Servings: 1|Difficulty: Normal

Nutrition Info: Calories 120, fat 3mg, fiber 3mg, carbs 6mg, protein 7g

INGREDIENTS

DIRECTIONS

Cup of 3/4 blueberries
1 tbsp low-fat butter peanut
3/4 cup of milk with almonds
1 mashed banana
Two Dates

1. Mix the blueberries with peanut butter, cream, banana, and dates in a blender, process properly, split into small cups and serve cold.

Apple Coconut Cupcakes

Ready in 10 minutes| Servings: 12|Difficulty: Hard

Nutrition Info: Calories 200, fat 4mg, fiber 4mg, carbs 12mg, protein 5mg

INGREDIENTS

DIRECTIONS

Four spoonfuls of coconut butter
1/2 cup of Applesauce Regular
Four eggs
Extract 1 teaspoon of vanilla
3/4 cup of flour with almonds
Two teaspoons cinnamon powder
1/2 teaspoon powder for baking
One apple, cut and cored

1. Heat a skillet over medium heat with butter, insert applesauce, vanilla, and eggs, mix, heat for two minutes, remove heat, cool, incorporate almond flour, baking powder & cinnamon, mix, partition into a lined cupcake pan, put it at 350 degrees F in the oven and bake for twenty minutes.

2. Split between dessert plates and cover with apple slices. Leaving the cupcakes to cool off.

Cinnamon Apples

Ready in 10 minutes |Servings: 4|Difficulty: Normal

Nutrition Info: Calories 200, fat 3g, fiber 4mg, carbs 8mg, protein 5mg

INGREDIENTS

Four big, cored apples
Four tbsp of grapes
1 tablespoon ground cinnamon

DIRECTIONS

1. 1. Stir with the cinnamon, pack the apples with the raisins, organize them in a casserole tray and put them in the oven at 375 Degrees F, twenty minutes to bake, and serve cold.

Pumpkin Bars

Ready in 15 minutes| Servings: 14|Difficulty: Hard

Nutrition Info: Calories 210, fat 2g, fiber 4mg, carbs 7mg, protein 8mg

INGREDIENTS

Two and 1/2 cups of flour with almonds
1/2 tsp of soda for baking
1 tbsp of flaxseed meal
Water, 3 tablespoons
1/2 cup of flesh from pumpkin, minced
1/4 cup sugar for coconut
Two spoonfuls of coconut butter
Extract 1 teaspoon of vanilla

DIRECTIONS

1. Mix the flaxseeds in a dish of water and whisk.
2. Sift the flour, baking soda, flaxseed meal, pumpkin, coconut sugar, coconut butter, and vanilla in another cup, combine tightly, scatter on a baking tray, push excellently, cook for 15 minutes in the oven at 350 º F, leave to cool, slice into bars and serve.

Cold Cashew and Berry Cake

Ready in 5 hours | Servings: 6 | Difficulty: Hard

Nutrition Info: Calories 230, fat 4g, fiber 4mg, carbs 12mg, protein 8mg

INGREDIENTS

Concerning the crust:
1/2 cups of apples, bruised
1 spoonful of water
½ teaspoon vanilla
1/2 cup sliced almonds
For the cake:
Two and 1/2 cups of cashew soaked and drained overnight
1 blackberry cup
3/4 cup of sugar of maple
1 tbsp of molten coconut oil

DIRECTIONS

1. Comb dates with water, vanilla, and almonds in your mixing bowl, pulsate well, move this to a working surface, straighten it and press on the bottom of a circular plate.
2. Comb maple syrup with coconut oil, cashews, and blackberries in your mixer, blend properly, scatter uniformly over the crust, store for 5 hours in the fridge, slice, and serve.

Cold Carrot and Mandarins Cake

Ready in 3 hours | Servings: 6 | Difficulty: Hard

Nutrition Info: Calories 170, fat 2mg, fiber 4mg, carbs 11mg, protein 8mg

INGREDIENTS

3 onions, rubbed
1/3 of a cup, pitted dates
Four Mandarins, Peeled
A handful of sliced walnuts
Coconut oil, 8 tbsp, melted
1 cup of cashews, drenched for 2 hours
Juice containing 2 lemons
Two tbsp of sugar coconut
Two spoonfuls of water

DIRECTIONS

1. Combine carrots with dates, walnuts, mandarins, and half the coconut oil in your mixing bowl, mix really well, pour in a cake pan, and distributed properly.
2. Adding cashews, lemon juice, stevia, water, and the rest of the oil to your food processor, and mix a little more.
3. Apply this to the mixture of carrots, scatter, chill in the fridge for 3 hours, slice, and serve.

Green Tea Cream

Ready in 2 hours | Servings: 6 | Difficulty: Hard

Nutrition Info: Calories 160, fat 3mg, fiber 3mg, carbs 7mg, protein 6g

INGREDIENTS

Fourteen ounces of coco-milk
2 tablespoons of powder for green tea
Coconut Milk 14 ounces
Three teaspoons of sugar from coconut

DIRECTIONS

1. Put the milk in a saucepan, add the sugar and green tea powder, mix, bring to a boil, boil for two minutes, switch off the heat, chill, introduce the coconut cream, blend properly, split into tiny pieces.

Chickpeas and Pepper Hummus

Ready in 10 minutes| Servings: 4|Difficulty: Easy

Nutrition Info: Calories 231, fat 12g, fiber 6mg, carbs 15mg, protein 14mg

INGREDIENTS

Ingredients:
- No-salt-added, drained and rinsed 14 ounces of canned chickpeas
- One tablespoon of paste with sesame
- Two red peppers fried, diced
- 1/2 lemon juice
- Four walnuts, chopped

DIRECTIONS

Directions:
1. Mix the chickpeas with the sesame paste, red peppers, lemon juice, and walnuts in your blender, process properly, break into bowls and serve as a snack.

Lemony Chickpeas Dip

Ready in 10 minutes | Servings: 4 |Difficulty: Easy

Nutrition Info: Calories 200, fat 12g, fiber 4mg, carbs 9mg, protein 7mg

INGREDIENTS

- Fourteen ounces of canned, washed, no-salt-added, rinsed chickpeas
- One lemon zest, grind
- Juice of 1 lemon
- Olive oil, 1 tbsp
- Four spoonfuls of pine nuts
- 1/2 cup of cilantro, chopped

DIRECTIONS

1. Incorporate the chickpeas with lemon zest, lemon juice, coriander & oil in a processor, process properly, cut into small bowls, scatter on top of the pine nuts and serve as a snack for the party.

Chili Nuts

Ready in 10 minutes | Servings: 4|Difficulty: Hard

Nutrition Info: Calories 234, fat 12mg, fiber 5mg, carbs 14mg, protein 7mg

INGREDIENTS

1/2 teaspoon flakes of chili
One white egg
1/2 tsp powder of curry
1/2 tsp powder ginger
4 teaspoons of sugar from coconut
A taste of spice from Cayenne
Mixed nuts of Fourteen ounces

DIRECTIONS

1. Integrate the chili flakes, ginger powder, curry powder, ginger powder, coconut sugar, and cayenne in a cup and stir together well.
2. Insert the nuts, swirl properly, scatter them over a rimmed baking sheet, place them in the oven and bake for ten minutes at 400-degree Fahrenheit
3. Split the nuts and serve as a snack in containers.

Protein Bars

Ready in: 10 minutes | Servings: 4|Difficulty: Hard

Nutrition Info: Calories 100, fat 3mg, fiber 4mg, carbs 8mg, protein 5g

INGREDIENTS

Four ounces of apricots, canned
Two Ounces of Water
Two spoonfuls of rolled oats
One tablespoon of Seeds of Sunflower
Two spoonfuls of coconut, shredded
One spoon of sesame seeds
Cranberries for 1 tablespoon
Three tablespoons seeds of hemp
One tbsp of seeds from Chia

DIRECTIONS

1. Incorporate the apricots with the water and the oats in your large bowl, process well, move to a cup, incorporate coconut, sunflower seeds, sesame seeds, cranberries, seeds of hemp, and chia, and mix until you have a paste.
2. Roll it into a log, cover it, cool it in the refrigerator, cut it and serve it as a snack.

Red Pepper Muffins

Ready in 10 minutes | Servings: 12|Difficulty: Normal

Nutrition Info: Calories 149, fat 4g, fiber 2mg, carbs 14mg, protein 5mg

INGREDIENTS

1 3/4 cups of whole wheat flour
Two tsp of powder for baking
2 teaspoons of sugar from coconut
A squeeze of black pepper
1 single egg
3/4 cup of milk with almonds
2/3 cup red pepper roast, chopped
1/2 cup of mozzarella, low-fat, sliced

DIRECTIONS

1. Combine the flour with the baking powder, coconut sugar, black pepper, egg, milk, red pepper, and mozzarella in a cup, stir properly, distribute into a lined muffin tray, put in the oven, and cook for thirty min at 400-degree Fahrenheit
2. Serve as a light snack.

Nuts and Seeds Mix

Ready in 10 minutes | Servings: 6|Difficulty: Easy

Nutrition Info: Calories 188, fat 4mg, fiber 6mg, carbs 8mg, protein 6mg

INGREDIENTS

DIRECTIONS

One Cup of a pecan
One Cup of hazelnuts
One mug with almonds
1/4 of a cup of coconut, sliced
One Cup with walnuts
Bits of 1/2 cup papaya, dry
1/2 cup, cooked, pitted, and chopped dates
1/2 cup of seeds of sunflower
1/2 cup of seeds for pumpkin
One Cup of raisins

1. Integrate the pecans with coconut, walnuts, papaya, hazelnuts, almonds, dates, sunflower seeds, pumpkin seeds, and raisins in a bowl, whisk them together and serve as a snack.

Tortilla Chips

Ready in 25 minutes| Servings: 6|Difficulty: Easy

Nutrition Info: Calories 199, fat 3mg, fiber 4mg, carbs 12mg, protein 5mg

INGREDIENTS

DIRECTIONS

12 tortillas of whole wheat, sliced into 6 wedges each.
Olive oil, 2 tablespoons
1 tablespoon of powdered chili
A pinch of spice from Cayenne

1. On a roasting pan, lay the tortillas, insert the oil, chili flakes, and cayenne, mix, put in the oven, and bake for 25 minutes at 350-degree Fahrenheit
2. Divide and serve as a side dish in bowls.

Kale Chips

Ready in 15 minutes| Servings: 8|Difficulty: Easy

Nutrition Info: Calories 177, fat 2mg, fiber 4mg, carbs 13mg, protein 6mg

INGREDIENTS

One cluster of kale leaves
Olive oil, One tablespoon
1 tsp of paprika smoked
A squeeze of black pepper

DIRECTIONS

1. On a baking tray, scatter the kale leaves, incorporate black pepper, oil, and paprika, swirl, put in the oven, and cook at 350 degrees F for fifteen minutes.
2. Divide into bowls and serve as a snack.

Potato Chips

Ready in 30 minutes | Servings: 6 |Difficulty: Normal

Nutrition Info: Calories 200, fat 3g, fiber 5mg, carbs 13mg, protein 6mg

INGREDIENTS

Two potatoes of gold, cut into thin rounds
Olive oil, 1 tablespoon
Two teaspoons of garlic, diced

DIRECTIONS

1. Integrate the potato chips with the oil and garlic in a tub, mix, scatter on a rimmed baking sheet, put in the oven, and bake for thirty min at 400 ° Fahrenheit
2. Split and serve into bowls.

Peach Dip

Ready in 5 minutes| Servings: 2|Difficulty: Easy

Nutrition Info: Calories 165, fat 2mg, fiber 3mg, carbs 14mg, protein 13mg

INGREDIENTS

1/2 cup yogurt that is non-fat
One Cup of sliced peaches
Pinch of ground cinnamon
A pinch of ground nutmeg, ground

DIRECTIONS

1. Integrate the peaches, cinnamon, and nutmeg milk in a bowl, whisk, split into smaller containers and serve as a snack.

Cereal Mix

Ready in 40 minutes |Servings: 6|Difficulty: Normal

Nutrition Info: Calories 199, fat 3mg, fiber 4mg, carbs 12mg, protein 5mg

INGREDIENTS

Ingredients:
Olive oil, 3 tablespoons
One tsp hot sauce
1/2 teaspoon crushed garlic
1/2 teaspoon ground onion
1/2 cumin seed, field
A taste of spice from Cayenne
3 cups of rice cereal Squares
One bowl of cornflakes
1/2 Cup of Pepitas

DIRECTIONS

1. Integrate the oil with the hot sauce, the garlic powder, the onion powder, the cumin, the cayenne, the rice cereal, the cornflakes, and the pepitas in a cup, mix them, spread them on a rimmed baking sheet, put them in the oven and roast for 40 minutes at 350-degree Fahrenheit

2. Split and serve as a snack in bowls.

Goji Berry Mix

Ready in 10 minutes| Servings: 4|Difficulty: Normal

Nutrition Info: Calories 187, fat 2mg, fiber 5mg, carbs 12mg, protein 6mg

INGREDIENTS

One Cup with almonds
One cup of berries goji
1/2 cup of seeds of sunflower
1/2 cup of seeds for pumpkin
1/2 cup walnuts, halved by two
12 dried and quartered apricots

DIRECTIONS

1. Integrate the almond with the goji berries, pumpkin seeds, walnuts, sunflower seeds, and apricots in a cup, toss, split and serve into bowls.

Artichoke Spread

Ready in 15 minutes| Servings: 4|Difficulty: Normal

Nutrition Info: Calories 200, fat 4g, fiber 6mg, carbs 14mg, protein 8mg

INGREDIENTS

DIRECTIONS

Spinach, 10 ounces, minced
Hearts of 12 ounces of canned artichoke, hardly any-salt-added, filtered and processedChopped
1 cup of milk of coconut
1 cup of cheddar, reduced-fat, shred
A squeeze of black pepper

1. Integrate the spinach with the artichokes, the salt, the cheese, and the black pepper in a bowl, mix well, move to a casserole tray, put in the oven, and bake for fifteen minutes at 400 ° Fahrenheit
2. Split and serve into bowls.

•••

Avocado Salsa

Ready in 5 minutes|Servings: 4|Difficulty: Easy

Nutrition Info: Calories 198, fat 2mg, fiber 5mg, carbs 14mg, protein 7mg

INGREDIENTS

DIRECTIONS

One Thinly sliced onion of yellow hue, diced
One jalapeño, diced
1/4 cup coriander, sliced
A squeeze of black pepper
Two peeled, pitted, and cubed avocados
2 tablespoons of juice with lime

1. Integrate the avocado jalapeno, cilantro, black pepper, and lime juice with the onion in a cup, swirl, and serve.

•••

Onion Spread

Ready in 40 Minutes|Servings: 4|Difficulty: Easy

Nutrition Info: Calories 212, fat 3mg, fiber 5mg, carbs 14mg, protein 8mg

INGREDIENTS

DIRECTIONS

Olive oil, 2 tbsp
Two onions of yellow origin, cut
A squeeze of black pepper
Low-fat Eight ounces of cream cheese
1 cup of cream of coconut
Chives 2 teaspoons, minced

1. On low heat, warm a skillet with the oil, insert the onions and the black pepper, swirl and simmer for 35 minutes.
2. Mix the onions with the cream cheese, coconut cream & chives in a cup, mix well enough and serve as a spread for the party.

Simple Salsa

Ready in 5 Minutes | Servings: 6 | Difficulty: Easy

Nutrition Info: Calories 142, fat 4mg, fiber 4mg, carbs 6mg, protein 7mg

INGREDIENTS

DIRECTIONS

One bell pepper yellow, cut into cubes
Two tomatoes, cubed in cubes
One slice of cucumber, cut into cubes
One tiny red, cut into cubes onion
Olive oil, 1 tablespoon
One spoon of red vinegar

1. In a mug, mix the tomatoes, cucumber, onion, oil, and vinegar with the bell pepper, shake, split into small cups and serve.

Spinach Dip

Ready in 10 minutes | Servings: 4 | Difficulty: Easy

Nutrition Info: Calories 200, fat 3mg, fiber 5mg, carbs 14mg, protein 6mg

INGREDIENTS

DIRECTIONS

Olive oil, 1 tablespoon
Spinach, 10 ounces
1 and 1/2 cups of dried, no-salt-added, drained and soaked chickpeas Rinsed

Directions:

1. Incorporate the chickpeas with the oil and the spinach in your mixer, process properly, split into bowls, and serve.

1. Incorporate the chickpeas with lemon zest, lemon juice, coriander & oil in a processor, process properly, cut into small bowls, scatter on top of the pine nuts and serve as a snack for the party.

Avocado Dip

Ready in 10 minutes| Servings: 8|Difficulty: Easy

Nutrition Info: Calories 187, fat 3mg, fiber 7mg, carbs 17mg, protein 8mg

INGREDIENTS

DIRECTIONS

Four cleaned and pitted avocados
One Cup of leaves of cilantro
1/2 cup of milk of coconut
Sliced 1 jalapeno,
1/4 cup of juice of lime
A squeeze of black pepper

1. Integrate the cilantro, coconut cream, jalapeno, lime juice, and black pepper with the avocados in your processor, process properly, divide into bowls and eat.

••

Chives Dip

Ready in 10 minutes|Servings: 4|Difficulty: Easy

Nutrition Info: Calories 211, fat 3mg, fiber 5mg, carbs 15mg, protein 6mg

INGREDIENTS

DIRECTIONS

Chives 2 tbsp, minced
1 shallot, diced
1 tablespoon of juice from a lemon
A squeeze of black pepper
Low-fat cheese 2 ounces, shredded
1 cup of milk of coconut

1. Mix the chives with the black pepper, cheese, shallot, lemon juice, and coconut cream in a cup, mix well, and serve as a dip for the party.

••

Dill Dip

Ready in 10 minutes|Servings: 6|Difficulty: Easy

Nutrition Info: Calories 181, fat 3mg, fiber 7mg, carbs 16mg, protein 7mg

INGREDIENTS

DIRECTIONS

Eight ounces of cream of coconut
Horseradish 1/4 cup
Two spoonfuls of dill
A squeeze of black pepper

1. In a bowl, mix the cream with the horseradish, dill, and black pepper, mix very well and serve as a party dip.

Chickpeas Salsa

Ready in 10 minutes | Servings: 6 | Difficulty: Easy

Nutrition Info: Calories 189, fat 3mg, fiber 6mg, carbs 14mg, protein 6mg

INGREDIENTS

DIRECTIONS

15 ounces of dried, no-salt-added, drained, and rinsed chickpeas
Four scallions, minced
Two red peppers fried, diced
One Cup of arugula baby leaves
Lemon juice 2 tbsp
Olive oil, 2 tablespoons
A squeeze of black pepper

1. Integrate the chickpeas with the red peppers, scallions, arugula, lemon juice, oil, and black pepper in a dish, toss, break into small bowls and serve.

....

Cilantro Dip

Ready in 10 minutes | Servings: 6 | Difficulty: Easy

Nutrition Info: Calories 188, fat 4mg, fiber 6mg, carbs 7mg, protein 8mg

INGREDIENTS

DIRECTIONS

Two heaps of cilantro leaves
1/2 cup of ginger, cut
Balsamic vinegar with Three teaspoons
Olive oil, 1/2 cup
Two tablespoons of amino coconut
Sesame oil for 2 teaspoons

1. Mix the cilantro with the ginger, vinegar, oil, amino, and sesame oil in your processor, process properly, split into small cups and serve.

Yogurt and Dill Dip

Ready in 10 minutes|Servings: 4|Difficulty: Easy

Nutrition Info: Calories 181, fat 2mg, fiber 6mg, carbs 11mg, protein 7mg

INGREDIENTS

DIRECTIONS

2 cups of yogurt without fat
1 clove of garlic, hacked
1/4 cup of sliced walnuts
1/4 cup of dill, chopped

1. Integrate the yogurt with the garlic, walnuts, and dill in a cup, whisk well and serve in cold water.

....

Broccoli Dip

Ready in 10 minutes| Servings: 4|Difficulty: Easy

Nutrition Info: Calories 189, fat 4mg, fiber 6mg, carbs 15mg, protein 7mg

INGREDIENTS

DIRECTIONS

14-ounce florets of broccoli
1 cup of cottage cheese that is low-fat
A squeeze of black pepper

Combine the cheese and black pepper in your mixing bowl, pulse properly, break into small cups, and serve.

....

Easy Salmon Spread

Ready in 10 minutes|Servings: 4|Difficulty: Easy

Nutrition Info: Calories 212, fat 3mg, fiber 6mg, carbs 14mg, protein 7mg

INGREDIENTS

DIRECTIONS

Horseradish for 2 teaspoons
Low-fat 8 ounces of cream cheese
Cut two tbsp of dill,
Smoked salmon for 1/4 pound, chopped
A squeeze of black pepper

1. Mix the horseradish with the cream cheese, dill, salmon, and black pepper in a cup, mix well and serve as a spread for the party.

COOK BOOK PAGE 237

Manufactured by Amazon.ca
Bolton, ON